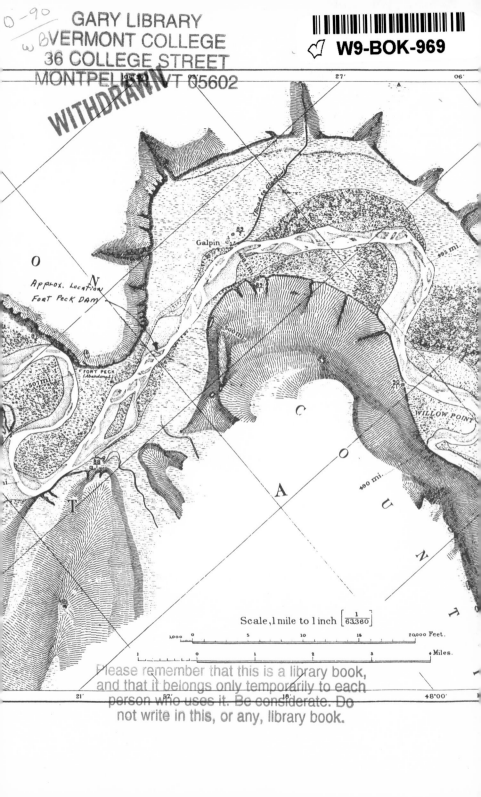

Galpin

O
N
Approx. Location
Fort Peck Dam

FORT PECK
(Abandoned)

T

C
O
U
N
T

A

WILLOW POINT

495 mi.

500 mi.

490 mi.

500 mi.

500 mi.

Scale, 1 mile to 1 inch $\left[\frac{1}{63,360}\right]$

1,000   0   5   10   15   20,000 Feet.

1   0   1   2   3   4 Miles.

Saying Goodbye

SAYING GOODBYE

A Memoir for Two Fathers

M. R. Montgomery

 ALFRED A. KNOPF, NEW YORK, 1989

THIS IS A BORZOI BOOK
PUBLISHED BY ALFRED A. KNOPF, INC.

The author would like to thank the following organizations for
providing the art used on the chapter opening pages: the operational archive at the Fort Peck Army Corps of Engineers
Area Headquarters for the Introduction and Chapters 4, 6,
and 7; the Montana Historical Society for Chapters 1 and 2;
Goodspeed's Book Store, Boston, for Chapter 3; the Great
Lakes Steel Corporation for Chapter 9; the Watanabe family
for Chapters 10, 11, and 18; the Boston *Globe* for Chapter
12; the Still Photograph Division, the National Archives,
Washington, D.C. for Chapters 14, 16, and 22; the Amador-
Pleasanton, California School District for Chapter 22. Art for
Chapters 5, 8, 13, 19, 20, and 23 came from the author's own
collection. The front endpaper is a Missouri River Survey of
1896, facsimile reproduction courtesy of the Beinecke Library,
Yale University. The back endpaper is a plan of the Fort Peck
Dam, courtesy of the Army Corp of Engineers.

Library of Congress Cataloging-in-Publication Data
Montgomery, M. R.
   Saying goodbye.
     1. Montgomery, M. R.—Childhood and youth.   2. Mont-
gomery, M. R.—Family.   3. Montgomery family.   4. Civil
engineers—United   States—Biography.   5.   World   War,
1939–1945—United States.   6. Japanese American physicians—West (U.S.)—Biography.   I. Title.
CT275.M5835A3 1989   929'.2'0973   88-45818
ISBN 0-394-57333-1

Manufactured in the United States of America
First Edition

For Florence

I will tell you a story with a meaning,
I will expound the riddles of things past,
things that we have heard and know,
and our fathers have repeated to us.

Psalm 78:2–3

Contents

	Illustrations	*xi*
	Acknowledgments	*xiii*
	Introduction	*xvii*
1	A Sense of Place	*3*
2	Uncrowded Country	*16*
3	Bear Paw Country	*25*
4	Notes on Engineers, Politicians, and Cost-Benefit Thinking	*42*
5	*Life* Goes to Its First Party	*54*
6	Down That Lonesome Paper Trail	*64*
7	"Goodbye, Boys"	*79*
8	Rumors of War	*94*
9	Destination: Scotland	*104*
10	An Orphan's Journey	*115*
11	For the Sake of the Children	*121*
12	A Right Way, a Wrong Way, and the Harvard Way	*129*
13	Fragments of Memory	*142*
14	An Official History of the British Bases	*152*
15	More Detailed Records	*165*
16	"A Severe Disappointment to Them"	*173*
17	"A Long and Weary Job"	*182*
18	"Serving the Country by Teaching"	*192*

19 "A Grand Bunch to Go Out With" *200*
20 "A Bit of Local Color for Your Book" *209*
21 California and the Pacific Theater *222*
22 A Personal Gripe *236*
23 Impalpable Dust *248*

Illustrations

Front endpapers: Missouri River Survey of 1897 □ Introduction: Pouring concrete, Spillway control structure, Fort Peck, Montana, 1936 □ Chapter 1: Chinook, Montana, ca. 1912 □ Chapter 2: Buffalo bone pickers in Montana □ Chapter 3: Northern Railroad Survey, Milk River at Chinook, Montana, Bear Paw Mountains in background, late 19th century aquatint and lithograph □ Chapter 4: Railroad spur line under construction □ Chapter 5: Photo collage by David Ryan □ Chapter 6: Inspectors of the Spillway Division, 1937 □ Chapter 7: Failed section upstream face of Fort Peck Dam □ Chapter 8: M. R. Montgomery, Sr., ca. 1937 □ Chapter 9: Quonset hut construction detail, Naval Construction Battalion Center, Port Huyneme, California □ Chapter 10: Dr. Lee M. Watanabe and his brother by adoption, George Watanabe, in Fresno, California, ca. 1918 □ Chapter 11: The Watanabe family, with Mary Anna (left), Florence, and Kendrick, January, 1942 □ Chapter 12: British Ambassador to the United States Lord Halifax (left), President James Bryant Conant (center), and Clarence Dykstra (right), first head of the Selective Service System, after Harvard University commencement, June 1941 □ Chapter 13: The author and his mother, ca. 1942 □ Chapter 14: The *Queen Mary* in wartime camouflage, anchored off the Rosneath Peninsula, 1943 □ Chapter 15: Victorian folly on Calderwood's farm at Rosneath, with surplus Quonset hut attached as a cow barn □ Chapter 16: Submarines at Base 2, Rosneath □ Chapter 17: Pipe-laying, 1943 □ Chapter 18: Dr. Lee Watanabe and four students at the Naval School of Oriental Languages, Boulder, Colorado □ Chapter 19: Kenneth Barge paying off the beaters after a hunt for driven grouse, Rosneath Peninsula, 1942 □ Chapter 20: Rosneath Peninsula from above Helensburgh □ Chapter 21: Pleasanton Elementary School, ca. 1945 □ Chapter 22: Australian infantry landing on Borneo from U.S. Navy ships, 1945 □ Chapter 23: M. R. Montgomery, Sr., 1945

Acknowledgments

As is always the case in matters historical, an author's greatest debt is to anonymous clerks and typists and keepers of records as well as to archivists and managers who have kept at least some part of the fabric knitted together over time. This book would not have been possible without the operational archives at the Army Corps of Engineers Area Office, Fort Peck, Montana, and the Naval Construction Battalion Center, Port Hueneme, California. At Fort Peck, Area Manager Ron Wallem and several members of his staff were not only gracious on my visits, but unflaggingly helpful by mail and telephone as we knitted up the loose ends. The same is true for the staff at the Historian's Office, Port Hueneme, where Carol Marsh stayed long hours so that I might make the most of a brief visit, and also continued to help afterward as new questions arose.

At the National Archives and Record Administration office in San Bruno, California, Kathleen O'Connor and Melvin Menegaux managed to cut red tape, sometimes literally, to move documents from storage to the reading room. Access to the records of the District Intelligence Officer, 12th Naval District, 1940–45, required the assistance of the successor agency, the Naval Investigative Command, and it was graciously forthcoming, thanks to Special Agent Joe Beene and his associates.

Records held in Washington, D.C., at both the Naval History Center, Old Navy Yard, and the National Archives were made available as efficiently as possible. Michael Walker at the Naval History Center was unusually helpful, and Richard von Doenhoff at the Modern Military Branch, National Archives, made that cumbersome system work as well as could be expected.

For access to the Margaret Bourke-White correspondence, I am indebted to Amy S. Doherty, university archivist at the George Arents Research Library, Syracuse University. The Montana State Historical Society provided photographs of the towns near Fort Peck. Ms. Mala Conrad of the Harvard University Map Collection not only located illustrative materials, but took a lively professional interest in eastern Montana, northern Borneo, and Dunbartonshire, Scotland.

One of the realities of history is that you can spend hours looking for something that simply no longer exists, and I particularly want to thank Mr. Kenneth Shanks of the Chicago branch of the National Archives, who deserves some kind of special award for bootless effort, as he tried so very hard to locate both Army Corps of Engineers and naval-district records that have been, he and I are now convinced, long since discarded. Some archivists located records with less enthusiasm than he, unsuccessfully, undertook his search.

Richard P. McDonough, my literary agent, was a constant source of enthusiasm from this book's first vague outline until the manuscript was finished. All agents make deals, but Dick makes books, too.

The standard historical works on the Great Depression and World War II which I consulted are too numerous for me to make a meaningful list, and the reader will find them, and more, in any large public or university library. However, one particularly significant work on the meaning of being an engineer in the early twentieth century might escape the curious researcher who would not expect to find a historical gem under "literary criticism." For many insights into my father's generation and profession and, for that matter, my mother's life as a "household engineer," I am beholden to Cecelia Tichi's *Shifting Gears: Technology, Literature, Culture in Modernist America*, published by the University of North Carolina Press in 1987. K. Ross Toole's *Twentieth-Century Montana: A State of Extremes* (University of Oklahoma Press, 1972) must also be singled out. It is a model revision of the romantic myths of Big Sky Country.

For logistical help, I am indebted to Loretta McLaughlin and Sean Mullin of the Boston *Globe*. Each of the several *Globe* employees who have written books owes much to the tolerance of William O. Taylor, publisher, who understands that writers cannot always live on short pieces and daily deadlines and must sometimes take long views toward distant horizons. Drs. Mohandas Kini and Larry Roth, Boston-area ophthalmological surgeons, are well aware of their special contribution, but I thank them again, here. John Scheuren, a retired civil engineer familiar with the difficulties of hydraulic-fill dam construction, provided insight into that arcane process.

My families—the friends and relations of M. R. Montgomery, Sr., and Dr. Lee M. Watanabe—shared their memories and mementos, the happy and the sad, without reservations.

And then there is my editor—no mere arbiter of punctuation, but a friend and an ally to all her authors—Elisabeth Sifton, who has the twinned gifts of empathy and optimism.

Introduction

I guess you could call me Junior. When my father died, I dropped the Junior; one is supposed to do that. We juniors are not very much in fashion, any more. There is hardly a man alive under the age of thirty-five who carries the complete patronymic burden so commonly shouldered before the postwar baby boom. We were supposed to be "chips off the old block," I guess.

Only the American Express company still styles me "M. R. Montgomery, Jr." I have not had the urge to communicate with them on the subject of my father's death. Sometimes it seems that if they edited the credit card he would never have existed at all. This is what my father would have called "a screwy idea."

Well, we all have melancholic days, and when the blackness comes on us, how many of us will attempt a cure with small doses of nostalgia? Go, if you have never been, to the National Archives in Washington, D.C., or to any of the dozen regional branches, and you will see that the major business there is not the nation's history, but family history. For every serious archival scholar there, a dozen people on private family business will be poring over microfilmed copies of the national census. True, some are Mormons, working on the salvation of ancestors, who, if they can be identified, will be included among the Latter-day Saints. And there are professional genealogists. But most of the readers, blinking at the slightly unfocused microfilm in the reading machines, are just ordinary people, trying to find a census with their parents' names, their grandparents' names. By and large, they are satisfied just to find the enumeration page. It is an act of remembrance, this verification that the ancestors in fact were once visited, counted, named.

We have a fascination with the physical reminders of times past. It is not mere greed or speculative investment or a hoarding instinct that makes Americans in particular such collectors of moderately priced antiques. Go to Manhattan, an island covered and re-covered with modern buildings, and you will find men and women thronging through shops littered with the detritus of our parents' generation, with Wurlitzers and plastic tableware and black dial telephones and even bits of buildings. These are antique stores freighted with carcasses of dead households, of the very houses, everything present but the dead themselves.

Several times, when I've had to travel to Washington on business, I have stolen some time to visit the Smithsonian Museum of American History. It is not just the nation's attic; it is your attic, too. On the second floor there is a diorama of some anonymous bit of ground located somewhere west of the 100th meridian. This is my attic. A windmill rises from the polished wooden floor, and if you press a button, the recorded sound of the windmill can be heard over the chatter of small children. It squeaks, and makes music if you understand it as music, and the eccentric gear transfers the rotation of the sails into the slow rhythmic thump of the drive rod, which pumps the water. This is not my song of memory but my father's. He knew how to build and repair a windmill. I am expert in replacing the O-rings in the Delta kitchen faucet, but I will stand and listen to the windmill until the tape stops and, if there is no pressing business, push the button again and walk away before the sound dies. Some day, when great improvements have been made in the delivery of domestic water supplies, there will be a display of Delta faucets and the O-rings and the small tool used to replace them.

My father's name was Maurice Richard Montgomery, and he was born in Chinook, Montana, in 1904. His father's name was Richard Maurice Montgomery, but this grandfather of mine was widely known in Blaine County, Montana, as M. R. Montgomery, or Maurice Montgomery, for he did not like the easy familiarity of nicknames such as Rich or "Dick." He did not reverse the order of his names legally, so I was spared being styled "the Third."

All males with the last name of Montgomery are eventually called by the same universal nickname. My grandfather and my father adopted it, and spelled it, still rejecting any common familiarity, "Monte." It seemed logical to me to close it with the naturally occurring last letter, and so, to my father's mild displeasure, I began writing it "Monty." I believe he detected a faint odor of rebellion.

Blaine County is, except in the opinion of its few remaining residents, just about as appalling a countryside as North America has to offer. Its largest body of water is the Milk River, named from the color rather than the sweetness. The Milk rises in Glacier Park, running white with the scoured stone flour typical of glacial creeks. But instead of settling and clearing, the Milk meanders north into Canada, and returns, staying muddy and milky for its entire course eastward, draining an alkaline badlands country that lies between the Missouri River breaks and the flatter wheatlands of Alberta and Saskatchewan. The Milk joins the Big Muddy, the Missouri River, 150 miles east of Chinook, over in Valley County. I was born there, in the town of Glasgow.

I say it is appalling country. It is not ugly in the ordinary sense

of the word; it has, rather, the look of a land that has been abused
by a capricious god, and all the scars left by human beings seem
less like wounds than like small and tentative diagnostic biopsies.
Road shoulders and the cut banks of highways seldom, if ever, need
to be mowed. Nothing grows, after the thin topsoil is graded down
and the primordial earth revealed. A few flowers will bloom just
at the edge of the blacktop, where they get an extra dose of water
from the infrequent rains that slide off the crown of the pavement
and irrigate the earth for a few inches before disappearing. In dry
years, and that is almost all years, ranchers have difficulty keeping
cattle behind the road-paralleling barbed wire, because the stock
can see the bright green herbs at the edge of the asphalt. Antelope
and mule deer come down to the highways, gliding over the wire
as though it were hardly there at all, and feed quickly, slipping
back into the sagebrush if one of the passing automobiles or trucks
slows down and makes the animals suspicious.

There are places where you can look at wagon tracks that are
surely fifty years old, the narrow, clean-sided mark of metal-rimmed
wooden wheels not used here since the gasoline engine and the
rubber tire became common. Maybe they are old chuckwagon
tracks, or a farmer's buckboard scars, made after the range was
fenced. People here tend to claim they're covered-wagon tracks,
but nothing grows in them, and it matters not at all if they are the
first, or the last, wagon tracks; they will stay forever.

Through Glasgow and Chinook ran the old Great Northern Railroad, now the Burlington Northern, headed from Saint Paul, Minnesota, to Tacoma, Washington, with a built-in curve around the
boundaries of Glacier National Park, stopping at special stations
for the two mammoth park hotels. There, near the headwaters of
the Milk River, is the Montana of the imagination, or the travel
brochure.

Though people from my part of the country might say they were
from Chinook, Choteau, or Havre, Harlem or Coburg (the local
town names are a mix of Indian tribes, French explorers, and, in
the case of the last towns to be founded by nineteenth- and

twentieth-century immigrants, European cities), they used to tell outsiders, persons not intimate with the political geography, including other Montanans, that they were from "the High Line." They meant James J. Hill's Great Northern Railroad, the only route to the West Coast built without subsidy, a matter of pride to the residents and curiosity to the historian, since if ever there was a railroad route that needed a subsidy, it was one through this arid, howling wilderness. There was scarcely a High Liner of my parents' generation who could even say the words without adding a comment on the entirely private-enterprise nature of the Great Northern. Fierce independence is every American's theoretical and philosophical birthright, I suppose, but seldom so much a fact of life as for these few people clinging to so many millions of desolate acres.

For most High Liners, life was not only dependent on the railroad, but lived within earshot of the trains hauling Midwestern corn and high-plains wheat to Tacoma on the Pacific, or east to Minneapolis, the flour-milling capital of the Northern states. Towns clung tightly to the railroad. With all the acres of open and inexpensive land, houses rose close to each other on orderly small lots. There is no such thing as Montana architecture. When my grandfather settled in Chinook in 1902, he built a substantial two-and-a-half-story shingle-style house, a sort of overgrown cottage in the style of A. J. Downing, the early-nineteenth-century landscaper, architect, and promoter of country living. His house would not have looked out of place in San Diego, California, or Winnetka, Illinois, and that was the point, that was the purpose. All along the High Line are towns that could be picked up entire and set down anywhere in America.

When Dorothy said, "Toto, I have a feeling we're not in Kansas anymore," everyone in the small theaters along the railroad knew exactly what she meant. The Technicolor land over the rainbow didn't look a bit like Havre, Chinook, Zurich, Harlem, Savoy, Coburg, Malta, Tampico, or Glasgow, either.

I grew up without a palpable memory of the Milk River country or the High Line, of antelope, wheat fields, or cottonwoods (the only tree one ever would see), being born too late and leaving too soon—carried out of the country in 1938 like a baby being rescued from a fire and taken to California, where, except for a few years during the Second World War, I was raised. After my father died, I admitted—I think that is the right word—I admitted to a great need to see the Milk River and the High Line and Chinook. I was not interested in Glasgow, my birthplace, suffering under the common delusion that I knew who I was. The first question was about my father. Who was he and why had he told me so little about his life? It has been pointed out to me, in the course of this investigation, that it is not only fathers and sons but wives and daughters and mothers who wonder who these strangers are that they have married, children they have borne, family known all their lives. These are questions for someone else to answer; this book is a somewhat more monomaniacal search.

So, this is a quest, not for what one might become if one found the grail or captured the whale, but for what one is, who the father was, to try to understand what happened. Something happened, of that I was always sure.

Once, a long time ago, a college instructor assigned a reading, one which has been given to however many millions of us who ever signed up for American History 101, or whatever they called it at your school. It was that classic and problematic book *Democracy in America*, by Alexis de Tocqueville, a young French minor-league nobleman who visited the United States before the Civil War, ostensibly to study the legal and criminal system in what was then the only representative democracy in the world. Tocqueville's work is roughly divided into lengthy observations of and conversations with Americans, and into philosophical and reflective essays on the meaning of democracy. It is the observations that are usually assigned, for professors have decided that college students are more interested in facts than in the musings of dead Frenchmen. But it was the reflective chapters that enchanted me, although at the time I did not understand why.

Americans, Tocqueville wrote, "owe nothing to any man, they expect nothing from any man; they acquire the habit of always considering themselves as standing alone, and they are apt to imagine that their whole destiny is in their own hands." Well, that's Montana in 1935, one hundred years after *Democracy in America* was published. For Tocqueville, Chicago and Green Bay were the outposts, the wilderness. Montana, which observes its centennial year in 1989, may have preserved some of the founding and frontier mentality, but so have we all. Tocqueville remains absolutely right about the *illusion*, the aptness to imagine, as he so gently put it, that we have our destiny in our hands. It is still the psychological underpinning of a great deal, including advertising campaigns for automobiles. But the illusion of independence, when it is acted upon, takes a terrible toll.

This is what Tocqueville wrote next:

"Thus not only does democracy make every man forget his ancestors, but it hides his descendants and separates his contemporaries from him; it throws him back forever upon himself alone and threatens in the end to confine him entirely within the solitude of his own heart."

For all the many years after I read those words, I believed that Americans did indeed suffer that condition. But during that time I was not so acutely aware that my father was thus confined, and so was his son. I suspect it may be so with you.

My argument is this: There is a peculiar form of the ordinary difficulty of the father-and-child relationship in this country. It arises in the twin doctrines, the paired values, of mobility and self-reliance. Loneliness is the price that democratic man pays for his independence. To overcome it, Tocqueville noted, we Americans are fond of associations: clubs, church fellowships, even the game of golf with regular partners. The most symbolic, I think, is Rotary, a club that requires perfect attendance, and to whose meetings all visiting, temporarily dislocated fellow Rotarians are invited, so that they can maintain that ideal of regular attendance. As we take solace in membership, so, as I have already noted, we look to artifacts in museums, in antique shops, and in archives, to verify that we have association across time itself.

All of us have some quirky bit of knowledge that represents, for us, a fragile link across the generations. Sometimes it is the almost ceremonial introduction to a commonplace bit of wisdom—"as my father used to say" or "as Mom liked to say." Sometimes it is a prayer in a foreign language, or a fairy tale from a distant country, one not learned from a book, something carried here and left with us. It can even be a rule of simple social behavior that is in fact not universal, yet still unquestioned, understood as the right way to behave or the proper thing to say in a given social context. I missed out on fairy tales, unlike my wife—who has always known the story of Momotaro-san, the Japanese hero-boy born from a peach, a *momo*, who was not only heroic but very good to his adoptive parents. Somehow, my quirky bit of knowledge is an old textbook definition of Portland cement. I got it wrong, by the way, which may have been my father's fault or mine; it doesn't matter any more.

My father was a civil engineer, and could build anything if you gave him the plans and the money—tall buildings, long bridges, airfields, anything at all. I was always incompetent at anything more mathematical than long division, so he could not teach me his craft. But once, even before I reached the age of long division, he taught me a formal definition of cement, that gray powder which is mixed with water and stone and sand to make concrete. This is what I learned: "Portland cement is a mixture of argillaceous and calcareous substances, heated to incipient fusion and ground to a palpable dust."

All that means is that it is a mixture of clayey shales and limestone rocks, melted in a furnace until it fuses together, and then it is ground into a very fine powder. He told me that "palpable" meant "very fine," something like baby powder or ashes, so fine that it would float when you sprinkled it on the surface of the water. It is true that cement dust will float, but between the two of us, or by just one of us, we got it wrong. The old Latinate definition should read "impalpable dust"; that is what it is. It is a dust so fine you cannot feel it when it is rubbed between your fingers; that is what "impalpable" means.

I wasn't mathematical or scientific, yet I always liked the words, although I seldom understood their technical meanings. There is little poetry in civil engineering besides "impalpable dust." I also enjoy the phrase for the natural slope that a pile of dirt, or sand, or gravel, will assume if it is simply dumped into a heap, or pushed over the edge of a high place and left to lie as it will. This is called "the angle of repose." That last word is an odd one, not much heard in ordinary speech, and usually reserved as that state for which we pray in regard to the souls of the dead. It is possible to overcome the tendency of dirt to achieve its natural angle, but that can also lead to problems, which is why civil engineers worry about something as odd as reposing dirt.

After my father was dead, and the dust, as we learned in Sunday school, had returned to the earth that gave it, I was moved to explore. I was not quite sure what for, you understand—just to look, to visit places, to try to make some sense out of his life, which was a life not unlike so many men's lives of his generation, a mixture of independence, association, and, finally, loneliness. Along the way, I stopped here and there looking for my father-in-law, who had died several years earlier. I think I have had some possibly foolish sense that, if I could place them in their proper context, I could, somehow, reconcile them to each other, and to us. So, they are both in this book, although my father will get most of the space, which is not unfair, simply a reflection of the differing amounts of mutual experience. I hope only to tell enough for each of them, so that, if you follow me, there is some alignment of their repose.

Saying Goodbye

1

A Sense of Place

There are two Montanas, as different one from the other as if they were on separate continents. One is the mountainous west, with pines and trout streams, meadows and waterfalls. The other, the genuine Big Sky Country, lies east of the Rockies and north of the Big Horns. Tourists race across it, headed from Mount Rushmore to Yellowstone Park, headed for the mountains, where there are trees to comfort by giving some shade from the sun, some softening of the landscape, some shelter from the wind. Visitors from California, who make up most of the state's tourists, skip it entirely, having seen enough desert between Reno and West Yellowstone.

Those of us from the eastern part of the state regard trees as Californians regard snow, a curiosity to be admired, traveled toward, perhaps even created for holiday festivities. We do not *expect* trees. They are something to be planted, or something that will grow naturally a few miles away, where the land is higher and cooler, more likely to catch the spare rain and even sparer snowfall of the high plains. In eastern Montana, we live below and above the two tree lines. The high hills and the sheltered valleys have trees naturally; ours are all planted, nursed, maintained. Where my family comes from, you can see a great distance, because there is nothing that grows taller than a man, save only the cottonwoods down in the dry creeks and the willows along the river bottoms, nothing taller than a man on horseback, or even an ordinary-sized man on his own two feet.

Just a few miles south of Jordan, Montana, there's a tree that doesn't belong. It's a big, lonely elm tree, miles from a creek bottom, up on the high bare ground by the Jordan–to–Miles City highway. The locals put a fence around it and painted a sign: "Rock Springs National Forest." It's the only tree for fifty miles in any direction, and in Montana, when you say "any direction," you're not kidding.

My father's brother Gordon remembered leaving home in Chinook and going to college at the university in Missoula, and being depressed, although the works of Freud and Adler were not quite available to him in 1918. He knew he wasn't just homesick, he told me: it was worse than that, there was something terribly wrong about Missoula, a town that sits surrounded by mountains on three sides, deep in the valley of the Clark Fork of the Columbia River, on the western side of the Continental Divide. He understood what the problem was, he recalled, when he took the train home at the end of his freshman year (the Montgomery family was rather too frugal to encourage Christmas-vacation homecomings). After connecting with the Great Northern spur line in Butte, he traveled northward, through the eastern foothills of the Rockies, until the line broke free of the hills and climbed out of the Missouri River Valley. He got off for a few minutes when the train stopped in Big

Sandy, north of the Missouri River, and realized what had been
wrong: with all those mountains and all those trees, he hadn't been
able to see anywhere. For someone from the plains, to see for only
a mile or two is like being locked in a cellar. If you can't see for
forty miles, you can't see *anything*.

Big skies, I am afraid, can make for both large and small am-
bitions. You dream big, but you cut a small figure in country
measured by the section, that standard square mile that can be
laid out so easily anywhere from the Ohio River to the Rocky
Mountains. The very vastness gives people a terrible desire to cut
it up in small, manageable pieces, to live sedate lives, to be intensely
respectable. Almost every small town in Montana had, even in the
dustbowl 1920s, a golf course. The putting greens were usually
raked sand, but it was called golf, and it was the same game that
gentlemen played in the country clubs of the big cities. I have one
of those small, square-format Box Brownie photographs of my father, aged perhaps sixteen, which would make it 1920, just as
Chinook is about to turn from a land-speculating, wheat-farming,
wheeling-dealing boom town into a dried-up, hard-scrabbling hamlet on the edge of nowhere. He is standing in front of the family
home, the solid, elephantine shingle-style pillars of the front porch
framing him. He is carrying a golf bag with a handful of mismatched
clubs peeking out of the top, and wearing a shirt and a tie and a
billed sporting cap. The photograph could have been taken anywhere in the United States, except that in a richer, older community he would have more and better-matched clubs.

The very pressure of the sky, the endlessness of the broken,
rolling landscape, the tenuousness of the small community poised
on the edge of a truly howling wilderness made respectability an
end in itself. Montanans, so soon come into the country, wanted
more than anything to be like other Americans, either to assimilate
if they were foreign, or to replicate the settled communities they
had left behind. You see, if you could not create a typical American
town, it would be an admission that you had somehow left the real
America behind, that you had made a mistake, that you had picked

the wrong country to farm, the wrong town to grow up with, the
wrong climate.

The potential for self-delusion in such a situation is considerable.
My father's father left San Diego, California, in 1898, on the
assumption that it would improve my grandmother's health to move
to a drier climate. And he never acknowledged that this was not
an excellent move. It was, I suppose, drier, but there is nothing
particularly salubrious about a northern desert with annual temperature swings of 150 degrees in moderate years from summer
highs to winter lows. My mother's family immigrated to another
part of eastern Montana, just about two hundred miles due south
of Chinook, between the northern and southern railroad routes.
They were all going to become millionaire wheat farmers. The very
names on the map should have discouraged them: the homestead
was on Big Dry Creek, near the crossroad village called Sand
Springs.

The earliest, and still-persistent, delusion of the eastern-
Montana settler was the fantasy that this dry land was appropriate
for agriculture. It can be done, in lucky years, or with irrigation.
The fantasy was not any collective madness, any spontaneous community insanity. The settlers were suckered into the countryside
by a mixture of railroad promotion and an apparently scientific
agricultural movement sponsored by the same railroad companies.
This was the Campbell System, the life work of one Hardy Webster
Campbell, director of model farming for the Burlington Railroad,
publisher of the annual *Soil Culture Manual*, and intellectual patron
saint of the Dry Farming Congress, whose annual meetings in the
early 1900s attracted up to ten thousand visitors. That most of the
members of the Congress were railroad executives, bankers, lawyers, real-estate agents, state publicists, and Chamber of Commerce employees should not surprise us.

With variations, but always with railroad support, the gospel of
dry farming promised to turn the forbidding high plains into a
second Midwest. The Northern Pacific and the Great Northern
had their own special expert, Thomas Shaw, who ran more than

forty experimental farms along the High Line, and preached the gospel of "plowing deep," which did unlock last year's soil moisture, but which also guaranteed next year's dust bowl, when the inevitable cycle of drought returned. Calvin Coolidge was perhaps correct, speaking for the settled East Coast, when he said that the principal business of the American people is business. But the principal business of Montana, from its very beginning, was self-promotion and, with the assistance of the railroads, the cynical deception of hundreds of thousands of small homesteaders. The railroads subsidized the "science" of dryland farming, paid for official publications issued under the Great Seal of the state of Montana, and mailed tens of thousands of railroad brochures to Easterners, each one followed up with copies of the state publication because, as a Northern Pacific executive noted, unlike his own promotional literature, "a book under the hand and seal of Montana is looked upon as an honest and accurate description of the country." The motto of Montana is more accurate, if wealth is what you want: *"Oro y plata,"* gold and silver. That it is written in Spanish, not Latin, is a curiosity. The Mexican influence on Montana is pretty much restricted to microwave-based chain restaurants. If you want an educated guess, since the actual origin of the state motto is lost to us, I suspect it was the old dream of the Spanish *conquistadores*, who set out from Mexico looking for the Seven Cities of Cibola, all built of gold and silver, *oro y plata.* A Montanan would naturally assume that they just quit too soon, down there in Colorado, before they got to the good country.

If the illusion of dryland agriculture seduced a hundred thousand homesteaders, the heartbreaking business of farming had some real competition for inducing a mild state of subclinical paranoia in Montanans. The other major source was "The Company," which meant the Anaconda Copper Company at the turn of the century, when they controlled the mines at Butte, the smelter at Anaconda, and the copper manufactories of Great Falls. It has come to mean, now that copper is no longer king, the Montana Power Company, which controlled the hydroelectric wealth of the state and most of

the good, private timberlands in the watersheds. Besides the two
Companies, the railroads appeared to have captured most of the
irrigated farmland, coal deposits, and oil fields. The average citizen
lived in a world where everything from the fickle weather to the
cost of transportation was controlled by omnipotent beings, and the
One was not necessarily more powerful than the Others.

Given such a world, the citizen had the choice of getting out or
denying, in the psychological sense, his situation. I would suggest
that the easiest way to make an enemy in eastern Montana is to
tell him, or her, what you think of the countryside. If that doesn't
chill the air, you could wonder aloud why anyone in his right mind
would invest money in downtown real estate. The ones that stayed
have not given up, and don't need any outsider's opinion on the
wisdom of their choice.

Little boomlets do appear, like the small, discrete thunderheads
that roll westward from the Rockies, the ones that drop veils of
rain, the rain that evaporates long before it reaches the dry prairie.
"Virgos," they're called, from the wispy garments of vestal virgins,
and, like those scantily clad maidens, they titillate, they promise,
and they deny. Near my father's hometown, they've had some little
oil booms. The newest office building in Chinook is the local title
company. Title searches are the stuff of mineral rights and bank-
ruptcy sales, so that even the worst of times is good for business.
I looked up the owner of the title company, figuring he would know
my family's long-gone land—it was his business to know where the
dead had walked.

"Your grandfather had two spreads," he said. "One was south
of town, and the other up north, in the hard country."

As he spoke, we were standing on a hilltop looking over the town
of Chinook. There were a few street trees, a few more shade trees
in front of the houses, and, down by the Milk River, a line of
cottonwoods. The ground underfoot was bare sand and burnt-
looking red rock; the grass was in small, brown bunches, and the
largest plants in sight were prickly-pear cactuses hugging the grav-
elly soil. North, where he had waved, the land stretched infinitely

to a smooth horizon. I looked at him and said: "The *what* country?"
"The hard country."

"You mean it gets worse?"

He looked at me, and said, very slowly, as one repeats things to
a small child: "It gets *hard*er." We got in his car, drove the few
blocks through town, crossed over the railroad tracks on one of
those unguarded, unsignaled crossings that make driving something
of an adventure along Montana's back roads, and headed north. It
got harder, all right. From the Milk River north, the land seemed
slowly to break up into dustier, rockier, steeper ground. There was
nothing so significant as a hill, but there was a constant precipi-
tousness. Up close, the hard country resembled the image of those
microscopic photographs that turn the edge of a razor blade into a
scorified mountain ridge.

Some poor son of a bitch had homesteaded it once, which was
fine, as long as all he wanted to do was raise two steers on his 320
acres. It's good grazing country, at 160 acres to the beef animal.
The Herefords on the hard country looked feedlot-fat, gnawing at
the scattered tufts of bunchgrass.

A few oil wells were pumping—this was when oil was twenty-
five dollars a barrel. They are probably capped now, and Chinook
is waiting for another cloud on the horizon. None of the oil is on
my family's old land. This is probably just as well, psychologically.
My grandfather didn't own the mineral rights, just the surface and
water rights. As in most of Montana, someone had gotten there
first.

Montana's small towns tended toward the homogeneous. Some
were ethnically singular, like Big Sandy, which is a town where
the population can still summon up a lilting Norwegian, if they
think no outsiders are listening. There were towns full of German
Mennonites who had picked up as a congregation and resettled,
Hungarian towns, French towns (including one over in western
Montana that is named Frenchtown but called, I'm afraid, Frog
Town). Chinook ran heavily to Presbyterians, which is not an
ethnic group, just a style. (The 1910 census for Chinook shows a

large population of people with Italian surnames, but closer inspection of the old enumeration pages reveals that they were all
bachelors, they all lived in boardinghouses, and they were all employed by the Great Northern Railroad. They were not expected
to settle down.)

Someone in the family—it was probably my cigar-smoking uncle,
Henry McKnight Montgomery, known as Mac—once remarked
that there were only two unusual people in Chinook. One was a
Jew, who rolled cigars for a living, selling them out of the store and
also on the passenger trains that made regular stops in Glasgow,
Chinook, and Havre. The other unusual person was a Catholic
priest, assigned to the nearby Indian reservation. They were both
bachelors, and used to be seen walking about town on clement evenings, discussing things. It was implied, and understood by me, that
they wouldn't have had anyone else, except each other, to talk to.

So, up there on the high plains, the world got divided into usual
people and unusual people. And the major definition of "usual"
was a combination of ethnic background and religion. In this respect, Montana was not unlike Eastern cities, in that people
clumped together into ethnic and therefore religious neighborhoods. It was just that the sparseness of the population meant that
what in the East were a city's ghettos or neighborhoods grew up
here as individual towns, scattered across the wilderness like those
little clumps of bacteria that grow on agar medium in high-school
biology classes.

Even among these pioneers, there was a sense of loss, which
was not all imagined. An understanding that something has gone
wrong, or will go wrong shortly, comes naturally in a country where
the temperature can drop seventy or eighty degrees in a morning,
where it can blow up a blizzard at the end of a winter that hasn't
seen an inch of snow fall on the dry land, a country where everyone
else has gotten there first—the Companies, the railroads, the real-
estate schemers.

That may account for what happened in Montana during and
after World War I, when it led the nation in paranoia. The whole

country, cheered on by politicians and propagandists, went through a war of German-bashing and a peace of Red-baiting, but Montana, out there in absolutely the middle of nowhere, was even more patriotically insane. My father was only a boy, but I think it left some imprint upon him.

World War I produced the first government-sponsored case of mass hysteria in the United States. It was not merely war against the Central Powers that the United States eventually entered, but war against the Hun. All across the country, with the prodding of the federal government's Committee on Public Information, Americans were encouraged to abhor everything German. On the amusing side, in long retrospect, it was an era when sauerkraut was renamed "victory cabbage." Unlike World War II, which was portrayed, on the European front, as a war against Hitler and the Nazis, not necessarily an anti-German war, the first war was an attack on all German-speaking peoples of Europe. It was, although without an event as shocking as Pearl Harbor, a campaign more like the one waged against the Japanese in the second war. The clear difference, and it should be kept in mind, is that the World War I propaganda campaign against the Germans was cultural *and* racial; the next one, against the Japanese, was simply racist.

The harassment of German cultural institutions was national, and it did not exclude the universities. The beer-brewing Busch family of St. Louis endowed a museum of German culture at Harvard University. Completed in 1916, the Busch-Reisinger Museum did not open until 1921, when the passions had subsided. German athletic clubs disbanded in the cities, putting away the medicine balls and the Indian clubs for the duration.

Montana, well peopled with a variety of European immigrants, was not satisfied with calling frankfurters "hot dogs" and hamburgers "Salisbury steaks." Nor were Montanans content with patriotic parades and war-bond campaigns. The state responded with measures far in excess of any taken in the other states, creating a mixture of centralized dictatorship and local vigilante groups. It started with the Montana Sedition Act of 1918, the first in the nation and the pattern for the federal Sedition Act (later to be repealed by a Congress that had come to its senses). A Council of Defense was created, and it heard hundreds of terrified immigrants deny any culpability in such widely rumored evils as the existence of a secret German air base hidden somewhere in the wooded parts of Ravalli County, west of Missoula. Counties and cities created Councils of Defense that had, and used, powers of arrest and detention, based on merest suspicion—all quite contrary to the United States Constitution and common-law *habeas corpus*. Though convictions in the regular court system were all but impossible, given the vagueness of the charges and the hearsay evidence, careers were ruined, small farmers driven off the land, and every man's hand was turned against his neighbor.

This was partly a pure class struggle, of Anglophones against other immigrants. To be Polish was nearly as suspect as being German, and Hungarians, after all, were part of the German empire. The nascent Irish nationalists were traitors, weren't they? It was class war, and the persecuted were, in that old Montana jargon, "honyockers." That's a hard noun to explain. Generally speaking, any foreign-born dirt farmer was a honyocker, but it helped to be poor, messy, and incompetent. When I was young, my parents would talk about people who parked cars in their front yard or didn't mow their lawns as honyockers. That was not the meanest epithet. About the worst thing a child could do was to make such a mess in the front yard that, as my father would put it, "It doesn't look like white people lived here." Given the utter absence of blacks in most of eastern Montana, then and now, the reference is to Native Americans, or, as my parents would say, "Indians."

But sedition and espionage were merely the beginning of the concerns of the Councils of Defense. Libraries had to be cleared of all books that said anything favorable about Germany, and that certainly meant all textbooks of the language and all music books with German songs, lyrics, and composers. Thrifty librarians took scissors and razor blades to mingled texts, in order not to lose an entire volume.

And this was not enough, not in Montana. The third order of the state Council of Defense forbade the use of the German language within the boundaries of the state, including sermons and prayers in churches that had entirely German-speaking congregations. Whole hamlets were depopulated, as German Mennonite farmers removed themselves to Canada. Even such ordinarily private acts as buying Liberty Loan Bonds and Stamps became the public's business. Farmers who could not or would not contribute to the Liberty Loans were hauled in front of County Defense Councils and badgered mercilessly. City and town Liberty Committees, without the quasi-judicial powers of the Councils, resorted to advertisements in local newspapers accusing people of being shirkers. On more than one occasion, they simply hauled men off the street, and beat them senseless as an example to the unpatriotic. The Montana legislature has not gotten around to repealing the Sedition Act to this day. You never know, in Montana, when you might need it.

Jeanette Rankin, Montana's Congresswoman, voted against American entry into World War I; she was to do the same in World War II. But that is just one of the possible ways to react to the insanity of unregulated patriotism. The other, I think, is to recognize the error of such foolishness as banning psalms in German, but to remain convinced of some larger yet unnamed conspiracy that somehow threatens America. In Montana, after World War I, the Defense Councils turned their wrath on Reds, Wobblies, and unionized miners. And the same year, in the summer of 1918, the first great drought struck along the High Line. In 1919 the influenza epidemic carried away one soul in ten, including my father's sister Jessie, who taught mathematics and science in the Chinook public schools. And in 1919 the drought moved south and east, covering the entire high plains, making a final mockery of the Campbell System. From Billings east to the Dakota line, the plains of Montana had reached their population peak; it would all be downhill for the next seventy years.

But what's been down so long begins to look like up to some of

us. Those of us who have left, or escaped, or been dispersed un-
willingly, are not sour on the state, even if we couldn't live there
any more, having seen Paris—or Peoria. And those who have stayed
are not buffoons or lost souls. Certainly it is rural, and getting
more so, unlike the rest of the United States. But there are no
peasants in Montana. They know a thing or two, as my uncle Mac
would say.

Driving through Garfield County, where my mother was born
and partly raised, you can go an hour, flat out, without seeing a
house. When she was a child, there would have been a house every
mile or so, on both sides of the road, and if you turned off on one
of the section roads—dirt tracks that marked the boundaries of
homestead sections—once again there would be a house a mile on
both sides of the road. Now, every twenty or thirty minutes, even
in the most desperate-looking country, there are farm roads with
cattle guards, and a standardized set of home-address signs on
galvanized metal shining by the gate. They give last names, and
the distance, to the tenth of a mile, from the highway to the ranch
house. Some people live twenty and thirty miles away from the
highway, off toward the Missouri, or the Musselshell, or Flowing
Springs, where the water makes for trees and pastures, small oases.

It is still America, if rather badly scattered. When they opened
up most of central and eastern Montana to homesteading, the last
big chunk in 1909, Montana had a dozen counties, some of them
as big as Connecticut or New Jersey. Eventually, because of the
local need for a courthouse and a land office closer than a four-day
ride, the state ended up with fifty-two counties, a lot of them with
total populations (Indians always excluded from the enumeration)
of fewer than a thousand souls. Towns did not spring up instantly—
it took a few years—but immediately, as soon as the land was
settled, there were school districts. The 1910 Census, the latest
one available to the public, the one found on microfilm at every
National Archive branch and in most large public libraries, enu-
merates eastern Montana in many more school districts than towns.
In 1910 my mother's family is not in Jordan but in School Dis-

trict 26. Unfortunately, the enumerator in District 26 had a bad batch of ink, and the forms, on microfilm, are endless lists of illegible gray scratches.

Headed east on Montana 200, a highway that bisects the state from the Rockies to the North Dakota border, one of those roads with no houses for an hour, travelers are not able to imagine, any more, that the area was once populated. I know this: I have tried to convince some people, as we rolled by the barbed wire, and I have not been persuasive. You cannot imagine houses on such land.

On 200, the townsite of Sand Springs is marked by nothing but an empty gasoline station and a post office that looks disused, although it may open on some days when we have happened, by accident, not to pass by. Twenty minutes and twenty miles east of Sand Springs, there is a single unpainted, or once-painted, structure on the south side of the highway. It sits quite alone. There is no gate in the barbed wire alongside the road, no visible track from the highway to the building. The windows are boarded shut and the front door is nailed shut. Out here, the wind works at old buildings with a geological patience, and the paint is gone, if ever there was paint, and the nailheads in the door are polished bright by blowing sand.

It is a one-room schoolhouse, once necessary when there were more people here. A duplicate is over in Jordan, set up next to the Garfield County Historical Museum. Once there were four of these scattered schools, plus a larger one in Jordan with a small dormitory next door for the children who lived too far even from the four rural schools. I am not claiming that Montana settlers were wholly education-minded, but they understood one thing, and that was that without education, without the ability to read and write and do sums, you didn't have a prayer. That is why there are no peasants in America, in the long run—due more to schooling than private land ownership or prohibitions against involuntary servitude. It might be a four-day ride to minimal justice or a marriage-license office in Montana, but it was, from the beginning, only a long walk to school.

2

Uncrowded Country

When I saw my father alive for the last time, I had not even thought of going to Fort Peck, of doing any kind of retracing, of trying to answer so many never-asked questions. His mind was fully occupied with the immediate, brief future.

We had achieved a kind of truce about questions. I wouldn't ask him many, and if he had anything to say, he'd say it. That sounds a little cold, but it was a satisfactory arrangement, for it solved any number of problems created by asking the wrong questions. I had long since discovered that he did not remember things that seemed important to me, that he really didn't like to talk about World War II, and that he was frustrated by the painful business of trying to explain engineering concepts to an utter layman or, when I was younger, layboy. I suspect one of the reasons I never tried to take high-school physics was my clear understanding, although not conscious, that getting help with physics homework would have been even more painful than help with Algebra 1 and Plane Geometry had already proved to be.

On that last visit, the summer he knew he was going to die, we were sitting in the living room of his house, making small nontalk. He had already shown me the list of his assets three times, so that I would somehow be useful to my mother after he was gone. He was watching the traffic, headed down the hill in front of the house, a lot of small cars, mostly Japanese-made, and many of them driven by women, everyone headed for work in San Diego, aimed at the freeway entrance a few miles west. He said, without any bitterness, and, as usual, without any introduction:

"We should never have moved here. There are too many people here."

At the time, I thought he meant this particular house, the second one he had owned in La Mesa, and in a less attractive part of town than the first. The old, big house was on a hill, and you could see all the way to the sometimes snow-capped Cuyamaca Mountains on a clear day. After having gone back to Fort Peck, I don't think it had anything to do with the house. I think he meant California.

All his life, after the war, he could never really quite believe that another 250 people a week would want to move into San Diego County, month after month, year after year. He really should have been a millionaire by the time he died. He always made good money, he had friends in the real-estate business, all he had to do was believe in the infinite growth of San Diego and speculate quietly in house lots or commercial property. But he simply could not believe that so many people would want to live so close to each other and pay him a king's ransom for property he had accumulated before they arrived. He had considerable imagination about many things, but not about the irresistible desire of people to spend money on real estate that is unacquainted with snow. Everyone who just missed the California dream has his own reason: being from Montana may encourage one to believe in some natural limit on the voluntary density of human population.

When it finally came time for me to return to Fort Peck, I was unprepared for the sparsity of it all: of people, buildings, cattle, roads, every human impingement on the country. I knew Montana, I thought, because I had seen the western part of the state, with cities and suburbs and great reaches of national forest where it was understandable that there were no people, these being lands set aside for trees and trout streams and wildlife. And I had seen some of the High Line, from Cut Bank to Chinook—that is, from west to east, where the small towns are strung along the highway like beads, not so very many miles apart. But that did not prepare one for a trek across the state from south to north, from down along the southern railroads, the old Burlington, the old Milwaukee, the old Northern Pacific lines that stay down toward the Wyoming border, cutting straight north toward the High Line, across the railroadless, nearly automobile-road-less, center of the state.

The least likely direction for visitors to approach Fort Peck is from the north, where U.S. 2 parallels the High Line. This is the northernmost of the east-west U.S. highways. By chance, we ended up in California living as close to U.S. 80, the southernmost, as my father had lived to U.S. 2. I was born one block off U.S. 2, in Glasgow. He died one block off U.S. 80 (now Interstate 8).

Fort Peck Dam is a short, twenty-minute detour south of U.S. 2, a highway used by a few tourists coming out of North Dakota and headed for Glacier National Park, but hardly a major one. Most of the tourists come out of South Dakota, headed for Yellowstone on Interstate 30, after they've seen the big sculptures of presidents at Mount Rushmore, and stopped by Deadwood to look at Wild Bill Hickok's last hand—aces and eights, the story has it—and maybe a peek at the mines in Lead—pronounced "lede"—and then off west to the Battle of the Little Big Horn and roll on to Old Faithful. But if you do come up from the south, from Miles City, you get a whole different outlook on what it means to say, "There are too many people here."

There isn't much between Miles City and Jordan, the village from which my mother escaped in 1928, and there's a hell of a lot less afterward, moving north to the dam. There's a little museum in Jordan, run by the Garfield County Historical Society. One of its main attractions is the one-room school my mother attended, built in 1910, when there was no legal entity called Jordan, not even a Garfield County, just a rural school district. Montana has about five times as many counties as it needs, local pride overwhelming common sense, and every dirt farmer wanting his own, convenient county seat. The other attractions are some dinosaur bones, all from the Big Dry Creek beds, and a collection of pioneer furniture. There are two kinds of pioneer furniture, the stuff you save and the stuff you throw away the minute you get a chance, so, of course, the museum gives a somewhat inflated view of pioneers, most of the furniture being solid Victorian stuff that would bring good prices in an East Coast antique store. And there's one coffee shop and two barrooms, in either one of which, on any day of any year, you can listen to complaints about the low price of wheat and the general cussedness of the weather.

As you come out of Jordan, headed east again on State Highway 200, civilization as you know it begins to peter out. At the turnoff to Fort Peck, where you would head north on State 24 to see the dam, there's a small roadside rest, built next to the Highway Department section garage. It has the usual amenities: a drinking fountain, toilets, a couple of tattered shade trees, and some picnic benches. A big faded black-on-white sign encourages you to make a detour "just an hour north" to see "Fort Peck Dam, One of the Civil Engineering Monuments of America and the World's Largest Earth Filled Dam." It is neither a monument nor the largest, and the sign is a mixture of typical Montana boastfulness and outdated information. I don't know if anyone ever actually takes the advice— an hour's detour isn't much—but, as you go by the sign, you're just halfway between Jordan, where no one ever went for the scenery, and Richey, which doesn't even have a pioneer museum. The only reason anyone ever goes down Montana 200 is to cut a straighter line across Montana than the Interstates provide, and detours are unlikely events when even gas stations are a hundred miles apart.

Up from Miles City, all the way on 24, is exactly the right way to go. For the hints of population and progress that seemed likely to disappear will do exactly that, evaporate on Highway 24 halfway to the dam.

The first to go are the electric wires, and with their poles gone, the telephone dives underground, buried next to the cattle fence, marked every half-mile by a solitary post where the cable comes up out of the ground so the linemen can check it. And then the fence disappears, and the highway rolls on without any boundary except the drainage ditches and a few green weeds growing just at the edge of the asphalt and in the bottom of the ditches. What little rain falls is effectively multiplied as it drains off the crown of the macadam, and small green plants flourish where the asphalt meets the dirt—annual sunflowers, mostly. There the deer and the antelope play. It is not pure wilderness. Occasional strips of flat land—we call them "benches"—are planted with winter wheat; every few miles a dirt road takes off east or west; sometimes a tin-roofed barn twinkles in a distant coulee. And three times, the tall steel towers of a Rural Electric Agency line cut across the highway at an angle, headed for an isolated ranch house.

Cars and pickup trucks appear suddenly in a visitor's rearview mirror, pass, and disappear as quickly over the next roll in the road. The speed limit is optional, in Montana. This is what the country looked like when my parents were growing up, save only the tar on the road and the electric lines. The telephone ran through the barbed wire, not part of the Bell system, just battery-powered, hand-cranked, home-made telephone party lines, one end at the livery stable in town, and magneto and battery telephones in the houses, out there on the wire.

My grandfather sent his five sons, usually two at a time, out to his small ranch near Chinook, to keep the stock alive over the worst of the winter. This would mean missing most of a school year, but they were smart boys. One was my uncle Gordon, who became, by a natural affinity for conversation that was unique in the family, its unofficial historian. He could describe the barbed-wire telephone in some detail, being a graduate electrical engineer. But what he liked to do more was talk about the party line. When the boys were lonely, they'd just listen on the line, and Mrs. MacLean, who lived on the line, would come on every evening. She'd crank up her Edison record player, and play them a song, over the wire, so that they wouldn't be too lonely. My uncle Mac was particularly fond of listening to the music. Gordon couldn't remember the names of any of the tunes. This is not uncommon in our family: I've heard us all sing hymns or whistle, and none of us could ever carry a tune.

Highway 24 heads more or less perfectly north. That's true north, not magnetic north, because it, like so many roads from Ohio to Oregon, is laid out to surveyors' standards, what country people call "section roads" whether or not they happen to mark the boundary of a land-grant section of 640 acres—one square mile, one thirty-sixth of a township. East-west section roads can run forever, but north-south roads have to be readjusted periodically, because the lines of true north converge at the pole. If two men started surveying due north, one from, say, Detroit and the other from Chicago, they would be approaching each other as they worked north across Canada, and, somewhere just south of the North Pole, one would see the other come over the horizon as they neared their meeting place at the top of the world. The surveyors have to make offset sections, compromising the reality of a square mile with the inevitable tendency of the north-south lines to approach each other. This convergence explains the presence of jogs in the road unforced by any natural feature as the surveyor makes his offset. Townships are laid out on a central north-south line and then measured out to the edges, and if there's a road on the central line, it is usually called Meridian Road. The most accurately gridded city in the world is Wichita, Kansas, which was laid out in one year, before anyone really moved there, just after the Native Americans had been relocated, and which has no major geographical features to alter the orderly tessellation of its city blocks.

The highway to Fort Peck does reel a little off pure north, skirting bluffs and benches, and then, as it approaches the oxbow of the Missouri, curves abruptly west to align itself with the east-west direction of the dam. The sweeping curve, rather than any road sign, alerts the northbound driver that he is participating in some major geographical event, and as the automobile comes out of the curve, the white concrete structure of the Fort Peck spillway glistens in the distance. At night, it is lighted with the first streetlights in sixty miles.

Most visitors from the south assume that the spillway, which carries the highway on its segmented columns, is the dam itself. We have a general concept, an archetype of a dam, in our mind. Dams bridge narrow gaps, are made of concrete, and are broad enough to support a two-lane highway. Spillways are usually built directly onto concrete dams, at one side or the other, where they can discharge excess water without damage to the structure. With an earth-filled dam, where a rush of water near the dam would erode it, one builds a separate and distant drainage to escort water safely around the softer material of the dam itself. It is this ancillary spillway structure, photographed in its half-completed state, that makes up the cover of the first *Life* magazine, published on October 23, 1936.

Visitors coming down to Fort Peck from the north, from Glasgow and U.S. 2, usually drive across the earth dam without realizing that they are motoring on the marvel of civil engineering that the state of Montana has encouraged them to visit. The countryside about the Missouri River is transected with glacial ridges, old bench-lines of the vanished inland sea, and the low earth dam seems to grow out of the landscape organically. One moment you are traversing the desert prairie, and the next moment there is impounded water on your right. In the distance (the earth dam is three miles long) rise the towers of the hydroelectric plant, and the more distant spillway is hidden from view by one of the larger glacial ridges. If you happen to be standing at the roadside, atop the dam, a motorist may stop and ask you for directions to the great structure, which has somehow been penciled-in on a vacation itinerary. A woman from Alberta, traveling alone with her pre-adolescent son, seemed perturbed, either that the dam was so unspectacular or because she had missed it. I directed her to the power-station visitor center, hoping that the dinosaur museum would make the detour worth her, and her son's, while. The dam itself, huge but earth-hugging, only slightly more regular than the geological benches it imitates, is probably more interesting viewed from space, along with other perturbations of the earth—meteor craters or earthquake fault lines.

The town of Fort Peck, with its remnants of the great years of construction, lies downstream from the dam, on the Glasgow side of the Missouri River. The town attracts few tourists, although it does gather in local residents for summer events: the Eastern Montana Fast-Pitch Softball Tournament and the summer theater season, when plays of an elevating or amusing character are performed in the old movie-and-stage building that was constructed in 1934 to provide what is now called "family entertainment" for the construction workers. Indigenous Montana entertainment, in 1934, consisted almost entirely of poker, paid sex, and whiskey by the drink, all three of which were illegal but hardly unavailable. Drinking is still popular, and there are electronic poker machines in all of the barrooms. Prostitution seems to have gone the way of the sexual revolution, or else there just isn't a large enough population, any more, to support it.

The theater is on the National Register of Historic Places, as one of the finest remaining examples of what is called American Craft Movement Chalet Style. They tried playing *Death of a Salesman* in the early 1980s, but no one came. People in Montana have troubles of their own, and they like musicals, comedies, and pretty girls in bright costumes.

The entire planned city was the creation of Henry Tanner, a Kansas City architect who had, like most of the residents of his city, gone bust once or twice in the Depression and ended up working for the Army Corps of Engineers. He is famous in the world of architecture not for Fort Peck, but for designing the Country Club development in Kansas City, which featured the first automobile-oriented shopping mall in the history of creation. It was not a suburban roadway mall. It was really just a shopping court, off a main street, but with parking for a couple of dozen cars. At that, it was a revolution in the American consciousness, for it assumed the right and duty of everyone was to drive to the store. Fort Peck was also automobile-oriented: each of the houses had a garage, although electrified ones were a privilege restricted to the twelve regular-army officers who lived in the dozen permanent houses.

Henry Tanner never got any real national publicity for his town planning. Indeed, it was the growth of the boom towns around Fort Peck City that got the attention; of these, Wheeler was the kingpin. It boasted paved roads, its own deputized sheriff's department, a municipal light plant, and the Riding Academy, which had nothing to do with horses and would, by a quirk of journalism, make Fort Peck Dam famous.

3

Bear Paw Country

Fort Peck City, my hometown, has the odd distinction of being the first planned community in the United States, discounting only such exotic places as military reservations or small religious settlements. Outsiders, thanks to Western novels and travel literature, tend to be mildly interested if they ask you where you were born and the answer is "Montana." They imagine we were all born within shouting distance of Old Faithful, or else on a cattle ranch. But some of us were born in government project housing, and most of the rest of us in small towns and inconsiderable cities, and have no values, habits, or attitudes that distinguish us from other Americans. Except one, which is that we might just be one generation behind the general trend. The last time I was home, you could get a glass of white wine in a hotel barroom, but I drove eight hundred miles without seeing a bottle of Perrier.

Fort Peck City, like the dam itself and the spillway, was drawn first and then built. Every detail of the community was as firmly fixed on paper as the geometry of the dam, before a shovelful was turned. Everything, all the way from street plans to such fine details as the cupola on the movie theater, was sketched, approved, and blue-lined by architects in the Kansas City, Missouri, office of the Army Corps of Engineers. Like housing built a dozen years later, after the war, the town was mass-produced, but with variations in external decoration to create the illusion of variety. The streets were curved, not rectilinear, to give an impression of spontaneity and to conform somewhat to the contours of the landscape. Today there's just enough of it left—a dozen homes and another dozen public buildings, and scattered buildings moved off the township site—to preserve the inspiration of this War Department version of the American dream.

My father's house was one of 280 temporary single-family dwellings. Every one of them is gone now, many hauled off the townsite and turned into utility buildings on the scattered ranches of Valley County and McCone County, to the south of the Missouri. Montana ranchers, having a surplus of space and a minimum of cash, never throw anything away, and collect anything that's not tied down. What once were homes have become chicken coops, tool sheds, and bunkhouses. On the two-lane state highway, just at the turnoff to Fort Peck, a small motel is composed entirely of old temporary houses, with their steeply pitched roofs and small, false dormered windows in the imaginary second story. The effect is of a set of miniature Swiss chalets that got lost.

Over in the town itself, the Swiss-chalet motif, mixed with some carpenter's-Gothic details, sets the style for the employees' hotel (still in business), the movie theater (now used for a summer-stock theater) that once showed movies twenty-four hours a day, catering to the laborers who worked three shifts all summer and most of the winter. Carpenter's Gothic decorates the old hospital (divided into apartments), the Lutheran church, and the town recreation hall. All these buildings look as if they've been picked up out of a well-wooded mountain resort and dropped, quite by accident, on a dry and barren plain. Besides these public spaces, a dozen permanent houses survive from the 1930s, built then for the army officers who managed the dam's construction, and still occupied by some of the Corps of Engineers employees who maintain the dam. These are designed in a style officially designated by the National Register of Historic Places as Cottage Picturesque. The picturesque part is a series of veneers applied to the street-facing sides of the two-story cottages. Each is different, unlike the temporaries. One has round cobbles mortared together, another dressed field stones, a third is brick, a fourth has exposed wood and stucco in the Queen Anne style.

The other remaining structure from the 1930s is a stolid two-story office with concrete walls and a tile roof, the Administration Building. Even here, the architect had the opportunity for minor detailing, for subtle additions that make it different from cheaper, modern construction. The exterior wooden forms were made of sandblasted tongue-and-groove boards, so that the grain of the wood is permanently captured in bas-relief on the concrete, and the grooves provide a series of parallel extruded lines that break up the smooth surface of the concrete. The effect—the grain and the bands of the grooves—is a way of denying that the building is simply concrete, by creating the illusion, a sort of physical memory, of the wooden forms.

In the full and commodious basement of the headquarters are the historical files of Fort Peck, as collected by the local office of the Corps of Engineers, plus a few rooms occupied by the offices of the Geodetic Survey and the Bureau of Reclamation.

When I told my mother that I would be visiting Fort Peck, I asked her if she could remember the street address of our house. She was not sure about the number but was quite clear about one thing: "It was on West Kansas," she said, "which was in the better part of town." That was the first, and so far the last, good thing I ever heard about Fort Peck from my mother.

It was also true. There were then, and are now, only a couple of dozen houses on that side of town. If you take the hotel and the Administration Building on two sides of the large grassy common as the center of town, East Kansas and West Kansas are somehow on the right side of the tracks. East Kansas was officer country, where the twelve permanent houses still stand. West Kansas had fifteen of the temporary houses, but they had endless back yards and were set much farther apart than the other 265 temporaries over on the other side of town. From a town planner's point of view, the permanent officers' houses had the best view, toward the river and the dam being built across it. The view from West Kansas, on the architect's plot plan, should have been of bare and endless rolling prairie. Perhaps, from the perspective of Kansas City, that landscape would be covered with purple sage and bathed each evening in the glow of the setting sun.

Recently, following a directive of President Reagan's Office of Management and Budget, federal towns like Fort Peck and the others built near other dams downstream on the Missouri are being reorganized into proper private-property villages. The residents, instead of paying rent, are being offered a chance to buy their government-built houses and join the mainstream. Most of the houses in Fort Peck were sold within two years, but there were, the last time I was there, five in a row that didn't sell, all on West Kansas, including the site of our old house at 1137. The reason is pretty obvious. There's nothing between West Kansas Street and the North Pole, and the winter wind blows directly on the front doors and living-room windows, howling down from Alberta, off to the northwest. And the afternoon summer sun beats on the same front doors and windows. It truly was the better part of town, but only as drawn in Kansas City.

West Kansas had other problems, as a neighborhood, back in the 1930s. The trouble with planned communities is that they have neighbors outside the pale, and the actual view from West Kansas was toward the most notorious of all possible neighborhoods.

When money for Fort Peck was authorized by the Public Works Administration in 1933, the Corps of Engineers envisioned a city occupied by older professionals, mostly civil engineers and other experts, and a large labor force composed of local residents and of unmarried or unaccompanied construction workers. The original town plan had called for vast dormitories where itinerant or single workers would be housed. That was not to be the case, for federal planning ran into state regulations.

Of all the possible sites where the Corps of Engineers could have spent money in the Missouri River Basin, from Kansas up through the Dakotas to Montana, Fort Peck was chosen as a favor to Montana's senior senator, Democrat Burton K. Wheeler, a staunch ally of any New Deal scheme to increase employment. But Wheeler also insisted that preference in hiring at Fort Peck be given to Montana residents. And Montana law, as it was applied to hiring for public-works projects, required that heads of families be given preference over single men.

So it was that more than two thousand married eastern-Montana dirt farmers who had never built anything larger than a barn or dug anything deeper than a well were hired to build the largest earthen dam in the history of the world. Local workers commuted, carpooling from Glasgow and Nashua, the only settled towns in the area, but the rest moved into shantytowns around Fort Peck City, the largest taking the name of the Senator who had brought them work, Wheeler. From 1137 West Kansas Street, you could see the lights of Wheeler glimmering above the eastern abutment of the dam. At the time of peak employment—the winter of 1938—Wheeler had 498 houses, eighty-three business buildings, two schools, and its own electric-light plant. It was nearly twice the size of Fort Peck City—and considerably livelier. Wheeler, you see, had all the whorehouses and most of the saloons. Across the highway from Wheeler lay New Deal—274 houses, twenty-one businesses, two schools, but no electricity. Park Grove, below the dam, had 278 houses, four schools, eighteen businesses, and a small diesel-powered electric generator. Across the river, near the spillway construction site, rose the town of McCone, in the county of McCone, perhaps the most desperate of all the boom towns, with just one barroom, one gas station, and one store. All told, almost fifteen hundred tar-papered, board-and-batten houses were scattered outside the more pristine confines of Fort Peck City, and they attracted more attention than the orderly government town.

Raw landscape, except to a geologist, has no significance. But if you wish to imagine the banks of the Missouri River studded with appalling hovels and also with orderly town streets, the riverbed and the benches near the river swarming with men and machinery, your vision of this place will be clarified by knowing the geography in some detail. Then, as you understand the lay of the land, certain events still unrelated will be apprehended in their real significance.

First, the Missouri River. Its headwaters, the Gallatin, Madison, and Jefferson rivers, rise in the Rocky Mountains north of Yellowstone Park and merge at the town of Three Forks; its principal tributaries below that are the Smith, the Judith, and the Musselshell. Below Fort Peck, the Milk and then the Yellowstone rivers join the main stream. West of the dam, the drainage area is 57,725 square miles, approximately one-third of the state of Montana. The Missouri is subject to great extremes of flooding—a mixed blessing that periodically destroyed riverside settlements but also created silted bottomlands, which are great producers of crops, particularly alfalfa and grains, in ordinary years.

The average flow of water at Fort Peck is 9,500 cubic feet per second, an ungainly measurement not meaningful to the average citizen. It translates into some 42 million gallons of water a minute. A typical garden hose delivers something on the order of 4.2 gallons per minute, so, if the trivial appeals to you, think of 10 million garden hoses all running at once. The river's maximum at spring flood rises to 685 million gallons a minute, or 163 million garden hoses.

The high plains of eastern Montana are composed largely of sedimentary rocks, and geologically rather young and soft ones—sandstones and shales. The land is somewhat folded and contorted, but upthrusts of completely metamorphosed and very hard material are widely scattered. The Missouri cuts and then tumbles most of its river bottom into sand and mud. To finish the dam, real rock, in the form of gravel and field boulders, was brought in ninety miles by Great Northern Railroad and a spur line from Cole, Montana. Quarried granite riprap for the dam's upstream face, placed to keep wave action and ice from eroding the soft-earth fill of the structure, was hauled 130 miles from Rattlesnake Butte, near the Canadian border, north of Harlem, Montana. The bulk of the dam itself could be, and was, found within ten miles of the dam, in the riverbed and ancient floodplain, both upstream and down. It was judged, at the time, to be adequate soil for construction.

With its sedimentary rocks covered only occasionally by deep beds of glacial till, eastern Montana is excellent country for hunting dinosaurs. When Barnum Brown arrived at the turn of the century to collect for the American Museum of Natural History, he rode horseback from Big Dry Creek down in Garfield County to the Missouri's bank in McCone County. He started, incidentally, just a few miles from my maternal grandfather's homestead. And while riding, looking for fossil-bearing outcrops, Barnum Brown counted 150 triceratops fossils in one day; the great three-horned skulls, poking out of the wind-eroded benchland, required no closer inspection than a glance from horseback for positive identification.

The Missouri drops slowly, cutting across this reasonably level plain, averaging just a foot of descent per mile. As slow-moving rivers will do, it cuts great loops across the land—oxbows, they're called, from the open oval shape of the wooden yokes of ox teams. Often, the river will cut back a straight line across the loop after an eon or two, making it an even more accurate representation of the oxbow, which has a removable spline that runs underneath the beast's neck to hold the yoke down on its shoulders. Fort Peck is on a great oxbow. The eastward-trending river makes a loop that runs due north, turns east and then south, back to the west-to-east general direction of the water's course. The site chosen for the dam is just as the river turns north, so that the dam itself runs east-west, parallel to the overall direction of the river. Fort Peck City, and thirteen of the fifteen shantytowns around the dam, are on the north and west side of the curving river; only two small ones are on the south and east side, enclosed within the oxbow. North and west also are the nearest permanent towns, Glasgow and Nashua, and the nearest railhead. To the south and east, there is nothing but a hundred miles of desolation, dinosaur bones, scattered ranches, and the hamlet of Jordan, halfway to Miles City.

If you were to draw a straight west-to-east line across the bottom of the oxbow, where the river would have run had it not meandered, you would be marking the path of an existing shallow depression, a gap in the rolling hills. Through this natural gap, which is almost certainly an old riverbed, the Corps of Engineers built a side channel, the flood-relieving spillway, which, as I told you, most everyone mistakes for the dam itself.

Of the local geography, then, remember that the dam runs east and west, and that Fort Peck, the administrative offices, and nearly all the employees are on the west side; of the geology, understand that the available material dredged up and poured in place to make the dam is a mixture of Missouri River mud and sand, the mud a fine and flocculent material mixed with sand and a little gravel, easy to dredge, excellent for making a solid and impervious embankment, but slow to drain its natural water, slow to set up, slow to firm into the world's largest hydraulically filled dam.

It used to be the world's largest *earth*-filled dam, when I was a child. Then the Russians built a bigger one, and now the Pakistanis have finished one even bigger. But it remains the largest pile of earth ever dredged, ever moved by pumping water, and, because of the difficulty of controlling the quality of a hydraulic dam, it will never be surpassed. It is not always the case that when we say, "They don't make them like that any more," we are lamenting a golden age of manufacture. No engineer in his right mind would suggest a hydraulic-fill dam in this day and age. Indeed, the very difficulties of properly constructing the Fort Peck Dam by the dredging method almost destroyed the project, took eight lives, and preyed on the minds of those civil engineers who believed, after the disaster, that it could and should have been prevented. It is precisely so that you can understand this calamity that I must write so much about dirt and rock and mud and sand, so that it is as palpable to the reader as it was to the dam builders.

That it was such a massive dam is something I knew as early in life as almost any bit of what in the late twentieth century we call "trivia." My father, who, I must say, was not given to casual conversation, did on occasion try to enter into my patently childish world. One of the books we owned, and the one I adored above all others at the age of twelve, was an adventure book by someone named Richard Halliburton. As far as I knew then, it had just been written, although a more adult understanding of it would have dated it accurately as a product of the 1920s. It was called *The Royal Road to Romance*, and included a picture of Mr. Halliburton standing on his head in front of Cheops' pyramid. I envied anyone who could stand on his head, and practiced frequently, with some minor success, in case I should ever get the opportunity to have my picture taken in front of one of the Seven Wonders of the World. Mr. Halliburton had his picture taken in front of most of the remaining Wonders of the World (ancient and otherwise). One of the most vividly recalled of the infrequent short conversations I had with my father concerned this book, or some idle chatter about it. Somehow the subject of Wonders of the World came up, probably in regards to Cheops' pyramid, and my father said: "The Chicago sewage system is one of the Seven Civil Engineering Wonders of the World. They made the Chicago River run backward." My father liked to include factual material in our conversations. After a pause, he added, "The Fort Peck Dam isn't."

And I said: "Why should it be?"

"Because it's the largest earth-filled dam in the world."

And I said: "Oh."

It has never even made the list of National Historic Civil Engineering Sites, which are a considerable cut beneath the Seven Civil Engineering Wonders. This is probably because of its location in a state of low employment, civil engineering or otherwise: the Historic Sites are voted on by the membership of the American Society of Civil Engineers. And it may be, in part, because it was not very cleverly designed or technically difficult to construct, although it is very large. And since the dam proper contains no Portland cement or structural steel, it gets no support from the cement lobby or steel manufacturers.

Besides Chicago's famous sewerage system, the other six Civil Engineering Wonders are the Colorado River Aqueduct, the Empire State Building, the Grand Coulee Dam and its associated Columbia Basin Project, the Hoover Dam, the San Francisco–Oakland Bay Bridge (not to be confused with the Golden Gate Bridge), and the Panama Canal. When you consider what else is missing from the list, I suspect my father was wrong to believe Fort Peck was a Civil Engineering Wonder. The dam is no more marvelous than the unlisted Brooklyn Bridge, or as useful as the honored Colorado River Aqueduct, without which there simply is no southern California. It is only a Montana Historic Civil Engineering Site.

In addition to the highly visible spillway structure southeast of the dam itself, visitors are attracted to the two tall towers that house water-driven electrical generators. The first one constructed is in the Art Deco style, as much as possible, including the sans-serif stainless-steel signwork and the metal cupola that tops the tower. In the base of this one, completed in 1943, a small museum of the geology and paleontology of the Fort Peck country is housed in a cool room, artificially lighted, buried well within the massive concrete structure. The generating building, solid as it is, emits a faint background rumble, somewhere at the bottom pitch of sound audible to the human ear, a noise as much felt as heard. This sound or feeling is caused by the slight eccentricity of the almost perfectly balanced generators, spinning in the outflow of the reservoir, turning the Missouri River into electricity. There are no gophers and no rattlesnakes near the generator, in what was once McCone City. Take it on faith if you must, but I tell you, it is the only part of the high plains lacking gophers or rattlers. The local residents attribute their absence to the constant, not-quite-audible noise from the electric generators.

In the center of the room stands a square table enclosed in a cube of glass, and on top of the table is a lovingly re-created bit of Montana more fragile than any National Parkland, longer-gone and less likely to return than the free-ranging buffalo herds. It is a triceratops skull poking up out of delicately arranged sand and sagebrush, gravel and bunchgrass, the three horn-bases, one shattered, pointing toward the sky. It is just what Barnum Brown saw from horseback, riding toward the Missouri from the general direction of Sand Springs, down in Garfield County, where the Big Dry Creek, the seasonal washed-out riverbed, cuts through the Cretaceous sediments. There are no more triceratops skulls lying out there, where the wind and the small rains and the windblown sand had cut away the soft rock and left the hard and mineralized bones. There are too many collectors now, too many four-wheel-drive vehicles, too many people who will pick up anything curious-looking, or break off a piece of the past to put in the back yard, by the barbecue grill.

The other display cases show fine things, but objects more typical of any small paleontology museum. What is unusual is that so much varied material could be picked up in a single part of the country, in the confines of the Fort Peck Dam and Spillway. The fossil record does illuminate, I think inadvertently, certain aspects of the construction of the dam, especially the difficulty of finding a firm foundation and a satisfactory building material. Most of the fossils are of marine animals and plants, for this part of Montana was once an often submerged, sometimes reappearing continental shelf beneath a great tongue of the ocean that ran north from what remains as the Gulf of Mexico, bisecting the old North American continent. West of this inland sea, in dinosaur time, the Rocky

Mountains were just beginning to rise, off in the direction of Yellowstone Park and the arid volcanic ground that is Idaho. So there are such oddities as lobsters the size of motorcycles, sharks great and small, seashells, the cemented bits of sea fans and coral reefs and great-chambered-nautilus shells as big as automobile tires.

But it was not always ocean, and before the great extinction of the dinosaurs some sixty million years ago, it was sometimes dry land. One eon it was beach, and then it became ocean again, and dried up after that, as the ocean rose and fell. What we call "benches" in this part of the country are often the petrified remnants of gently sloping beaches between the dunelands (now also petrified into sandstone cliffs) and the deep-water sediments now transmuted into shales and clays. The largest skeleton of the tyrannosaurus ever found was taken from these sparse soils at Hell Creek, a tributary of the Missouri just northwest of the dam site. Dozens of smaller carnivores—the jackals and hyenas of the age of dinosaurs—are buried here. These smaller ones are various sizes of dromeaosaurs, and their teeth are scattered through the sands and gravels, as are those of the sea-dwelling sharks and crocodilians.

After the dinosaurs began to disappear, perhaps affected by the same shifting world, the tongue of the ocean dried, and there were fifty or sixty million years of high plains; the teeth and the bones changed from reptilian to mammalian—woolly mammoths and dawn horses, long-extinct rhinoceroses, all grazers and browsers. In other parts of North America, great and monstrous changes in the landscape were commonplace, sediments were buried, stacked, folded, contorted, metamorphosed, and sometimes planed away by glaciers or thrust up by growing mountains thousands of feet above their original layment—by such means are incongruous corals and seashells found on mountain peaks. But eastern Montana tended to lie where it had been deposited, less changed by the passage of sixty million years and the gradual movement of the continent than other, equally northern lands. Wisconsin, for example, either is all ancient bedrock and glacial till, scraped clean a dozen times by advancing and retreating glaciers, or is ten-thousand-year-old post-glacial soil; there is no middle ground in Wisconsin. About Fort Peck, to the contrary, when my mother was a girl, triceratops skulls gleamed in the sunlight.

The old ocean bed, there for the longest of all imaginable and discoverable times, produced the greatest volume of eastern Montana's geological layers. Not by itself, not by the process of depositing hundreds of feet of plankton skeletons (as the ocean makes limestones), not so actively did the old ocean make the soil of Fort Peck, but more passively. Classic ocean sediments, besides the calcareous limestones, are shales and sandstones, created by the flow of water from dry land bringing simple mud into the ocean, as it does in the deltas of great rivers. When these seasonal floods are petrified, they become sandstones and, most particularly, the layered and splittable shalestones of commerce, roofing shales and flagstones and bluestones—the stuff of landscape designs and New England roofs.

But much of eastern Montana's ocean sediment does not have that layered look, caused by the annual deposition in time of spring floods, nor do they have the gradation produced by flowing rivers that deposit the largest material near the shoreline in gravel conglomerates and sandstones and then carry the finer materials farther to sea to become shales—as one can see in the muddy plume of the Mississippi, carrying would-be shale deep into the Gulf of Mexico. Not here. To the west, a part of the continental plate buckled and slid underneath the surface, creating volcanoes, and much of the sediment of the old ocean is volcanic ash, blown out of massive volcanoes that arose near what are now the Rocky Mountains and Yellowstone Park.

All those volcanoes are long gone, ground back under the earth by the same diving plate that created them. The ones still visible were created as the subsiding plate moved westward—the extinct volcanoes of Idaho and eastern Washington, the still-active volcanoes of the Cascades, including Mount Saint Helens, the Washington volcano that astonished America by depositing a few inches of ash on distant cities just a few years ago. Its ashes were carried eastward by the prevailing westerlies, the same winds that blew 60 million years ago.

The calderas (from the Spanish word for "kettle") left after the final explosion and collapse of the western volcanoes make adjoining, sometimes overlapping, circles, easily visible by a passenger aboard any airplane travelling from Bozeman or Billings toward Salt Lake City or Seattle. Some are dozens of miles in diameter, and make the partial blowout of Mount Saint Helens look like a pimple by comparison. Yellowstone Park is in such a caldera, but a very recent one, two or three million years old, a caprice of nature that sprang up after the front line of fiery mountains had moved three hundred miles westward to the shores of the Pacific Ocean. Driving into Yellowstone, you do not recognize the encircling mountains for what they are, the jagged teeth of a blown-out volcano. They are eroded, weathered ("spalled," as construction men say of aging concrete), covered with vegetation, softened by running water and wind.

Humankind has never experienced volcanic explosions like the ones that filled eastern Montana with ash. In modern times, fabled Krakatoa, the great volcano near Java, killed thirty thousand souls outright when it blew in 1883. Fire and ash took some lives, the rest were drowned in tidal waves fifteen feet high. Krakatoa changed the weather of the world for a decade, which makes it the prime parameter for calculating any dust-caused postnuclear winter. It created the blizzards of 1888, the year of no summer. But you could stack entire Krakatoas in the old Montana calderas the way you put apples in a basket.

So, then, for a few million years, at the end of the age of dinosaurs and in the age of their declining, the western volcanoes spewed ash day and night and blew apart most horribly, showering the eastward plains and the east-lying inland sea with the finest of small-particled ash. Two particular mineral formations resulted— one found in great volume, the other more scattered and, like most rarer things, more valuable. Both derive their names from the type-place where they were first collected, both Montana names. Taken together, these minerals caused most of the difficulty in building the Fort Peck Dam, and when culprits were required to explain certain catastrophes yet to be related, these two conglomerations of ancient volcanic ejecta took all the official blame.

Bentonite is the rarer material, named after Fort Benton, near Great Falls, a few hundred miles west and upstream from Fort Peck. Fort Benton is the head of all possible navigation, even by flat-bottomed riverboat, on the Missouri River, and so it was the westernmost outpost, the first place where furs could be transferred from horseback to raft and riverboat to be carried down to the fur sales in Saint Louis. Bentonite is a white material, usually found in thin seams between other sediments, and it is composed of an extraordinarily fine, crystalline ash rarely ejected by volcanoes. It is the perfect raw material for manufacturing drilling mud, and wherever it can be found near the surface in reasonably thick seams, and whenever American oil and natural-gas exploration activity is high, it will be mined. Mixed with water, bentonite makes a slurry of extraordinary slipperiness, and serves to lubricate and cool the drill head and, as a dense but liquid matter, to float the drilling debris upward and out of the drill hole, much as another very heavy liquid—mercury—will cause lighter metals and minerals to float to the top. It is all specific gravity and permeability, and bentonite drilling mud is very densely heavy and very permeable. All mud, by definition, is such fine dirt that it becomes greasy when wet, and bentonite is the slickest dirt in the world.

The seams of bentonite in eastern Montana permeate a larger class of volcanic silts—shales and slates. Dried mud is not a rock, to put it in simple but hardly trivial terms. Becoming a rock requires heat and pressure and time; the heat is created by the pressure of overlying rock and soil, and the time is unimaginable millions of years. The most characteristic and problematic shale in the area of Fort Peck is called Bear Paw shale, after the isolated small mountain range that pokes up out of the plains just south of Chinook, in the center of the big Blackfoot reservation named Fort Belknap. The Bear Paws are high enough to trap some cool air and rainwater, and there are pine trees and small brooks with trout in them, two biota wholly unknown a few thousand feet below, where it's all cottonwood, catfish, and buffalo carp. If shales are by definition a rock, Bear Paw shale is misnamed. It is the youngest of the massive banks of volcanic sediment, the last layer applied to the floor of the old inland ocean, and very slightly buried by later windblown dunes become sandstones, and by shallow loess soils. So lightly covered was it that no great pressure and thus no serious heat were applied to it.

In large measure, Fort Peck Dam sits on Bear Paw shale, and the enormous concrete spillway is cut through it. It is a desperately difficult foundation. It was also invisible, if not unknown, when the dam site was first casually surveyed in 1933, for it either was completely buried under the rubble of the Missouri River's old floodplains or had disguised itself. Say, rather, it was transmuted, for whatever rocklike qualities Bear Paw shale possesses, it loses them rapidly on exposure to open air. As I say, it is hardly a rock at all, but more of a plastic material, still containing a residue of the ancient ocean in which it was deposited, more glued together than truly petrified; and the glue, improbably, is water.

Dug from the earth that has covered it these last sixty or seventy million years, Bear Paw shale is hard but penetrable, like dried-up schoolroom modeling clay or a bed of soft coal. Left out to dry for even an hour, or overnight, a chunk of Bear Paw shale will harden perceptibly, with a glazed and cracked surface, lightly dusted with a fine ashen coating. It seems to have improved, to have hardened, to be more of a rock, but if you drop this newly dried, hard lump into a glass of ordinary tap water, it crumbles instantly; if you reach into the glass and feel the shale, it slips between your fingers, more a lubricant than a bit of earth. The simple act of dehydrating and then rehydrating the shale is thoroughly destructive. Outcrops of Bear Paw, exposed by running rivers or glaciation or wind, simply erode back into the land until something collapses over them and covers them again. The engineers at Fort Peck found ways to deal with the Bear Paw shale;

they learned to cope with it, to protect it, to build on it; but they never trusted it or admired it.

Bear Paw shale caused a number of deaths at Fort Peck. Although it appears, when cut into by machinery, to be a solid mass, it is faulted with microscopic cracks and planes of shearing, and workmen on two or three occasions were simply crushed when a solid-looking wall of shale "calved," like an iceberg falling off a glacier. Those are the deaths recorded in the official papers of the Corps of Engineers. By far the larger number of deaths, not recorded as work-related, were caused by tunneling operations in the Bear Paw. Beneath the dam itself run four outlet tunnels, two of which provide heads of water to the electrical turbines, the other two being simple drains, or outlets, to remove stored floodwater and return it to the river. All four tunnels, each a mile long, were cut through the Bear Paw, using modified coal-saws. Although the shale is imperceptibly fine, when ground up it is abrasive, and the common cause of death was what the nurses in the Glasgow hospital came to call "tunnel pneumonia." The tunnel miners, with lungs already distressed by coal mining or hard-rock mining, would contract a pneumonia—this was years before penicillin or useful sulfa drugs had been developed—check into the hospital, and be dead in twenty-four hours. Ordinary pneumonia patients took a few days, sometimes a week, to die.

Geology, I wanted you to know, is not a science without human consequences.

4

Notes on Engineers, Politicians, and Cost-Benefit Thinking

The primary function of the Fort Peck Dam, after you scrape away all of the official explanations, was to keep Franklin Delano Roosevelt on the good side of Senator Burton K. Wheeler, Democrat of Montana, who had been a staunch supporter of every early New Deal program. That the dam made it possible for my parents to afford two children, of which I am the second, is of no historical importance, except as Mary Lorraine Montgomery (born 1936) and the author (born 1938) are exemplary of several hundred eastern-Montana children born to parents

who because of the dam could afford at least minimal medical care
and baby food, right there smack in the middle of the most depressed
countryside in the most tendentious years of the Great Depression.

The Works Progress Administration was the source of the funds,
as it was for flood control and irrigation dams throughout the South
and Far West, as well as everything from improved roads to high-
school gymnasiums and even music auditoriums. How the dam
happened to come to Montana, besides the desire of the President
to cosset Senator Wheeler, is a story that begins with a political
organization in the state of Iowa, that rich farmland on the east
bank of the Missouri River, hundreds of miles downstream from
Fort Peck. Iowa farmers wanted the advantages of stable river
levels, which would allow them to plow and plant on the ordinarily
dry, rich ground of the maximum floodplain of the Missouri, these
being benched and terraced bottomlands flooded only in years of
maximum runoff. However, in those days, the Army Corps of Engineers was not interested in, was not congressionally charged with,
agricultural considerations. Its business—and in this it was a fore-
runner of the Department of Defense's Interstate Highway Program—was to provide navigable rivers for the transportation of
foodstuffs and military equipment in times of national emergency.

So it was with a small eye on cheap barge transportation and a
wide-open eye on flood control that the Missouri River Navigation
Association of Sioux City, Iowa, organized ten thousand Midwestern farmers into a lobby dedicated to building a major dam
somewhere high above them on the river. It was a questionable
deal, and would have seemed so then if it could have been seen
from some yet unimagined orbiting satellite. Approximately a
quarter-million acres of downstream farmland in Nebraska and
Iowa would be spared occasional flooding, while a quarter-million
acres of Montana bottomland would be inundated for all eternity,
or until the dam broke, whichever came first.

This project was to be justified, however, following the long-
standing mission of the Corps of Engineers, not as flood control
per se but as providing for the storage and scheduled release of

enough water to maintain an average dependable minimum depth of six feet at Sioux City, for transportation. After the project was approved and funded, on the direct authority of the Works Progress Administration (meaning with the President's signature and not by an act of Congress directly), the Corps concluded that it could probably maintain a minimum of eight feet on the Missouri during "navigation season" (meaning those months in the summer and fall when the Big Muddy wasn't covered with ice from bank to bank). Roosevelt thus managed, with a single project, to cosset his best Western ally in the Senate and mollify tens of thousands of Depression-hurt farmers in the central Midwest.

The other usual improvements created by dams are hydroelectric power and irrigation. The Fort Peck dam has yet to irrigate an acre of cropland, except as an accidental byproduct of maintaining stable flows below the dam. This is because, in large part, the United States as a whole, during the Depression and today, produces more northern crops—wheat and barley, alfalfa and sugar beets—than it can use, export, or store. And the Missouri River Navigation Association wanted flood-free land down south, not more competition up north.

As for hydroelectric power, that was just as simple a case of politics as putting the dam in Montana rather than at any of the several available sites in North Dakota, places where dams were built under Republican administrations after World War II. (Had Roosevelt chosen a North Dakota site, it would have trapped even more floodwater, including the Milk in Montana, which debouches into the Missouri just downstream from Fort Peck, and the Yellowstone, Montana's second-largest river, which drains much of northern Wyoming and southern Montana, including the Little Big Horn.) There was to be no electric generation, originally, because Montana Power, The Company, said there shouldn't be public power in Montana; if you wanted power you'd buy it from them.

I need to digress here, further into the future. In May 1940 a power-generation station was added to the Fort Peck project, the same month my father was called to active duty in the United

States Naval Reserve in preparation for what Roosevelt regarded as an inevitable entry by the United States into World War II. (I don't mean to imply that he called my father up and asked him to get on the team, but only to say that they thought alike on exactly one thing and only one thing ever in their lives, and that was the necessity to oppose the Nazis and the Japanese actively. All else is summed up in the fact that Franklin Delano Roosevelt was usually referred to in my household simply as *"That* Man.") The electrical-generation project, too, was a preparation for war. In fact, a generating station had always been, not secretly, but quietly, planned into the project. Two of the four outlet tunnels that carried the stored water underneath the dam, returning it on a scheduled program into the Missouri, were sited so that they could be used to run generators. They were not so identified on the original plans, but they were located deliberately for that purpose, a hedge against the future, when power generation would be politically possible and economically, or militarily, necessary.

Electrical power for the construction of the Fort Peck Dam—carried on 150,000-volt lines—was purchased from The Company's private hydroelectric plant on the Great Falls of the Missouri, and brought east 288 miles to Fort Peck. The transmission lines were as political as the basic decision: one-half were made of copper, placating the other Company, Anaconda Copper; the other half were made of aluminum, which, through Alcoa, had its own lobby in Washington. When electric generation was added to Fort Peck, to be completed in late 1943, the lines that once brought power to the project were simply reversed, and Fort Peck's electricity went back west to the expanded mines and booming wartime lead and copper smelters in Helena, Great Falls, and Butte. Many of the brass cartridges and lead-cored bullets so generously expended on Japanese and Germans were made with Fort Peck power. And after the war, The Company having lost little political clout, the power was shut off to Great Falls and exported eastward, across the border into North Dakota. A few years later, with tempers mollified, the Fort Peck generators were connected to the Western power grid, serving small towns in Montana, the Dakotas, and Wyoming. Some of this electricity is used for purely federal purposes within Montana, including irrigation pumping on Indian reservations. The old strength of The Company is now partly illusion, unless you want to run for office.

It was, by accident of politics, then, that the Fort Peck project came to eastern Montana, but it could not have been sited better if the sole purpose were to drop ten thousand jobs in a place of appalling poverty. Rural poverty is difficult to see from a passing train or through the windshield of an automobile, and Valley County's poverty was practically invisible, as it was throughout eastern Montana. The last dirt farmers to survive the great droughts of the 1920s and the collapse of commodity prices that lasted into the 1930s were widely scattered, miles from train lines and highways, and from electric lights and telephones, hidden in the coulees.

Statistics were largely unavailable; relief agencies were not professional number-crunchers in the 1930s; indeed, they barely existed except as dolers of food and listers of rare job offers. I have no way of expressing how devastating it was to be poor in Valley, McCone, Blaine, Garfield—the four counties closest to the Fort Peck project. But there is one telling example from Valley, which counted, in 1933, just eighteen hundred farm families scattered over five thousand square miles. Of the eighteen hundred, more than half were getting weekly food relief from the American Red Cross, and the Red Cross responded, then as now, only to disasters, not to mere privation. In simple terms, half the farm families in the county were literally starving, or—I can say this, knowing something of them—at least half of them were willing to admit it.

My father wasn't starving, or my mother, either, in 1933, when That Man decided to authorize the world's largest earthen dam, but they were not immune to the fourteen-year-old depression that had settled on the plains.

My mother was raised on a dirt farm—which means no running water, no indoor toilet, and no electricity—in Garfield County, in the exact middle of the most godforsaken country in North

America—halfway between Jordan, which has no river to match the name, and Sand Springs, which is exactly that, a series of spring holes that are usually dry. The country there is eroded by the upper end of Big Dry Creek, also very accurately named except for a few weeks a year in spring thaw, when it can drown an elephant. My mother got out by one of the two ways a pretty, intelligent girl can get out. She picked going to school. There was no adequate high school in Jordan, a county seat in name only, so she went down to Miles City and worked as what today is called an "au-pair" girl, a nice way of saying that you get to wash a lot of dirty clothes and dirty floors, and go to high school. After she graduated, she stayed on, still doing housework, and attended a two-year registered-nursing program at the local Catholic hospital. When it was done, she had a chance at economic and social respectability. You still had to be lucky, in Montana, to get a job. Hers was with the Bureau of Indian Affairs, nursing in the government hospital at Lame Deer, on the Northern Cheyenne reservation.

The Northern Cheyenne had a half-million acres of mostly inhospitable eastern Montana; except for the small water of Rosebud Creek, it is barren enough. The government provided a ten-bed hospital. Five hundred thousand acres sounds like a lot of land, but the immediate neighbors of the Northern Cheyenne are the Crow Indians, who have about 2.25 million acres (a reservation the size of Connecticut, in round figures). If you wonder why one tribe has five times as much as the other, it's pretty simple: the Crows were on Custer's side, however diffidently, at the Battle of the Little Big Horn, and the Cheyenne were on the other.

My father, a civil-engineering graduate of Iowa State University, class of 1928, was running a road crew for Winston Brothers, a Minneapolis contractor working for the state of Montana. Repairing country roads was about the only private civil-engineering work available in 1932. He came down the road (it's State Route 442 today) with a repair crew, and the rest would be history if this were history, so the rest is a family memoir. They were married

on January 1, 1933, and moved into my mother's apartment, an
ell attached to the grocery store (one could more romantically call
it the trading post) in Lame Deer. And then Franklin Delano
Roosevelt, the Works Progress Administration, and Burton K.
Wheeler accidentally made them virtually rich, by eastern-
Montana standards.

That is a mild overstatement, although simply to be employed
in 1933 was a remarkable stroke of fortune. I always assumed that
a civil engineer would make a decent wage, as I was partly raised
in the middle of the post-war California building boom. But, a few
years ago, when I started this act of remembrance, all I knew was
that my father had worked on the Fort Peck Dam. I started tele-
phoning around the country, trying to locate the physical records,
the actual archives, of the project. One day, on the telephone with
the Omaha (Nebraska) District Office of the Army Corps of Engineers, speaking with their official historian, I explained what I
was looking for, and that it was important, to me, because my
father had been a civil engineer and had some official position, I
thought, on the project. And the historian was most unsure that
any scrap of physical evidence was left that would mean anything.
"Civil engineer," he said; "hell, so were a lot of people. Work was
hard to find, and they had civil engineers running rods."

He said it kindly enough, but I knew that "running rods" is just
about as low as you can get on the engineering ladder. It means
holding the level rod, or the plumb bob or surveying rod, while
someone looks at it through a transit, or a level; even looking
through the optical instrument is not really proper work for a
graduate civil engineer. A long time ago, my first job in construction
was running rods, and I was fourteen years old and couldn't have
engineered a goldfish pond in a frost-free environment. What the
man said about rodmen didn't sit quite right, and I didn't believe it.

After the war, our family ran into other civil engineers who had
worked on Fort Peck—they tended to recognize each other—and
we children would be introduced. I remember one in San Diego,

a Mr. Doxie, who ran a small neighborhood butcher shop that had the most fascinating piece of machinery I had ever seen and may ever see, a drum with rubber fingers that plucked poultry. All in all, I was fairly confident that if someone ended up plucking chickens, he might have just run rods at Fort Peck, but there had to be more to it than that; otherwise we Montgomerys would have ended up plucking chickens, too, which seemed then, and seems now on some days, a worthwhile occupation.

If the choice of Montana for a major make-work WPA project was political, the precise location followed a process begun in the Coolidge administration. In 1927 the Corps of Engineers began a navigation survey of all of America's major river systems, and in 1928 the Flood Control Act extended its authority and provided for continuing surveys. It was not yet authorized to build dams for flood control, but as part of its mission to provide river transport the Corps could study and recommend flood projects. It was the WPA, and orders from the President, that sent two officers, a Lieutenant Colonel R. C. Moore and a Captain H. Wyman, Jr., up the river from Kansas City to Glasgow, Montana, by train, with a set of river survey maps and the urge to build a dam. There were, in those days, nothing but section roads south of Glasgow, straight-line dirt roads bordering homesteaders' square parcels of land. The idea of government men bringing money and jobs was enough to get the mayor of Glasgow, Leo B. Coleman, and Sam Rugg, secretary of the Chamber of Commerce, to volunteer to drive the two engineers over twenty miles of dusty section roads to the banks of the Missouri near old Fort Peck.

As the engineers pointed across the mile-wide valley and said, "There's the dam site," the apocryphal words of Mayor Coleman were, "My God, man, it would cost a million dollars to build a dam across there!" A million dollars, of course, was one of those mythical numbers, like the Biblical forty for counting years or the Biblical sixty for counting large numbers of objects. That is what he meant by a million dollars, simply a very large number indeed. Until then, the largest dollar figure in Mayor Coleman's experience was the relief budget of the Red Cross in Valley County, running at an average of a hundred thousand dollars annually, most of it for food and clothing.

Before the dam was finished, the actual dollar amount for its construction was somewhere over $170 million.

Coleman and Rugg and the engineers motored back to Glasgow, and the engineers obliged the mayor by drawing him a rough plan of the dam on brown wrapping paper, sketching out its almost unimaginable bulk in cross-section and plan view. The story made the next day's edition of the local newspaper, the Glasgow *Courier*, October 29, 1932, three years to the day after Black Tuesday's stock-market collapse. And no one paid any real attention. One reason was that no one had ever tried to build much of anything in a Montana winter. Spring would be soon enough to worry about, or hope for, jobs in Valley County.

Reading through the small histories of Fort Peck, scattered in journals of Western history and specialized engineering magazines, one comes across differing opinions of the value of the project. Navigation, as I've mentioned, was what we can call the "benefit of excuse," while the obvious benefit was what spending $170 million would do not only for the economy of Montana, but for manufacturers of earth-moving equipment, steel, Portland cement, and all the other physical components of the process and the completed structure. The great and permanent cost was the flooding of 275,000 acres of land from the dam site two hundred miles upstream, and it was unusual land, not the ordinary bare and dry high plains. It was the good crop and cattle land of the Missouri Valley. On that old and flat alluvial plain grew a substantial part of the only agricultural success story in Montana in the 1920s and early 1930s. Small irrigated fields, with water pulled by home-made weirs from the river, were green with alfalfa. To this day, to a Fort Peck enthusiast, the mere word "alfalfa" brings a scowl. All you have to do when someone like George Nicholas, who runs the hotel in Fort Peck, starts talking about what a wonderful project the dam was, is say "alfalfa," and the beginnings of a headache are etched on his forehead.

Alfalfa, a perennial cousin of the clovers, is a reliable hay crop if it can be irrigated, and Montana alfalfa was and is also harvested for seed. The same years that the Red Cross was handing out jackets and flour and coal in drought-stricken Valley County, the farmers down in the breaks along the Missouri River and those with water rights to the tributary Milk were selling hay and shipping a half-million pounds of alfalfa seed. It is hard now to imagine a couple of engineers drawing a line across a river and dislocating a hundred homesteading families who made up a large percentage of the only successful farmers in the state, but it happened, and there wasn't even a single lawsuit, just some minor bickering about the prices paid for the land.

We have forgotten, in this service-industry, computer-driven age, that only a few decades ago engineers carried authority, great civil works were not regarded with suspicion, and changing the landscape was the patriotic thing to do. There were popular novels about engineering, and they were not about the rape of the land, but about heroic deeds. *The Winning of the Barbara Worth*, the saga of irrigating California's Imperial Valley, stayed on *The New York Times'* best-seller list for three years, 1928–1931. Given that enthusiasm for public works in the nation's collective consciousness, an enthusiasm that began with the conquering of Panama and the building of the great canal, it is clear that Fort Peck was more than jobs; it was, in a very real sense, just one more act that celebrated and fulfilled the manifest destiny of America. The two most widely known palindromes in English—those backward- and forward-reeling sentences—are an odd pair, on first examination. One is about Napoleon and the other is about a U.S. Army civil engineer, George Goethals. Napoleon's, of course, is "Able was I ere I saw Elba," the palindromic epitaph of a failed megalomaniac. The engineer's is a triumph: "A man, a plan, a canal. Panama!"

Indeed, the idea of opposition to Fort Peck is, technically speaking, an anachronism. It would not be that age—raised on *The Winning of the Barbara Worth*, on the eradication of yellow fever by an army doctor, and on a civil-engineering feat that cut a continent in half at its waist—a generation at home with erector sets and Lincoln logs and that most famous of all fictional engineers, Tom Swift, juvenile inventor of ingenious devices—not that age which would regard men with slide rules and surveying instruments as a threat to the environment. Engineers controlled Mother Nature; that was their duty and their destiny.

The project had three avowed purposes in the spring of 1933: navigation, irrigation, and power. As we noted, local politics killed power until defense considerations overrode parochial ones, and Congress, which liked to vote on irrigation projects one by one, since they tended to be located in individual congressional districts, denied the WPA any authority to spend money on irrigation. "Porkbarrel" projects lose their appeal when control of them shifts from a gaggle of congressmen making deals of mutual satisfaction to a faceless agency.

But the dam was built, and then justified. The tendency of the Corps of Engineers today is to credit it with all possible benefits, including ones not even imagined in 1933. Navigation is a minor industry on the upper Missouri today, so the constant flow of water has been rechristened as a major benefit, because it allows cities in Nebraska and Iowa to dump considerable sewage in the river, where it is subject to what engineers call "in-stream sanitation"— dilution and aeration just in time to allow the next city downstream to start the process over again.

Flood control, the one benefit that really has justified the dam, is still difficult to put a value on. When the whole Missouri River Basin was deluged in 1952, flood storage in Fort Peck kept the crest at Omaha a foot and a half lower than it would have been and possibly averted a greater disaster; but taming the Missouri, if such is possible, required three more post–World War II dams, downstream and east of Fort Peck, at Garrison, Oahe, and Fort Randall, effectively turning the upper river into a chain of lakes in North Dakota and flooding another million acres of once-productive farmland. But all that is after the fact, and the primary benefit in 1934 was work itself. Yet I do not think it is an exaggeration to say that this project did more than make work, though there was plenty of that in the Works Progress budget. Fort Peck, by its very nature as a major piece of complex, professional civil engineering, symbolized the business of getting America moving forward again. It was no Panama Canal, to be sure, but it was of that family, of that ilk.

5

Life Goes to Its First Party

Wheeler and the other dozen encampments near the Fort Peck construction site sprang up almost overnight in the summer of 1934. Not only had the army overestimated the number of single men who would want barracks-style living, but it had greatly underestimated the number of service-industry workers that would descend. I realize that painted ladies give a whole new meaning to the concept of service industry, but if that idea was understood at all in Montana in the 1930s, I'm sure they would have been included. Fallen Women, bartenders, ribbon clerks, barbers, bouncers, midwives, preachers, and card dealers, along with several thousand construction workers, overwhelmed the neat plans of the War Department's engineers.

Fort Peck City had its clear class distinctions: the permanent houses were for regular army; the 280 temporary houses were for men like my father, who would direct the work of laboring men; laborers and craftsmen would live in 134 barracks buildings, with a capacity of 3,216 double bunk beds for 6,432 men sleeping in something very like regular-army open squad rooms; single foremen, the noncommissioned officers of construction work, were allocated private rooms in collegiate "dormitory blocks" with indoor plumbing. For the barracks there were separate outside washhouses with toilets and showers, which, considering the weather in Montana, may have encouraged what became a semiannual event: fumigating the barracks buildings for bedbugs. The barracks were kept at a reasonable distance from the single-family homes, the women's dormitories, and the Fort Peck Hotel, which provided transient housing and private rooms for better-paid inspectors, including my uncle Donald, who complained regularly about the food and the noise. Later he married Olive and set up single-family housekeeping. "Poor Olive" is what she was always called after he divorced her and left Montana for good.

Because the plan for military-efficient housing ran smack into the rules of the Montana Welfare Commission, which controlled the hiring of unskilled and semiskilled labor at the dam, the army of six-thousand-odd single workers never enlisted, and there were two results: about a third of the barracks and mess buildings were converted to family apartments in 1935; and Wheeler, Delano, Minot, Lakeview, Wilson, Valley, Park Dale, Idlewild, Willow Bend, Park Grove, New Deal, Midway, Square Deal, Cactus Flats, and McCone City sprang up.

It was these boomers that put Fort Peck on the cover of the first issue of *Life* magazine. Although the army had planned for decent housing, the miscalculation about the workers' family status made the boom towns inevitable, and there were rumblings, back east, about the failure of the army's scheme. The height of employment and the greatest crowding in the garish, sprawling boom towns happened to coincide with the invention of *Life* magazine.

Henry Luce's *Time* and *Fortune* magazines were successful, but he wanted a major photo journal that would tell the real story of what he liked to call the "American Century," the final conquering of the West and the growth of industry across the continent. The original intention for the contents of the first issue of *Life* included a cover story on the greatest dam, reclamation, and irrigation project in America, a vast public-works effort that would symbolize the American Century, that meant jobs and industry and the successful struggle of man against the elements. But it was not Fort Peck that they were thinking of in New York City; it was Bonneville, in Washington State, a project that really *was* one of the Seven Civil Engineering Wonders of the Modern World.

Luce raided his other publications for *Life*'s staff and, because it was to be a photo-essay journal, brought in one of his greatest free-lance contributors. This was Margaret Bourke-White, a successful advertising photographer who had worked regularly for *Fortune*—documenting great machines and factory buildings, taking portraits of industrial giants. She was perfect for the Bonneville job, for she could make machinery appear powerful on the page and capture in portraits the stern-jawed men who led America forward. She was hired full-time for *Life*, and her first assignments were to be Bonneville and, then, the All-American Canal that was under construction to bring Colorado River water to the Los Angeles Basin. The All-American was, in many ways, the logical final chapter of *The Winning of the Barbara Worth*, and would make not a desert bloom, but a Los Angeles boom. Wheeler, Montana, however, interfered with the well-laid plans.

In September 1936, as the final story conferences were being held in *Life*'s still-unfinished offices, Ernie Pyle, the roving correspondent of the Scripps-Howard newspaper chain, followed up on rumblings that Franklin Roosevelt's New Deal dam in Montana was not exactly a model of social planning. The front page of the old New York *World-Telegram* carried his feature column on Mon-

tana's boom, and it was read by Daniel Longwell, *Life*'s picture
editor.

> You have to see the town of Wheeler to believe it.
> When you drive thru [simplified spelling was popular in the New
> Deal, surviving today in road-sign neologisms like "thruway"], you
> think somebody must have set up hand-painted store fronts on both
> sides of the road, a back ground for a western movie thriller, but
> it's real. . . . Wheeler is a slopover from the government-built city
> at Ft. Peck dam, it is not on government property, hence is free to
> go its own way. . . . It has a half a dozen all-night taverns, and
> innumerable beer parlors.
> At night the streets are a melee of drunken men and painted
> women, as they are called in books. . . .
> Back behind Wheeler is a separate village where the women of
> easy virtue live. The town has an unprintable name. Everybody
> calls it by this name. [Unprintability is in the eye of 1936. It was
> called the "Riding Academy."] They say a thousand women have
> heard the call and drifted in for the easy reapings among the dam
> workers.

Backward reeled Daniel Longwell's mind. The Wild West Lives!
Deadwood! Tombstone! Dodge City! Miss Bourke-White was directed to stop at Fort Peck on her way to Bonneville and see what
was going on, photographically speaking.

She wrote to an old friend, just before departing for Montana,
saying that she looked forward to the "opportunity to work with
creative things like this—real life rather than attractive poses. . . .
The time comes when taking a perfectly dressed girl stepping into
a slick automobile seems to have no more meaning. I am delighted
to be able to turn my back on all advertising agencies and go on to
life as it really is."

Miss Bourke-White, who was living with the Southern novelist
and essayist Erskine Caldwell, had already investigated "life as it
really is," taking the then sensational photographs that accompanied his essay on Southern poverty, "You Have Seen Their

Faces." She was hardly unprepared for Wheeler, sociologically speaking, but not quite ready for Montana in general, particularly the vast scale of the state. She was most annoyed that she could not fly to Fort Peck, being an early adopter of airplane travel as a time-saving device.

She was still a bit of a neophyte at candid photo journalism, even after her work on "You Have Seen Their Faces," photographs taken in 1935 and 1936. Thus, in spite of her pre-eminence at carefully set-up photographs such as she had produced for advertising agencies, and her equally static photos for *Fortune*, she was nervous about this first assignment for her new employer. After the long flight from New York to Minneapolis, and the longer train ride to Glasgow, and the bus to Fort Peck, she snapped a few photographs in Wheeler and Fort Peck City and airmailed them back to New York: "See if my flashbulb effects allright," she scribbled on borrowed note paper. "Then *write* me a description of the pix, how they look, etc. . . . Most interesting here. Shall get many more night life pix before I leave. *Rich Possibilities*," she underlined.

No matter how attractive the brothels and bar-rooms of Wheeler were, Bourke-White was on assignment for Henry Luce, and that meant documenting his American Century to *his* satisfaction, and his world was not at all one entirely populated by hookers. She photographed strong-jawed, pipe-smoking, topdog Major T. C. Kittrell, the project manager. Unable to capture the sprawling earth-fill dam from the ground, she hired an airplane and took a classically dull photograph of it, enlivened only slightly by the low light of a Montana sunset. And she met my father.

She took a single photograph, mislabeled then and yet again recently in Vicki Goldberg's biography of Bourke-White, as "Fort Peck Dam." It is not the dam at all, but the concrete piers for the highway bridge at the spillway. She met my father because he worked on the spillway and because he had small feet. She had arrived at Fort Peck in a gray Paris suit and high-heeled shoes. She borrowed my father's L. L. Bean rubber-bottomed boots, and took the standard industrial photograph of the bridge structure, including a couple of workmen standing just off-center under the looming towers. The men were brought to the site, before the day's second shift began, as props to establish the scale. This photograph, severely cropped and misidentified as the dam, was on the first cover of *Life*. According to my mother, Margaret Bourke-White was not wearing stockings when she borrowed the boots, which is certainly hearsay and even more certainly not intended as a compliment. My father may have told her that. Women, except for the extraterrestrial Miss Bourke-White, would no more go to the construction site than to the Riding Academy. I do not recall that either of my parents ever explained that the photograph was taken at the spillway. For most of my life, when asked to identify Fort Peck, my birthplace, I always said, "It's the dam on the cover of the first *Life*."

Women from Fort Peck City did not spend much time in Wheeler's better sections, either, although it had stores and laundries and beauty parlors. Wheeler was unto itself, and served workers, not professionals. For some reason, by the way, *Life* misidentified Wheeler as New Deal in most of the editorial copy. New Deal, directly across the Glasgow highway from Wheeler, was a considerably quieter boom town.

Margaret Bourke-White found some of the painted women on Wheeler's streets to be extremely camera-shy, which is understandable, since their parents probably thought they were typists or filing clerks at the government office. She did find some subjects, though, including three employees of Ruby Smith who smiled at the camera. Bourke-White, still unused to street-scene candids, cut off the tops of their heads in the negative. They are smiling because they have just made a little rhyming joke. She asked for their names, and they said: "We're just three destitute prostitutes."

Photographing *inside* Ruby Smith's cathouse was another proposition. Bourke-White was loaned Major Kittrell's car and driver by the Corps, and when she asked to be taken to the biggest whorehouse in town, the driver, Gene Tourtlotte, agreed, but suggested she should wait in the car while he went inside to ask if she could come in and make photographs. This event produced the classic Bourke-White story, Wheeler-wise. While she was waiting for the driver, a drunk, noticing a well-dressed, quite attractive woman outside Ruby's place, approached the car, tapped on the window, and said: "You got a man, honey?"

"He's inside," Margaret Bourke-White said calmly.

"Lord," the drunk muttered, "you are about the most even-tempered woman I ever even heard of."

Gene Tourtlotte, the driver, was an ingenious fellow, and talked Ruby Smith into letting a photographer, and a woman at that, into her place. Two years later, almost to the day, he saved Major Kittrell's life, by driving most expeditiously away from the tragic collapse of the Fort Peck Dam. That is what we call the Big Slide, an event that made the dam notoriously famous among civil engineers but has nothing to do with Margaret Bourke-White, whorehouses, or *Life*.

Her nightlife photographs were, with no humor intended, regarded by the staff back in New York as the first example of what became a magazine staple: "*Life* goes to a party." The essay in captions that accompanied her photographs was written overnight, on deadline, as the prints came off the studio dryer. Archibald MacLeish cobbled a story together that identified prostitutes as working girls or waitresses, and that did not point out that her flash picture of the taxi dancers in Wheeler precipitated a full-scale brawl when the bulb went off. With the girls and their "dates" advancing on Miss Bourke-White, a flying wedge of construction workers led by Gene Tourtlotte escorted her out of Ruby's joint. She had become close friends with Tourtlotte, in part because she carried a pint of rye whiskey in her photo case, and the two of them would tone up for a shoot with a quick shot.

PEGGY [MacLeish telegraphed the morning after the first issue went to bed] THOSE PICTURES OF FORTPECK ARE MAGNIFICENT YOU ARE JUST AS SWELL AS I THOUGHT YOU WERE CONGRATULATIONS AND REGARDS   MAC.

If the first-issue story tried to walk the line between nightlife and the American Century, it made someone nervous in New York, as the introduction made clear to the reading public. The first page acknowledged that the contents were not quite as planned, and perhaps not quite as the reader expected.

"If any Charter Subscriber is surprised by what turned out to be the first story in this first issue of LIFE," the editors explained, so were they. They had hoped for little more from Montana than "construction pictures." But her documentation of Western frontier life was, at least to the editors, "a revelation." They certainly knew what Wheeler was like; that was all in Ernie Pyle's column. That she had invented the photo-essay on her first *Life* assignment was the real surprise.

The first telegrams to Bourke-White from Daniel Longwell were congratulatory: "FORTPECK PICTURES EXCELLENT NIGHT LIFE PERFECT STOP HOPE YOU GETTING SOME HUMAN TOUCHES ON THE OTHER BIG PROJECTS NEW SETTLERS ETC THINGS TO CONTRAST WITH BIG BUILDING STOP. . . ." (The other projects around Bonneville were deluged with fall rains, which were preventing her, day after day, from working, just as the first issue was coming off the presses.) "NEW SETTLERS" was part of Longwell's sense that history was repeating itself, as conquest by engineering replaced conquest by gunfighting, but he didn't want a repeat of the perfect nightlife she'd found in Wheeler.

Responding, a few days later, to her problem with the weather delays at Bonneville (which he thought was in Oregon), he did not encourage her to go out and meet the real people again. But he knew better than to give orders to this independent, hardly even-tempered prima donna: "YOU WILL HAVE TO USE YOUR JUDGEMENT AS TO WEATHER AND SUBJECTS TO GUIDE [YOU] STOP YOUR FRANK-LIN ROOSEVELTS WILD WEST AT WHEELER MONTANA RAN AWAY WITH THE FIRST ISSUE STOP" And then he made his plea, with some Western Union misspellings, for a more Lucean product: "ITS MAGNIFICENT BUT CAN[T] MAINTAN PROLETARIAN STRAIN THOR-OUGH OUT YOUR SERIES NEED SIGNS OF PROSPERITY INDUSTRY BOOM

ETC NEED INDUSTRIAL BIG ACTIVITY ASPECTS NOW STOP THINK YOU
OUGHT TO DO COMPLETE JOB WEATHER PERMITTING. . . .
LONGWELL"

My mother would have agreed. After all, there was nothing
particularly unusual about Wheeler, whose lights twinkled in the
distance beyond her front porch; it was full of whores and drunks,
just like any other Montana town, only they were somewhat more
numerous.

Today the boom towns are completely gone, burned, salvaged
for lumber, buried, plowed under undulating fields of winter wheat
where rectangles of stone mark destroyed footings, where shallow
circular depressions remain from filled-in cellar holes. Even the
Famous Buck Horn Saloon is a replica. The original, the last building in Wheeler left standing, burned in a winter fire in 1983, and
pellets of lead from celebrations past were found in the ashes of
incinerated two-by-fours. It's still a hell of a barroom, where people,
I think, tend to act out the drama as it was written for them, back
in the 1930s. They still dance, either to the juke box or, on weekend
nights, to live music. They still will give you that old Montana
highball, now only slightly tonier, thanks to the progress of the
culture thereabouts—that old highball being "a shot on the bar,"
which goes like this: you turn around, back to the bar, lay your
head back, open your mouth, and the bartender just pours. Recently
it's been "margaritas on the bar," a two-handed pour of sweet-and-
sour bar mix and tequila, but it's still shots on the bar, and deadly.

It wasn't all fun and sex and drinking. Over in McCone City,
south of the river, one or two dugouts are left of the hundreds of
these hobbit-holes that men and women lived in, made babies in,
died in from the ravages of "tunnel pneumonia." Dugouts are another old Montana tradition for the first houses in a territory. You
still see them, on back roads, including over by Roundup, in the
central part of the state. To make a dugout, you just dig a hole
into a coulee's side, roof over the top, sod it to keep out the cold,
and live that way until things get better, the job is finished, or you
give up and leave.

What remains, then, for the traveler down time who is looking for some inward lost and peaceful place, where he is a baby and his father is young and the world's work is waiting to be done? Wheeler's gone, Fort Peck City is almost totally modernized. There is such a place, as it turns out, somewhat to his surprise. It is the basement of the Army Corps of Engineers headquarters, where paper is saved.

6

Down That Lonesome Paper Trail

The administration of Fort Peck Dam, and the management of the town of Fort Peck until it was "privatized" by the Reagan administration in 1986 and put on the market, has remained a task of the Army Corps of Engineers, although all of the management, after construction ended, was in the hands of Department of the Army civilian employees. As the numbers of employees declined and the military officers left, it was downgraded from a Corps of Engineers District to an "Area," an undefined term that implies a certain senescence.

The original headquarters building, stripped of two vast temporary wings that once housed more than two hundred resident engineers and inspectors plus an equal number of clerks and typists, holds down one end of the town's central square, a grassy knoll that resembles many a New England village green or campus quadrangle. Headquarters is solid, monolithic, poured-in-place concrete, with a dormered second story and vitreous tile roof. The design is called "colonial"—not New England colonial but Southern-mansion style, lacking only the ubiquitous brickwork of Washington's, Baltimore's, or the Delmarva Peninsula's great houses. The architect's eclectic chalet style foundered on the army's sense of what a headquarters represents.

In my search for documents about my father's life, the Corps of Engineers records seemed a logical place to begin, but it quickly became clear that what passes for an archival system in the federal government is a capricious mix of collecting and disposing. Records of the regional offices of the Corps should be located, by ordinary administrative procedure, in the closest office of the National Archives and Records Administration. Midwestern records from the Kansas City, Omaha, and Minneapolis district offices should be in Chicago, and for all one knows may be there now, in one of those warehouses of cardboard boxes that are our nation's alternative to a viable archival system. The problem with the National Archives is simple: they are overcollected and understaffed, and burdened by a daily invasion of genealogy researchers. Regional Corps records, in unlabeled, unorganized, boxes, may well be there in the Chicago NARA Branch, but they were effectively unavailable.

However, in conversations with the Corps office in Omaha, I learned that some kind of archive was located in the headquarters building at Fort Peck. This was only hinted at. On several occasions in the past, each of the Engineers' Area and District offices has been ordered to send all old documents and photographs to the appropriate NARA regional offices, where they were to disappear into the thicket of unprocessed cardboard boxes. But in Fort Peck, I was told, "you will find a surprising amount of old material." Agencies and branches of the military services sometimes escape these orders to destroy, dispose of, or relocate their historical rec-

ords by maintaining what are usually called "operational archives,"
meaning supposedly useful material for day-to-day operations or
training purposes. On the telephone, Ronald Wallem, area manager
for the Corps at Fort Peck, allowed as how they had a pretty good
operational archive and I was certainly free to use it.

But what was I looking for? The physical reality of the spillway
structure, recognizable even in its finished state as the image on
the cover of *Life* magazine, had been reason enough for the trip.
But the archive was another matter.

That task would come in the morning. First one had to sleep in
the Fort Peck Hotel. The walls are as thin, the paneled doors as
loose in their frames, as when Uncle Donald lived here and complained about the noise. In the middle of the first night, I awoke,
rigid with fear, certain that someone was in the room, breathing,
next to my bed. It was another sleeper, in the next room, the soft
rasping breaths slipping through the walls as easily as if they were
radio waves. I took an odd comfort in the intruding sound, once I
understood it as human and peaceful.

The headquarters archive is divided into two parts. There is the
genuinely useful, consisting entirely of rolls of plans—drawings
showing everything from buried water lines to the dimensions of
buildings, waterworks associated with the dam, the spillway structures, the diversion tunnels, the power station, and very accurate
surveys of the dam itself. The one thing one does not want in any
great engineering project is movement, and the dimensional data
kept in the plan room, plus the fixed survey markers, allow one to
keep a close and accurate eye on the sleeping dam. Across the
basement hallway from the frequently used plan room is the paperwork archive, consisting of 168 numbered but mostly unlabeled
boxes of correspondence, reports, and miscellany. In addition, there
are two dozen boxes of eight-by-ten black-and-white photographs
documenting the construction of the dam and the spillway. The
photographs are arranged in chronological order, from early construction in the spring of 1934 until the completion of the dam
in 1939.

Ron Wallem unlocked the door to the paperwork-and-photo archive and said he hoped I'd find what I was looking for, in a tone of voice that indicated his doubt. My exact emotion is probably mediated by time and events, but it was hopeful, not unlike that ancient joke I remembered then about the small and optimistic boy who pawed his way through the room full of horse manure in search of the causative pony. Such thoughts tend to come over me in otherwise serious moments, and I recall looking at the shelves of dust-covered boxes, if not at the first moment then sometime during the first day, and thinking that there had to be a father in there somewhere.

The boxes were simple two-cubic-foot packing boxes, not the so-called Hollinger boxes familiar to librarians and researchers. Hollingers are the hard gray cardboard boxes with flip tops, which hold half a cubic foot of paper.

When you have no idea where to look, you just start with box number one, carry it over to a table, wipe off the thin coat of dust, open it up, and start reading. The contents of the first box, the first dozen boxes, the first sixty boxes, were most discouraging.

All military organizations, and the semicivilian Corps of Engineers is no exception, write "official histories" of their projects, their operations, their battles. At the end of the first day, all I could say with certainty about the history of Fort Peck Dam was that the army had very high standards for typists. For the boxes were jammed with monthly, yearly, and completion histories. There were duplicate, triplicate copies, and these carbons, even on onionskin, with the inevitable blurring, were of remarkable quality. Every history, every monthly report, was flawlessly typed with very few erasures, and those quite difficult to detect. Here was an army that marched on typing.

I was really just looking for a name. It made no sense to pore over the details of construction of the outlet tunnels, or the setting of sheet piling, unless I knew they were somehow related to whatever it was, exactly, that my father had done. Toward the end of the day, it was becoming a most uninstructive activity. In the first

fifteen or so boxes, there weren't any names at all, except the
occasional signature block of Major Kittrell or Captain Someone.
There weren't even any lieutenants in the official record, and the
army has always had lieutenants; it is in the nature of things.

Bored, or eyestrained, I would open one of the boxes of photographs, where each print was in a numbered envelope. In with the
print was the original eight-by-ten-inch negative. Now, the prop-
erties of a large-view camera are useful for documenting vast land-
scapes. You get an exceptionally fine quality of focus, achieved by
using the ground-glass plate at the rear of the camera, so that the
photographer is looking not at a reflection of the image, as in a
modern reflex camera, but at exactly the product of light and lens
that will fall on the negative. (It is upside down, by the way, which
is how babies see the world until their brains can reprocess the
image on the retina and make it correspond with the reality of
gravity.) I suppose I was looking for a face, but the official photographs were as discouraging as the collected paperwork. There
were no people in them, either. Small and distant human figures
appeared occasionally, but the photographer had in mind an entirely
different purpose from showing people. Pictures of the dam showed
as much as a third of its three-and-a-half-mile length, and very
small machines and even tinier men could be seen scrabbling away
at the soil like ants in a vegetable garden, completely dwarfed within
the large view. In close-up photographs of some ingenious device
or a dredge boat or a concrete structure still wrapped in wooden
forms, there were no people at all.

The greater number of the photographs were posed, apparently
during lunch breaks or between shifts. This is understandable.
For many years, Kodak sheet film has been coded by a pattern of
notches on the edge of the negative sheet. The notches showed
that the film used at Fort Peck was one of great clarity, with an
extremely fine grain and thus relatively slow film speed, ASA 100
or so. I'd estimate the typical exposure, using a very small aperture
for maximum clarity out to infinity, even shot in burning midsum-
mer Montana sunlight, would be at least one-thirtieth of a second.

In such photographs working men would be blurred forms, their moving figures smearing the desired precision for the project's photographic record.

Photograph number 36-2348 (the first two digits are the year of the century, the second figure is the serial count, beginning in 1934 with number 1) was the first photograph I found with not only recognizable human beings but their names typed carefully on an attached caption. It shows the twelve players, the manager, and the coach of the 1936 Fort Peck Championship Baseball team, the Spillway Builders, Inc. They were an extremely rough-looking crowd.

One of the annual reports of the town management division for 1936 noted that Fort Peck could profit from more effort at landscaping, and described the successful scheme of awarding small cash prizes for the best vegetable gardens, the best lawns, the best flower gardens. Neither the winners nor the amounts of the prizes were mentioned. Turning to another box of photographs, bored again with the endless reams of official paperwork, I came across the first name I recognized. It was a façade-on photograph of one of the temporary houses, with a neatly trimmed lawn, flower beds by the house, and more flowers lining a gravel walkway from the unpaved street to the front door. The caption indicated that the winner of the 1936 beautification prize was Mr. C. D. Hurst. He is not in the picture; the only living thing is a white cat lounging in the corner of the yard. This man, I knew, would be "Chick" Hurst, who also ended up, with his family, in San Diego after the war. Chick and Gladys Hurst were from Anaconda, the copper-smelting town. In the 1930s there was very little growing in Anaconda, since the fumes from the smelter killed most green plants. I would not have guessed the Hursts would win a lawn-and-garden prize, although when I knew them they did keep a neat and floriferous front yard. But in San Diego everyone had a garden, once.

By the end of the day, the explanation for the absence of names in the official summaries, reports, and histories was made painfully clear. In a box of random administrative correspondence was a mimeographed memorandum of October 26, 1938, titled "History of Fort Peck Project" and sent to all division and section heads. Written by the Historical Section, it noted, "It is difficult or impossible to obtain accurate information of Section activities after demobilization . . ." and ordered the collection of historical material immediately. "Employees whose knowledge of Section activities is of value . . . should submit written reports to the Section before leaving. . . ." By the fall of 1938, various parts of the project were almost complete, including the separate spillway and the diversion tunnels. The second page of the memorandum gave directions for the outline and contents of each official history. The general organization would be:

A.   Contractors.
B.   Government inspection force.
C.   Hired labor force.

In all cases, the memorandum ordered:

Refer to charts, omit personalities.

That is a very military concept, I know now, and a very American one. We deliberately created, after the experience of World War I, a military of interchangeable parts, exchangeable ranks and ratings, so that any infantry sergeant or enlisted seaman or officer could be reassigned to a comparable position. The military history of Fort Peck reflected that. Work would be done not by individuals, but by classes of individuals—with the exception of such senior officers as the District Engineer or a section head. I had already seen a table of organization for the diversion tunnels, and it listed every government inspector down to low-paid sub-sub-assistant inspectors by title, but without a single human name attached. It is difficult, at this remove, even to hint at how outraged I was to discover that the Army Corps of Engineers had set out, quite deliberately, to erase my father's name, and everyone else's, from the records.

Indeed, up to that point, the only document I had discovered (except those few photograph captions) with a list of names on it was the collection of depositions given by the survivors of the Big Slide—each man's description of the collapse as taken by the board of inquiry. A cover sheet included the names of the men killed in the Slide. There was also a summary report of all the fatal accidents that had occurred between 1934 and 1939, but without names, simply with causes of death. I looked at the historical memorandum again, copied down the section on the exclusion of names, ordering the reference to tables of organization, and left the archive for the day. Outside headquarters, automatic sprinklers played on the grassy central common. I walked around it, taking the long way around three sides of the grass, to the Fort Peck Hotel. It was too frustrating a day even to hurry for a beer. Taking that route around the central common, you walk by the largest of the dozen permanent houses built for the officers at the beginning of West Kansas Street. That was Permanent House No. 1, residence of District Engineer Clark Kittrell, who, according to the official histories, I muttered out loud as I walked by, "built the whole goddamned thing by himself."

The next morning, after another bad night's sleep in the aspirating hotel, I went back to the basement and continued without much enthusiasm through the boxes of records. There is a gentle kind of amusement in reading official histories. The Town Management Section's history described the temporary houses as "well-insulated." The insulation consisted of one-inch-thick cellulose-board, known universally in Montana as "beaverboard." It does look, and feel, like wood that had been masticated by that same rodent. Close reading of the official history turned up the information that about half of the houses, because of shortages, were protected only by half-inch beaverboard. My mother remembers coming into our children's bedroom and seeing frost, formed by condensation from our breath, growing an inch or two out of the wall, on horizontal icicles attached to the nailheads. I suppose we had the half-inch stuff.

Leafing through the boxes of photographs for the year 1937, I came upon one of the spillway gates, the Margaret Bourke-White *Life* cover subject, but with the structure complete. The great white, dinosaurlike towers were by then much obscured by the continuation of the construction. Photographed a year after her *Life* assignment, the towers were already carrying the liftgates and supporting a completed railroad track and highway roadbed on the once-bare projections that loomed on the magazine's cover. With all their parts completed, the towers were less attractive and not at all mysterious.

And for the first time, around the middle of 1936, an entirely different kind of photograph began to appear. As a specific piece of the dam and the associated structures neared completion, the official photographer gathered the government inspection crews together and took a group portrait. Here were the diversion-tunnel gate inspectors, the sheet-piling inspectors. Here was also a photograph of the town's hospital doctors (but not the nurses) standing solemnly in front of the clinic building, of the teachers at the school, of the firemen, and of the entire police force, twelve men, posed with a 1935 Ford sedan, each of them carrying his nightstick.

Less than a half-hour later, I saw my father's face, younger than I am now, looking at the camera with a small, half-embarrassed smile just like the one in nearly every other photograph ever taken of him. He was unused to smiling on command. The photograph was titled "Spillway Inspectors," and dozens of them were lined up in two rows, with a military officer standing at the left, slightly apart from the rest. Behind the men loomed the completed concrete gate structure.

So then I knew my father was a spillway inspector, and because he stood near the left, two persons removed from the military officer (counting along the front row), perhaps he was somewhere near the top. That was entirely speculative, but it is in the nature of people to arrange themselves in a hierarchy. In any case, they were not lined up in the classic military manner, by height. Quite a way down the line, far to the right, was Uncle Donald, identified on the typed caption as "D. Montgomery." This would have been just before he married Poor Olive, and he is startlingly good-looking, which may have been where the trouble started.

The pace of research picked up considerably once it became clear that only Spillway Section material was going to have even a chance at relevance. I started pulling boxes halfway off the shelf, prying open the flaps, and inspecting them quickly for their contents. A few were labeled, and, if they looked unpromising, were dismissed immediately. Toward the very end of the very last shelf, on the serially numbered 142nd box, there was a handwritten, smudged-pencil label: "spillway stuff."

This turned out to be an unusually disorganized collection of almost random paperwork. There were drafts of letters, rather than the neater, chronological carbon copies of correspondence. Someone in the Spillway Section had been less compulsive about throwing things away than the other filing clerks. Folded twice so that it would, thus quartered, fit in a file folder was a classic military table of organization for the Spillway Section, in gray line on yellowing plan paper—not a blueprint, which is a reversal of a drawing, but an Ozalid print, which makes a positive duplicate. The lonely box at the top contained the name of "John R. Hardin, Capt., C[orps]. of E[ngineers]., Chief, Spillway Section." But unlike all the other tables of organization, this one listed every position by name as well as title, and by salary. As of October 11, 1936, "Maurice R. Montgomery, Asst. Engr.," was second in charge of the Spillway Channel. He was making twenty-nine hundred dollars annually, which also put him at the second-highest level of all the civilian engineers. Money, more than titles, tends to hold up over time as a status mark. The average wage for the inspectors' force was about eighteen hundred dollars, or thirty-four dollars a week, less even than that of the tradesmen on the project, who made a dollar an hour. My father's substantial salary explained, I suppose, how we got to live on West Kansas, in the better part of town; or else the better part of town went with the better part of the salary scale. The official histories do not explain how housing was allocated among the inspectors and foremen and section chiefs.

Somehow this table of organization, clearly labeled as "Historical Data, Organization and Personnel," had survived the general ban on "personalities." And although it was absolutely unique, as a table, it was quite typical of the spillway office's way of doing business. Boxes 142 and 143, the two remnants of the Spillway Section, are the only ones in the entire archive that have even a remote flavor of personality, simply because some office correspondence was saved, while everywhere else it had been summarized and discarded.

You should not imagine that there is anything exciting in the interoffice correspondence of civil engineers, but when memory fades, there is at least the reality of paper. Reading through the surviving papers from 1936 and 1937, I learned that my father had been involved in supervising more than the physical construction. He was relied upon for what we can call, in a convenient shorthand phrase, "process controls." That is, he was responsible for ensuring the quality of raw materials in the concrete structures, the mile-long spillway channel, and the associated permanent roadways. In civil works as in most manufacturing projects, there are theoretical standards; the difference in construction is that you are making a single product, and it is supposed to last for decades. But almost all construction materials for such massive jobs are found on the project site or nearby ("near" in civil engineering means fifty or a hundred miles). So one is required to balance the optimal, theoretical sand and gravel with the reality of Montana dirt or, in the case of bituminous cement, Montana crude oil.

I found several two- and three-page, typed single-spaced memoranda to the spillway army engineer, Captain Hardin, written by my father. They are, on inspection, short courses in civil engineering. They attempt to reconcile the theoretical with the practical. Most of the memoranda are intended to justify changes from the original specifications as not reducing the quality of the final result. They describe the precision of the testing apparatus, specify the inspection methods, and frequently point out the wisdom of relying on proven techniques rather than abstract standards for laying pavement or pouring concrete. One set of these new inspection standards, my father wrote, "are based on the work of Stanton and Wheems, [as it] is used by the Montana Highway Comm." Appeals to authority, like textbook authors Stanton and Wheems, are frequently made, but also reference is made to standard practices as opposed to theoretical ones.

Subtle problems, including the cussedness of alkaline rocks, which would rather absorb water than oil, and thus contribute to the eventual degradation of the road surfaces, are solved in the memos. Captain Hardin's concerns about whether the civilian contractors are supplying as much material as they're charging the government for are attended to, and it is concluded that normal settling in the jouncing dump trucks is compacting the material between the contractor's quarry and the job site and that this is allowable, since the material would have been compacted by rolling in any case. Such is the romance of engineering—writing long reports at night, spending days watching gravel trucks and road graders at work.

I gather that my father was indeed working overtime, producing the memoranda and still supervising the daily construction. As I have said, it was 1936 when my father applied for a commission in the United States Navy Civil Engineer Corps (Reserve), and the strain of his Fort Peck job is evident in his enlistment medical examination. Musculature was "excellent," but he was "underweight, working overtime." At five feet nine and 130 pounds, he was not the family record-setter for thinness. Uncle Gordon, at six feet one, played tight end for the University of Montana football team at 125 pounds.

The recurring theme in the memoranda, which may account for their having survived, is that they tend to deal with compromises, with adapting Washington's or Kansas City's standards to local conditions. Many describe negotiations with civilian contractors, as in the search for the missing truckloads of material that turned out to be not missing but simply compacted. For several such changes in specifications, or prices to be paid, or manufacturing procedures to be followed, there are handwritten notes at the bottom, of which this exchange of May 7, 1936, on the flash point and permeability of bituminous asphaltum is typical:

> [From Captain Hardin to Chief Engineer Steiner] Have started change order as indicated. Have Montgomery look over to see if anything has been overlooked.
> [Steiner to Hardin] Montgomery O.K.'s the spec[ification]s as they are. I see nothing out of line.

A few years ago, when I visited Fort Peck, they were replacing the roadway that had been built with the change-ordered bituminous asphaltum. There was nothing wrong with the asphalt paving, but another, unexpected, difficulty had caused a problem; as usual in eastern Montana, the villain was the underlying rock formation, the curious Bear Paw shale, that ubiquitous material through which the spillway was cut, the power diversion tunneled, on top of which the one-time World's Largest Earth-filled Dam was built. Bear Paw shale, as you know by now, is not quite a rock, but an untransformed sediment, still high in moisture. When tested in the laboratory, it behaves very much like a rock, capable, in pressure tests, of bearing five tons of weight per square inch. This turns out to be somewhat theoretical, and was so proved by the construction of the two-mile-long spillway channel.

When the spillway channel was cut, some thirteen million cubic yards of dirt and rock had to be removed. Some of it was used to create hauling roads and to fill under the temporary railroad grade, but most of it was simply moved to one side and piled up in mountains the size of football stadiums. The shale, during the intervening fifty years, slowly shifted under the weight of the excavation's overburden. It crept, if that is the right word; it demonstrated its plasticity; and the spillway service road and the cut-back banks of the spillway itself moved a few feet up and away from the piles of excavated spoil, just as an obviously plastic object, like a child's balloon, will swell in one place when it is compressed in another. So, Montgomery was right to see nothing wrong with the specifications for the roadway, and not even he suspected, or could control, the quirky geology of eastern Montana. The concrete he poured in the spillway structure is in almost perfect condition. I walked on it, fifty-one years after it was poured. Almost no one gets to walk on the spillway, except for maintenance workers, but a few of us were given this special permission because we were filming a short movie for the Montana Arts Council, a documentary on the dam, the spillway, and in some smaller part my father and me.

Under the general heading of "Everything Connects," it turned out that the owner of, and bartender at, the Famous Buck Horn Saloon was quite familiar with the quality of my father's work on the spillway. We were filming him, and his wife, and afterward I asked him how he ended up in Fort Peck. He had come to Montana as a materials inspector for a construction outfit, and one of their jobs was to drill cores into the concrete at the spillway, to see if it was maintaining its strength after forty-odd years of Montana winters. One of the tricks with concrete coring is to miss the steel reinforcing, which does not cut easily with a core saw. "We got the plans," he said, "and measured it out, and we never hit a piece of steel, which is not usual in this business." The concrete, by the way, was hard as the hinges of hell, strong as the devil.

Climbing out onto the spillway structure, actually walking out on the narrow downstream flanges that surround each spillway gate and direct the water onto the spillway channel, reminded me of all those summers I would get out of high school or college and go back to work for my father. It seemed as if every time I got to a job, in late June, the building was already at least three floors off the ground, and I would have to crawl out on something considerably higher than a horse, which is too high off the ground for me anyhow. So it was while we filmed at the spillway, this middle-aged body walking catwalks a hundred feet above the hard concrete below, going down long ladders, and then trying to walk out on the narrow water-control flanges and look cool and collected for the cameraman. For many years, in high school and college, I had to look cool, too, and suck it up and start out across a beam that was a hundred feet off the ground, looking calm and collected for the other workmen, who, already acclimated to heights, were watching the boss's son on his first day. I had to bluff a lot, back then.

7

"Goodbye, Boys"

For most of my life, forty years now at least, I had been aware of the Big Slide. That disaster is formally called, in government inquiries, "Failure of the Upstream Face of Fort Peck Dam." It was not that we talked of it regularly in our family or that anyone ever asked questions about it. It was one of those underlying themes—I think every family has one. Each of us has his or her own set of dates. They are our watersheds of time. Things happened before them or after them—we moved, someone died, babies were born. For my wife's family, it was leaving California, just before the exclusion and incarceration orders that affected all Japanese-Americans on the West Coast.

The earliest conversation I can recall about the Slide went like this, and I have a very vivid recollection of it. We had moved to California after the war, and I was nine years old, approximately the age when small boys become minimally useful, as opposed to amusing or annoying. We were planting trees on our windswept hilltop lot, all different kinds of fruit trees, which is the sort of thing a Montanan does quite automatically, except these were tenderer trees than we would have planted at home—lemon, lime, orange, apricot, plum. The climate was too warm for apples, or we would have planted them, too. We tend to plant things you can make pies out of, rather than flowering trees. Flowers grow in beds and are really women's work. Men plant trees.

I was helping my father, which consisted mostly of running back and forth turning the hose off and on. We, maybe it was I, ran too much water into the shallow, dished hole that would hold the bare-rooted tree. It could not stand in the soft mud, and my father said this: "We'll have to wait. There's too much water, just like the Big Slide." We watched, as the dry California dirt began to absorb the water out of the mud, and he continued: "They built the dam too fast, and the water didn't have time to settle out. It felt like jelly when you walked on it."

I asked, "Why didn't they wait?"

And he said, in a tone of voice I could generate in him myself by doing something foolish and unhelpful, "Because those army engineers in Kansas City thought they knew everything."

After a while, when the mud was stiffer, we finished planting the tree. It was all very successful, by the way, this tree-planting business. We ate a significant amount of apricot jam and plum jelly when I was a kid.

It never occurred to me to ask why a dam, particularly an earth-filled dam, would have water in it. "Mud-filled dam" is not what one expects, after all, but that was indeed what it was.

The ordinary method of building an earth dam is this: Two fundamentally different kinds of soil are dug up, transported by truck, and shaped into a dam with rollers and graders. The center of the dam, the vertical middle layer, is made of impermeable dirt—very fine sand and clay soils—so that water will not pass through easily. This waterproof membrane is called the core. If water were to find a pathway through the dam, and flow, slowly at first, and then faster, as it eroded a larger path, it would undermine the dam. To give the dam strength and resistance to the elements, the upstream and downstream faces and the top are made of coarser sand and gravel. In engineers' speech, the combined exterior faces of the dam are called the "shell." On the upstream face, rock called "riprap" is placed, to protect the dam from erosion by waves and ice. That is how most big earth-filled dams in the United States have been constructed.

The Fort Peck Dam, however, was built by a dredging process. This choice of method had two precedents. A number of flood-control and irrigation structures on the Missouri and Mississippi rivers had regularly been built by dredging: levees (artificial banks), weir works, and diversion structures. And the largest dam ever built by the Corps of Engineers, the Gatun Lake dam, which provides a constant water source to operate the Panama Canal locks, was partly built of dredged fill—twenty-five million cubic yards of it. These are called "hydraulic-fill" structures, because water is the tool used to transport the material, just as you might say a wood-frame house was "hammer-built."

By the 1930s the Corps of Engineers was expert at the process of dredging. Their basic charge, on the Missouri and Mississippi, was to maintain navigable depths by dredging and to build flood-control levees by piling the dredge spoil into long embankments paralleling the rivers. It was the logical, probably inevitable, method of choice for Fort Peck, but a hazardous one.

The four dredges in operation at Fort Peck sank their giant cutting drills into sections of the Missouri River bed, above and below the dam site, and pumped its mixture of water, silt, sand, gravel, and small rocks through pipelines to the dam site. The mixture would be about half water, carrying the soil, and half usable material. The essence of the engineering problem was some-

how to separate the fine, waterproofing material for the core of the
dam from the coarser but stronger sand and gravel that would make
up the outside faces of the structure. This was accomplished by
pouring the dredge material out of pipes at the periphery of the
slowly rising dam. The larger and heavier rock would fall first,
settling near the outlet from the dredge pipes, and then the finer
sands and smallest gravels were carried a few feet farther away
from the edge of the structure, where they settled to the bottom.
And finally the finest materials, tiny sand grains and particles of
clay, were carried in suspension to the center of the dam, where
they precipitated very slowly, making the core. The top of the dam,
at this point and all through the construction phase, was a muddy
lake of dredge-carried water. This water was pumped out of the
lake, back into the river, downstream from the dam. In engineers'
jargon, the lake was the "core pool," sitting over the fine sands
and clays that would congeal into the waterproof core of the finished
dam.

There is another way to make a hydraulic-fill dam, one used in
Massachusetts for the Windsor dam of the Quabbin Reservoir,
which supplies water to greater Boston. This project is a contem-
porary of Fort Peck, begun a few years later and completed, like
Fort Peck, just before World War II. The method of placement is
the same and the theory is the same, but instead of material being
dredged directly out of the riverbed, a variety of carefully selected
material—sand, gravel, and fine silt—is mixed together in huge
boxes with sufficient water to allow it then to be pumped from the
"hog boxes" to the dam site. (They were called "hog boxes" from
the idea of a pig wallowing.) What that system gives you, as con-
trasted to dredge-and-fill methods, is much more accurate control
over the percentages of the different materials in the mixture passing through the pipeline to the dam. Although the Corps of Engineers made frequent and thorough tests in the borrow pits at
Fort Peck, it was hardly as precise a process as mixing separate
batches of washed sand and gravel and clay. The process controls
are much more elegant in a hog-box mixing-and-pumping process.

Understanding how Fort Peck was built, you can imagine how the dam might have shook like jelly when you walked on it or when machinery rolled along the beaches of the core pool. The stability of the structure depended on several things: the quality of the dredged material, the accuracy with which it separated and sorted itself into core and shell, and the rate of construction. If it were built too fast and the core and the shell never properly dewatered, you would end up with the world's largest mud-filled dam.

Hundreds of engineers and inspectors supervised the dredge fill of the dam. The raw materials at the dredge heads were studied, with samples taken by drilling and coring even before the dredges were brought to the borrow area. The differential settling rates in the core pool were analyzed daily, to make sure the sands and gravels were settling into a proper shell and the impervious clays were precipitating into the central core. The whole structure, all three and half miles of it, was surveyed weekly from fixed points at the two ends to ensure that it was upright and stable. What could not be known by objective means was what was happening down in the core and underneath the entire structure.

There is another universal problem with building dams, as opposed to simply constructing a building or even as dramatic a project as smashing a sea-level canal through the Straits of Darién—something the Army Corps of Engineers once proposed doing with a series of nuclear explosions. (A test of the explosive excavation system, using conventional explosives, was conducted on upper Fort Peck Lake, leaving an oddly rectilinear bay behind.) And the problem is, what do you do with the river? The first choice is to build an artificial channel to one side of the dam, and close it in after the structure is completed, returning the river to its original course. The other is to divert the water through tunnels under the structure. At Fort Peck four tunnels were bored and completed in 1937, so that, the entire summer, nonflood flow could be handled through them. With the river diverted, the Corps was able to proceed at maximum speed to finish the dam during 1937 and 1938, so that it would be ready to hold back the expected spring runoff floods of

1939. (The filling reservoir easily held the spring excess of 1937 and 1938.) The tunnels are still there, still in use, and except for one brief month in 1975, when an inch of water poured over the top of the spillway gates, the entire flow of the upper Missouri is held temporarily in the Fort Peck Reservoir, and returned to the river through the diversion tunnels. The spillway, my father's contribution, remains a hypothetical necessity.

Shortly after the tunnels began carrying the river underneath the dam structure, the channel for the old river was closed, and construction of the dam, building it up to 250 feet above the original riverbed, continued at a rapid pace. It is in the nature of engineers in general, and supervisors of vast work-relief projects in particular, to take pride in the numbers of men employed and the speed and efficiency of the construction. So it was here; by the summer of 1938, the dam was approaching its intended maximum height, with dredges running twenty-four hours a day. And the lake, with the diversion tunnels partly closed, began to fill, lapping against the upstream face of the dam.

The final goal, an elevation of 250 feet above the old level of the river, was within reach by the fall of 1938. The original plan called for dredge fill to the two-hundred-foot level, followed by fifty feet of dry, packed earth. But the dredges had proved so efficient that the plans changed, and dredge filling proceeded to 225 feet, saving only the last twenty-five feet for a dry fill, to be topped by the Glasgow-to-Jordan highway, Route 24.

As the dam rose, it narrowed toward the top. The slope of the rear, downstream side of the dam is very shallow: from the center of the dam to the downstream end of the banked dirt is over a half-mile. The upstream slope was designed to be on a sharper slope, roughly a quarter-mile from the white line of Route 24 to the upstream "toe." The ratio of height to width is significant. The upstream slope, as designed, had a slope of four in one; that is, for every foot of elevation there were four feet of width. The rear was more conventional: for every foot of rise, eight feet of width. The army's only other great hydraulic-fill dam, the Gatun Dam at the

Panama Canal, had shallow slopes both upstream and down. Gatun is approximately a hundred feet high (about a third as high as Fort Peck), and the sloping faces were identically built on the shallow angle of one foot in nine. When the Fort Peck Dam did partially collapse, it was the steep upstream end that slid, while the downstream slope stood firm. These are technical and theoretical matters, but if the reader merely understands that the construction of a huge earthworks is complicated and difficult, I am satisfied.

So, then, the stage was set for the tragedy. The dam was nearly completed, the summer flow of the Missouri River throbbed away underground, diverted into tunnels, tamed and controlled. And the rapid construction, the great dredge-and-fill exercise, continued. The men were working two shifts a day, from dawn to just after dark.

This was my father's version of what happened. It is almost completely inaccurate, you should understand at the outset. And why do I tell you a story that is not true? Because the difference between rarely remembered and seldom told anecdotes and historical fact is one of the subjects we are puzzling through, here.

He told me, once or twice, about the day of the Big Slide, and his essential account was as follows. Workmen had warned the army engineers that the dam was unstable; heavily loaded trains were wobbling on the temporary railroad lines running across its upstream face, where railcars were dumping the riprap for the outside skin of the dam, and this indicated that the structure itself was unstable. And then, the day of the Slide, he told me, two carloads of army engineers drove out on to the dam to see what these complaints were about, and as they did, it began to collapse. One carload was swept away in the Slide and the men drowned in the lake above the dam; the other was saved, because the driver, instead of taking time to turn his car around, just threw it in reverse gear and backed away from the crumbling face of the dam.

This was not an eyewitness account, as I always assumed it was. It was not until I started on this book, and had my father's navy personnel file in hand, that I found this out. At that point I could

actually date our family's exodus from Montana to California. The
Big Slide occurred on September 22, 1938. By then we were living
in California, where he had moved us after the completion of the
spillway project, and where he was working on another army flood-
control project, the Hansen dam in the Ventura mountains north-
east of Los Angeles. This one, by the way, was also an earth dam,
but constructed by the commoner and safer method of rolled-fill,
rather than dredged-fill. He would, however, have known something about the complaints arising from the instability of the railroad tracks, because his last job, after the spillway and before
packing us out of Montana to California in the summer of 1938,
was managing the Snake Butte quarry, where the granite riprap
was blasted loose and loaded on the trains. Problems with the tracks
at Fort Peck would have affected his scheduling of deliveries, and
he would have had daily opportunities to talk to the train crews.

However, no carload of army engineers drowned. In an odd way,
for he was not a vindictive man, that was pure wishful thinking on
his part. But there *was* a car that escaped by backing up. The driver
was Gene Tourtlotte, the same man who had driven Margaret
Bourke-White to Ruby White's whorehouse. The passengers were
some local army engineers, including Major Kittrell, overall head of
the operation. They did back up for a half-mile, as the dam crum-
bled in front of them and almost underneath them; that is true.

Here is what happened. All the information is in the operational
archives at Fort Peck. It is all quite beautifully typed.

On the morning of September 22, 1938, as the first dredging
shift came to work, the men noticed that the surface of the core
pool was almost overlapping the upstream crest of the dam. It was
never supposed to come within six feet of topping over the crest.
Since no dredge fill or dredge water had entered the core pool since
eight-thirty the evening before, this was inexplicable. They surveyed against known bench marks, and the surface of the core pool
had not risen: it was exactly where it had been the previous day.
If that was true, then the upstream face of the dam must have
slipped downward. For the rest of the morning, they worked to

check all the elevations, and discovered that the dredge pipe that ran across the upstream face was almost two feet lower than it had been when the last shift left on September 21. The pipes on the downstream face of the dam were exactly where they should have been. The dam was settling only on the upstream side; it was "shearing," in engineer's talk. This was when the call went to Major Kittrell, and he started out, motoring from the west end of the dam, nearest Fort Peck City and his headquarters building, a long three-mile ride across the top of the dam toward the east abutment, where the core pool threatened to overtop the upstream crest of the dam.

They continued to survey, with the dredges shut down. The distance from the surface of the core pool to the solid core at the bottom of the pool was normal. If the dam was slumping, it was only the upstream structure, the shell, that was moving. The sand and gravel and riprap facing were sinking, and sliding outward, creeping upstream.

This is what happened to Ray Kendall, who was making one of the survey checks; this is part of his deposition to the investigating officer:

> [I] Was having trouble setting up the [surveyor's] level when I noticed a small crack in the ground underneath my feet. . . . In a few seconds it got considerably deeper and longer.
>
> I noticed Douglas Moore . . . and Nelson VanStone down on the road. . . . Recognizing the danger, [they] were waving and yelling. . . . That was the last I saw of Moore, however VanStone (to the best of my memory) ran back to the road and close to Moore's car. . . . That was the last I remember seeing VanStone.
>
> I looked at my watch to make a check on the time of the slide. It was 1:21 p.m. Then I glanced at the two draglines which were . . . 400' away. They began to tilt over and go down very fast, then, I realized the great danger. Just a few seconds later the dragline seemed to have sunken 100 feet.

George Bondy was working on the dragline, which is an old-fashioned piece of earth-moving equipment: a large crane with a

free-swinging bucket suspended from the tip and then tied back to
the base; you drop the bucket onto the ground, and then drag it
back toward the crane with the cable—hence the name. The two
draglines were being used to trim the upstream shell of the dam
to the precise angle required in the plans. What George Bondy was
doing, as his wife explained to me fifty years later, was trying to
get it freed up. Somehow it had sunk into the usually solid shell
of the dam and was stuck, its crawler tracks buried to the hubs in
the sand and gravel. Bondy and the dragline operator gave up,
temporarily, and quit for lunch just before the dam went.

Ray Kendall found himself being swept away, not by water or
by an avalanche of mud and dirt. The very ground he was standing
on, the entire face of the dam as far as he could see, was moving
out into the lake in one solid piece. He was running across the
quarry rock, the final finished upstream face of the dam, turning
his ankles, falling, and as he ran across it, the riprapped face of
the dam moved a quarter of a mile straight out into the lake in less
than three minutes. When the slide stopped, he was standing on
a newly formed island, a solid, stable chunk of the dam itself that
was eleven hundred feet away from where it had been when the
slide started: "Realizing I was on safe ground I looked at my watch
and it was 1:25 p.m. With a big lump in my throat, I almost knew
that my fellow workman was not as fortunate as me."

Kendall crossed the river of water draining out of the core pool
to a section of the face which still stood intact:

> I climbed to a high point of the hill to get a better view of the
> tragic scene. . . . I picked up a transit [a surveyor's instrument
> with a very high-powered telescopic lens] and went back to the
> scene hoping that I might spot Johnson or someone else that might
> be in distress. I searched the terrible scene for bodies but all was
> in vain. Rescue Parties carried on the search.
>
> Thus ending the most tragic scene in all my life.
>
> [signed] *Ray Kendall*

Douglas Moore and Nelson P. Van Stone, Sr., whom Kendall saw just before he began his terrified run across the moving face of the dam, were killed. So were six other men.

I mention Van Stone's full name because it implies, it requires, that there is, or once was, a Nelson P. Van Stone, Jr., out there somewhere. He would be about my age, if not a few years older. Van Stone, Sr., was thirty-one when he was carried out into Fort Peck Lake, where his body still lies under hundreds of feet of mud and sand and reservoir water. The area where he died was covered with additional fill, after the Slide, to reinforce that section of the dam, almost five million extra yards of earth-filled dam, placed at the shallow angle of one foot of rise for every twenty-five feet of length.

Ralph E. Anglen's deposition confirmed Ray Kendall's fears. Anglen was an oiler—that is, a maintenance mechanic—on one of the two draglines that Kendall saw fall into the lake. Mrs. Bondy does not recall if it was the same one her husband was working on. But it was the dragline near which Kendall saw Van Stone and Moore. This is what Anglen saw:

> At about 1:15 p.m. on September 22, 1938, I was working on dragline No. D-11 when Mr. Nelson P. Van Stone came running up the slope of the upstream face of the dam yelling. I looked around and it looked like the corepool was going to run over the edge of the dam. I then looked down the slope and saw the slope cracking near the railroad track. I started to run west and down the slope with Mr. Van Stone in front of me. The slope seemed to rise in front of us while the part we were on dropped fast. Mr. Van Stone had turned east [away from the center of the slide]. As I dropped he went out of sight and I heard him say, "Goodbye boys."

Anglen found himself in the lake, covered with mud, alive. "I came up near an island," he added, "and I saw a pair of boots washed by me."

Oiler Anglen had that peculiar retentive mind for detail which

many construction men do have, but I was not exactly prepared
for his account of Van Stone's last words. They are quite believable:
you or I might scream or pray or curse, but men of Van Stone's
generation had a model to follow. It is, in ways, the standard
American heroic model, and you can pick your own hero: more
than one horse thief has stood on a gallows or sat on a horse with
a noose around his neck, and said something close to what Nelson
Van Stone said, but it is more generally the soldier's exit line, and
examples are almost endless.

Let me give you one that by its very obscurity makes that point
clearly. The following account is from among the hundreds of
personal memoirs written by Civil War veterans, this one by New-
ton Martin Curtis, *From Bull Run to Chancellorsville* (published by
G. P. Putnam's Sons, New York, 1906).

At the Battle of Glendale in the Civil War, also known as the
Battle of Charles City Road, near the James River in Virginia, the
16th New York Brigade was guarding the Charles City roadway
when they were attacked. On the evening of June 30, 1862, the
rebels shot Eland A. Woodruff, Private, who "survived his wound
half an hour; as he was carried to the rear, he said, 'Good bye,
boys, I can't be with you any longer.' "

Nelson Van Stone knew how to behave. I have thought about
that often. When my father was dying, much more slowly, of
cancer, he behaved very much the same way.

The eight deaths in the Big Slide are accounted for in the official
records of the Army Corps of Engineers, as are all fifty-nine deaths
that occurred at Fort Peck. The official judgment of the cause of
death is, "unavoidable." Whether the Slide itself was unavoidable,
as the army concluded, or was caused, as my father believed, by
the dam's simply being filled too fast, making it waterlogged and
unstable, is a question that was never resolved by all the investigations into the Slide. These official inquiries, which took two
years to complete, blamed the Slide on the underlying earth foundation of the dam, the Bear Paw shale, which, as we have noted,
was a difficult material. Bear Paw shale formations usually contain

strata of bentonite, and these were present in the foundation of the dam, far below the filled material. Bentonite is, in the arcane Latinism of civil engineering, "an impalpable clay," meaning very fine indeed, and extremely plastic.

So the official army explanation for the failure of the upstream face of the dam was this: Undetected seams of bentonite, located below the foundation of the dam, were saturated by water from the forming lake and the drainage water from the dredge-filled dam itself; saturated, swollen, and lubricious, they provided a slippery surface upon which the bottom of the dam slid out into the lake. The weight of the dam itself squeezed the saturated bentonite until it broke out of its natural place, like toothpaste when the tube fails, and it worked its way through the shale, making a thin but extensive slippery surface underneath the dam, and on this greasy material the foundation of the dam slid away.

The army specifically denied that the construction method itself, the rapid dredge-filling, and the resulting inevitable saturation of the dam by water, could have been an error. None of the investigators questioned the very shape of the dam, with its steep upstream slope, although the redesign, after the Slide, created a "bigger footprint," which would lie more solidly on the foundation soils below the dam. But rather indirectly they did consider the question of too-rapid construction. At the instigation of one investigator, the late Arthur Casagrande of Harvard University, the army allowed that the material in the upstream face might have been partially liquefied by the pressure of the core pool's water and thus have had little or no stability. The water pressure, to put it simply, would have been great enough to float the individual grains of sand in the dam, keeping them from locking together as they would normally, destroying their capacity for friction, one against another. As with most things that go wrong, there is more than one cause. There seems surely to have been a failure in the foundation, apparently caused by the slippery bentonite, but the speed and the distance, the sudden and catastrophic nature of the failure of the upstream face, may have been accelerated by saturation. Saturated

sands do not necessarily liquefy; that usually is caused by some
sudden motion, like an earthquake or, in this case, an abrupt
shearing or failure of the foundation soils. The dam might have
failed in any case, because of the problems with the foundation,
but it might not have been so massive and swift a failure, had the
sand not been potentially liquefied. That liquefaction, or the pro-
pensity toward it, was what my father meant when he said the
whole dam would quiver like jelly.

There are very few survivors of the engineering corps responsible
for the construction at Fort Peck, but I have spoken to one of them
who was a shavetail lieutenant in 1938 in charge of inspecting the
core material and the dredging process. We had a cordial conversation until I asked him if there were any indications, before the
Slide, of problems with the integrity of the dam. I asked if anyone
had tried to warn him or warn the Corps, and he said no. And
then he said this: "I suppose it was a combination of things. But
why are you trying to dig up dirt, blame some good engineers?"
That was about the sum of our talk.

The well-understood difficulty with hydraulic fill, whether it is
monstrous Fort Peck or something more imaginable, like the Quabbin project in Massachusetts, is simply to drain the core properly.
Excess water is pumped out, or relieved by small temporary spillways from the core pool back into the riverbed, but that is only
the visible water. The real danger is standing, permeating water
in the core and shells. To measure water levels inside the dam,
engineers install perforated pipes, and add to them, as the dam is
built upward, so that you have a series of small wells; it is simple
enough, either mechanically or by a remote electrical sensing system, to measure the water level inside the dam. It is the same as
measuring groundwater anywhere, except more critical. There is
no mention of these measurements in the army's various accounts
of the Slide. Perhaps they were so normal as to be unnoticed—or
perhaps they were not taken. It is almost inconceivable, considering
how critical they are, that an official explanation would not at least
assert that they were taken and were normal, that the shell of the

dam was not waterlogged. The logical first statement in any reasonable explanation would be: "Groundwater levels within the shell of the dam were normal and safe." But it isn't there.

When the Corps rebuilt the dam, they changed the design completely, building it with a much flatter slope on the upstream side, generally of seven and eight to one, with some areas as flat as fifty feet of width for every foot of rise. Thus it came to resemble more closely its engineering precedent, the Gatun Dam, with its symmetrical nine-to-one slopes. We can say with assurance that an error of initial judgment is implied when the reconstruction is a complete redesign. If the fault lay in poor foundation material, one solution would have been simply to dig down through it to hard and unweathered shale, and start over again. An alternative solution would have been to pile enough material directly over the faulty foundation to press it down firmly: the shallow-slope redesign is an attempt, and altogether successful for four decades, at this latter solution.

My father's death certificate is dated September 22, 1981, forty-three years to the day after the Slide. It had been, by all our memories, at least thirty years since he had mentioned it to anyone in the family. But in the last few days of his life, apparently because of a metastasis of the cancer to his brain, he became somewhat unsure of exactly where he was. He was in the hospital, of course. He would try to get out of bed, struggling against the gentle restraints. He absolutely had to get to a telephone, he kept saying, and warn them. The dam was unsafe, he had to call them, or something terrible was going to happen. They were building it too fast. It was all wrong.

This was the last thing he could remember. It was his final and unfulfilled professional responsibility.

8

Rumors of War

That my father was not exactly enamored of the Army Corps of Engineers was a matter of style as much as substance. When, in his mind, it came time to volunteer to serve in the nation's defense, he had no intention of spending any time in an army uniform.

On more than one occasion, he told a version of this story: The regular army officers would come up from Kansas City or Omaha to go hunting, and the local workers would "lassoo the deer and tie them up and they'd shoot them out of the cars." That is pure exaggeration. Montana cowboys are pretty good with a rope, even today, when tough modern roping is pretty much confined to rodeos and bucking-stock shows. But they never did lassoo mule deer.

That is just not in the nature of the beast. On the other hand, shooting deer or antelope out of car windows is a Montana tradition among a certain class of citizen and visitor, right along with stealing horses, salting gold claims, and committing highway robbery. It is the downside of what the British call "field sports," and there are still outfitters in the West who guarantee kills, and the guarantees are seldom called. You may not be able to lasso a mule deer, but it's no great trick to herd one by a tenderfoot's stand. As for shooting from automobiles, deer have only recently, and by no means universally, learned that automobiles are as dangerous as men on foot.

What his frustrations on the job were, as far as they were caused by the Corps of Engineers managers at Fort Peck, I have some idea. There is a faint tone of impatience in some of his surviving Spillway Section memoranda. One in particular, summing up the difficulties of pouring concrete to accurate dimensions, points out that if the "need for accuracy to less than ¼ inch in 25 feet had been made clear to the contractor, some unpleasantness could have been avoided." The unpleasantness would have devolved on the shoulders of M. R. Montgomery, Assistant Engineer and Chief, Concrete Inspection, rather than some distant, office-bound, and rarely visiting army contract-specification writer.

The matter of working for the army was straightforward necessity. My father had been graduated from Iowa State University in 1928, with a degree in civil engineering and membership in the honorary engineering society, Tau Beta Pi. He was not eligible for the one people have heard of, Phi Beta Kappa, because of an insufficient number of courses in the liberal arts. He did not really want to be a civil engineer—he would rather have been a doctor—but his father refused to give him any support through college unless it was for studying civil engineering. Of the five brothers, the three who went to college all studied civil engineering, although Uncle Gordon sneaked in some electrical engineering, and he retired as soon as possible, thanks to some inherited real estate from his father-in-law, and took up full-time fly-fishing. Uncle Donald got out of engineering after doing his time at Fort Peck and divorcing

Poor Olive. He became the manager of a pea-packing frozen-food plant. My father did take bacteriology—and got an A—in the fall quarter of his sophomore year, but then quit dabbling with premedical studies. His college transcript indicates an unexceptional course of progress, with a cumulative average of a little over 90. (The worst grade he got was a 77, a B−, in extemporaneous speech.)

In May 1928, after graduation, he returned to Chinook and became the general manager of Montgomery and Son, Contractors, which was then renamed "Montgomery and Sons." The original "Son" was Uncle Paul, the oldest child, who was a carpenter and not quite a high-school graduate. Paul worked until he was seventy-five, and was probably the last man in Montana to build a log house that wasn't delivered to the job site in precut packages from a log-building company. He thought it was a damned silly way to build a house, but if that's what the customer wanted, he'd cut the trees down and built it for him. I helped him shingle a barn roof one summer, on his son-in-law's place, and he worked exactly ten hours a day with two ten-minute breaks and a half-hour for lunch. He was over seventy then, and sounded like a nailing machine if you shut your eyes, so regular was his pace. Uncle Gordon said Paul could shingle ten squares a day. A square is short for a hundred square feet, and a thousand square feet of shingle is one hell of a day's work. Gordon went fishing while we shingled, which I didn't mind at all. Paul didn't mind, either; he knew that Gordon had long since quit trying to keep up with him.

My grandfather died suddenly in December 1929, and that was the end of Montgomery and Sons. In my father's terse words on an application for a commission in the United States Navy Reserve: "Was Partner in company until Death of Senior Partner Dissolved Firm." He worked for three years as a resident engineer in Montana for Winston Brothers, the Minneapolis contractor doing highway work all along the route of the Great Northern Railroad. Finally, even that ran out. The state of Montana had been flat broke since the mid-1920s, and you couldn't sell highway bonds very easily in the absolute bottom of the Great Depression. That is how he ended up at Fort Peck, a job he appreciated from an engineering professional's point of view and as a recently married man. The job did not engender any affection for the chain of command, including Franklin Delano Roosevelt, up there at the top.

As I mentioned, the records of the Spillway Section, now housed in the basement of the Administration Building at Fort Peck, are unusually mingled. The usual official reports and monthly summaries that were typical of all the divisions of the project are there, along with what seem, at first glance, to be random memoranda that should have been disposed of years ago. Most of these were written by my father, or have his name on them somewhere.

These various papers make up a short history of changes made in the basic specifications for components of the Fort Peck project—whether structural concrete or bituminous paving for the roadways—or else they are alterations of the contracts between the private contractors doing the work and the Corps. As such, they fall into that vast category of frequently saved government papers—the ones that can be used, in the vernacular, to cover your ass.

They were also the only pieces of paper—and I quickly made electrostatic copies—that I had seen for many years with a single word on them written by my father. We in the family were not very good at writing letters and worse at keeping them. So it is that at the age of fifty I found myself considering the implications of the Bitumen Index and the proportion of crushed material smaller than one-quarter inch in diameter on the long-term stability of certain bituminous asphalt roads in Fort Peck, Montana. I will not force the same task on the reader.

One of the little-recognized roles of a government inspector is to assure that private companies manage not only to meet specifications, but also to make a profit, operate economically, and succeed. There are touches of this issue in the Montgomery memos, including almost but not entirely patient explanations of how things are done in the real world, as opposed to the orderly world of the Corps of Engineers. After explaining how to eliminate an entire set of truck scales and a weighmaster (one man for three shifts a day) by simply weighing the purchased material at the asphalt-batching plant and making sure it got delivered, my father concluded his description of this simpler, cheaper procedure by writing: "This system has been used successfully for a long time on highway work."

More than anything else, the Corps's penchant for volume, yardage, speed would have annoyed my father. For several years, during high-school and college vacations and for two straight years after college, I had the opportunity to work for him, and he ran efficient, safe, high-quality jobs. He understood, and certainly had a chance to learn, the difference between apparent speed and real progress. He poured a million yards of concrete at the spillway, to use the standard engineer's possessive locution about work they supervise. Yet I know it annoyed him that the army engineers were so concerned about volume to the detriment of the final project. This annoyance surfaced in an unusually lengthy description, for him, of a continual problem: pouring concrete so fast that the forms could not take the pressures.

> The forming crews made efforts to strengthen forms each time . . . but it seemed almost impossible to install enough tie rods or braces to withstand the pressures which could be built up by rapid pouring and the thorough vibration which the concrete received.
> The last few walls . . . were poured more slowly with generally satisfactory results, but one complete form failure during a pour . . . clearly demonstrated the wisdom of tempering the desire for "yardage" with a reasonable consideration for the type of pour being made. Needless to say, at the height of the trouble considerable friction developed between the forming and pouring [crews] . . . each group blaming the other for the difficulties encountered.

The tone is important. It is his engineer's understanding that problems can be solved if people will keep their eye on the product and the process, not on such trivia as "yardage" or other meaningless measures of raw effort. The Corps's preoccupation with

simple measures and sheer quantity frustrated his careful engineering mind. It is the construction equivalent of an infantry general's trying to make a reputation by capturing ground he has not
the strength to hold against counterattack, or even maintain un-
challenged, given the vagaries of supply lines.

He admired workmen who kept at a steady pace, and disliked
those who even gave the appearance of inattention. He once fired
the best carpenter I ever worked with, the cleverest and fastest
man on the job. It was, in part, my fault. This fellow was waiting
for me to get back up to him with some more material, so we could
finish out some small details in the form work. And while he was
waiting, he took his handsaw and played it, which you can do by
bending it and then striking it with your thumb, so that it moans,
sounding something like a cat in heat. He twanged his saw, unfortunately, just as my father walked by, and his check was waiting
for him when we broke for lunch. Accidents were not exactly
accidents, to my father; they were failures.

The one time I got hurt enough on one of his jobs to go to the
doctor, he pointed out to me, later, that if I hadn't filled the
wheelbarrow all the way to the rim with wet concrete, I could have
pushed it more easily, and it wouldn't have tipped over and tossed
me into the trench, and I wouldn't be sitting there trying to eat
dinner with ten stitches in my upper lip. I told him it only hurt
when I laughed.

I had always understood that my father joined the navy reserves
sometime before World War II. It came up, as best I recall, when
he talked to me about planning ahead, something he regularly
encouraged me to do. He had known there was a war coming, and
by taking a commission had ensured he could do what he did best,
rather than being caught up in a confused bureaucracy in the
emergency. My assumption was that he had enlisted in 1940 or
perhaps as early as 1939, after the war in Europe had begun.

Hardly so. On November 20, 1935, he wrote the Commandant,
13th Naval District (Seattle), and inquired about the United States
Navy Civil Engineer Corps (CEC). He had, at this point in his

life, never seen an ocean. The resident CEC officer in Seattle, a
Captain Walter H. Allen, responded, "I have read over with interest your record of education and experience as contained in your
letter. . . . As far as I am able to judge you are qualified for the
Civil Engineer Corps Reserve and I suggest that you put in your
application for the rank of Lieutenant Junior Grade. It should be
accompanied by a few letters of testimony as to your character and
engineering ability."

My mother was not surprised when he announced that he was
going to try for a navy commission. "It preyed on his mind," she
told me when I started on this book. "He was convinced there was
going to be a war. We'd go play bridge with people and he'd talk
about it, that's all he'd talk about." This insight into historical
determinism, if that is what it was, put him considerably ahead of
various world leaders.

I do not think it was a deep understanding of the menace of
Hitler and European fascism. Even *The New York Times*' editorial
board, let alone a civil engineer in the Missouri River Valley, could
regard Hitler as a necessary evil who was saving Germany from
inflation and Red revolution. And Mussolini? I have heard members
of my family say that at least he made the trains run on time. This
is not a joke in Montana, where people expect trains to make
schedule. But in November 1935? I do think the influences are
traceable. My father had, after all, come of age in a state that had
banned the speaking of German in public during the First World
War, from a small-town culture that saw considerable evil at work
in the outside world, back east, over there. At Iowa State, a land-
grant college, he had taken mandatory military training from officers
who had fought the Boche. And there were great rumblings already.
In October 1933, when he went to work at Fort Peck, Hitler had
withdrawn Germany from the League of Nations. In the summer
of 1934, there was an aborted putsch in Austria, and the incipient
Nazi movement had precipitated the murder of the Austrian quasi-
dictator, Dolfuss. I suspect that, beyond a general pessimism, it
was Hitler's May 1935 occupation of the Rhineland, and the utter

failure of the French to resist it, that convinced my father that
nothing would stop Hitler short of a major war.

In any case, he was obliged to find recommendations as to his
character and professional excellence.

The letters have a peculiar flavor. He got all of his recommendations of character from lawyers, proof, if any were required, that
1936 was a long time ago. A Mr. Fredlund, clerk of the Blaine
County court, "always found him as a man of commendable qualities, possessed with a clean moral character, industrious of habit,
conscientious and reliable in his dealings and worthy of the highest
esteem and confidence . . . [with] an unimpeachable reputation,
for honesty, truth and integrity, and he is regarded as a good, true
and loyal citizen." (This admirable person was one of no more than
a thousand inhabitants of the seat of Blaine County. Messrs.
D. J. Sias and D. L. Blackstone (so resonantly named), also both
attorneys at law, were the requisite second and third character
witnesses. It goes not without saying that all three were Masons,
as was my father.

Getting professional recommendations was a little trickier. As a
contract employee of the army, he had to ask that branch not only
to recommend him to the navy, but also to permit him to abandon
the army in case of war or other national emergency. But the
approval, and the recommendation from his direct superior, Captain John R. Hardin, was forthcoming, and nothing remained but
to pass the physical examination.

While Chinook, being a county seat in oil, gas, and ranch country, was overpopulated with lawyers, it was evidently short on
preventive medicine and quality dentistry when my father was a
child. Besides measles and mumps, which are understandable, he
had had smallpox, which has been preventable by inoculation since
the middle of the seventeenth century. As an adult, he was normal
and healthy, although underweight, having lost ten pounds in the
winter of 1935–36 because of "hard work." The serious physical
problem was dental. By the age of thirty-one, he had already lost
twelve molars to extraction. The human mouth is given twenty-

four molars to start with, including the wisdom teeth; not only were half of his gone, but the dozen that had survived were directly over or under the empty spots, leaving him no paired molars in either jaw. This is summed up in the physical exam in a quite remarkable understatement as "insufficient opposing molars," and his initial application was denied.

But, upon his promise to acquire appropriate bridgework and create a sufficiency of teeth, the defect was waived, and he became a lieutenant (JG) on May 1, 1936. He dreaded the dentist's office, that I know, and the promise to get his dental insufficiency repaired could be regarded as a truly patriotic commitment. I suspect that the wording of the certificate of commission—which says that the President of the United States was "reposing special Trust and Confidence in the Patriotism, Valor, Fidelity and Abilities" of the commissioned officer—was some comfort, especially the part about Valor. He never told me that big boys don't cry, but he certainly did once say that big boys had to go to the dentist. One of the few specific genetic traits he and I share is an unresponsiveness to the analgesic effects of ordinary dental anesthetics.

For these insights into his health and the assertions as to his character, I am indebted to the United States Navy, and the care with which the records of officers, beginning with the earliest correspondence about enlistment, are kept. An "Officer Personnel File" contains a sometimes bewildering pile of minutiae, most of it financial, and every last travel order; it also contains quarterly "Fitness Reports," which are in a sense the officer's personal property and are not forwarded to his various commanders when he changes stations. Each fitness report is independent of the previous ones.

Although the personnel files are kept in great privacy, they are available to the officer or, after death, to his heirs. Today they are kept in Saint Louis, Missouri, at the National Personnel Records Center, by the millions. Obtaining one, for a parent's military career, requires one to provide the death certificate, which, even well after the fact, is a difficult piece of paper to hold, let alone to read.

Although my father's records turned out to be incomplete, especially for a few critical months during World War II, it was as precise a chart of those mysterious waters as one might make from a single ship's log. It contains very little information about the world at large, but very accurate information about where he was at a particular moment. If you had to sail from Nantucket to New Guinea, and had no more information than the ship's log of a single but successful voyage, you could do it, though perhaps inefficiently. South America might be nothing more than the smell of land on an offshore breeze, Easter Island would pass unseen, but faithful adherence to the daily position of the ship's logbook would be enough, even to enable you to pass through the Straits of Magellan and cross the vast reach of the South Pacific between Patagonia and distant Oceania. Only if you were to add other material, maps and charts and so forth, would you see what fearsome shoal waters were narrowly avoided, what unnecessary distances had been traveled. But even without such additional charts, you would not get lost.

9

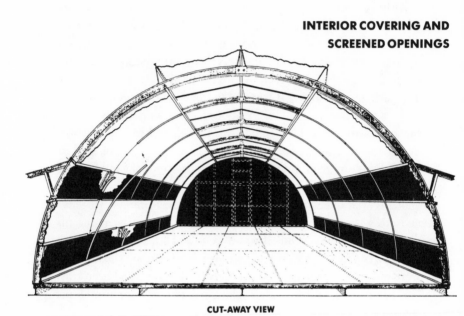

CUT-AWAY VIEW

Destination: Scotland

The last job my father had at Fort Peck, after the Spillway Section disbanded, was managing the rock quarry where the riprap for the upstream face of the dam was blasted, sized, and shipped by the trainload. Thus it was his rock that Nelson P. Van Stone, Sr., scrambled across before the slide buried him in the reservoir. The quarry was at Rattlesnake Butte, a chunk of primordial granite sticking up out of the broken country between Havre and Chinook, 160 miles northwest of Fort Peck. Working at the quarry put him back within a few miles of where he was born, and our family lived for a few months in the old Montgomery home in Chinook. A "butte" is a geological structure defined any number of ways; there are special and local definitions which make for good arguments among residents of different parts of the West. It's not a mountain, and it's more than a hill—that much is universal. It's certainly not a mesa. A mesa is flat-topped and sticks straight up out of the plains, as the name, Spanish for "table," implies. A butte, generally speaking, sticks up abruptly on one end, and tapers back into the general lie of the land at the other. Rattlesnake Butte would have been an island in the sea about sixty million years ago; the rattlesnake part is self-explanatory.

Rock, like real sand and clean gravel, is still a scarce commodity in eastern Montana, a country built on softer sedimentary rocks laid down in that old inland sea. My mother was terrified of the rock quarry. One could hear the blasting a dozen miles away, on a clear day, and feel the ground shake in Chinook. During the time my father was the quarry manager, there was a fatal accident, although I have no idea whether it happened on his shift. It is duly recorded in the list of fifty-six fatalities, and the cause is described as "failure to obey instructions, entered blasting area." There is also a photograph of the scene in the official files, which shows a large chunk of quarry rock resting against, rather than lying inside, a railroad car.

In July 1938, when my older sister was a toddler and I was a lump in diapers, we left Montana. The Army Corps of Engineers was managing a vast flood-control dam-and-canal project in the Los Angeles Basin, and my father's immediate superior at Fort Peck, another civilian civil engineer, had moved to Tujunga, a small town in the hills north of Los Angeles, and, as soon as a slot opened up, arranged to bring my father down. That got us out of Montana and introduced us to such strange things as lemons growing on trees. In Montana, and I suppose all across the central plains, cooks use a recipe for something called mock-lemon pie, which is a vinegar-and-sugar pie with Ritz crackers layered in the filling to give it some body. Except for a few years during World War II, my family had permanently graduated from snow and mock-lemon pie to sunshine and the real thing.

The move to California had a more important result than freedom from blizzards. It put my father within a few miles of the Pacific Ocean and made him handy, so to speak, to the bustling navy installations in San Pedro and San Diego. By the winter of 1938–39, as the Japanese consolidated their hold in China, the navy was already looking westward from California, and government funds were beginning to shift from politically based public make-work projects to the stirrings of a national defense program. My father took his navy correspondence courses, attended reserve drills and lectures, and wrote an occasional letter to the Commandant, 11th Naval District, Los Angeles, reminding him of his availability. By the spring of 1940, he was awaiting orders to active duty.

It would be events in Europe, however, that controlled all our lives. It is difficult, now, to imagine a tabletop radio in Tujunga spitting out the live broadcasts of William Shirer from Berlin. In March 1939 Czechoslovakia became part of the Reich. September 1939 saw the German invasion of Poland. And then came the Phony War—England and France at a state of declared war with Germany but without any fighting—and nothing happened until May 1940, when the Blitzkrieg swept across France and the Low Countries to Dunkirk. On October 1, 1940, five full months after the war in Europe began, we were swept up from the dusty hillsides of Tujunga and plunked down on Coronado Island in San Diego Bay. We were then the family of Lieutenant M. R. Montgomery, Civil Engineer Corps, USNR. The task my father had been called to active duty to perform was upgrading the Naval Air Station at North Island, the military two-thirds of Coronado Island and still a major military airfield. This occupied him from August 1940 to April 22, 1941. Mobilization for defense, if not for war, was now the policy of the U.S. Navy. What my father half-feared and half-desired had become true—there was a world at war, he was not going to spend it in the Army Corps of Engineers, and he would maintain his profession, he would build things, not destroy them.

This is, incidentally, about the time when the world became memorable for the three-year-old child I was then. The outside of the house is white stucco. There is an ocean nearby. Father is a fairly mysterious creature who leaves early and comes home late. I have only one precise memory of him from the spring of 1941, before he disappeared from all but the imagination until the fall of 1943. He departed without, to be honest, creating any anxiety I was aware of. My excuse for not noticing he was gone is simply that I was only three.

It was not so simple for my mother. This is what happened. On the first day of April 1941, my father received secret orders to be, in the language of such things, "detached" from the 11th Naval District, San Diego, and report to the Chief of the Bureau of Yards and Docks, Washington, D.C. Beyond that he knew nothing, and when he would know, it would remain secret. In a bustling but peacetime navy town, handsome lieutenants had been known to disappear for less reason, and my mother found herself in the position of having lost a husband and being unable to explain it to anyone. As the war progressed, this became more usual and people became accustomed to it, but not in April 1941. When I asked her about it just a few years ago, my mother said, "My friends thought your father had left me, and I couldn't tell them where he had gone. Finally, I just had to leave, and I did."

We went home to Montana. When my mother had wanted to go to high school, she had kept house in Miles City for the Shore family, who owned the clothing store. (When I say "clothing store," I mean the kind where they sell men's suits *and* ladies' dresses; it's still there, but now it sells only women's clothes.) The Shores were our friends, in some sense, but theirs was also the house where my mother had picked up after the boys and done the laundry and cooked and cleaned. That's where we went. Her parents were still living on the old dirt farm in Jordan, but Jordan was impossible. It was tough enough to move back into a house where you'd lived as a servant, but that dry farm was the place from which she had escaped and could never live again. We visited once—it must have been in the summer of 1941, before gas rationing—and I remember that there was a kerosene lamp in the bedroom; whatever else I

did, I was not to touch it. Moths beat against it, I remember that,
and fell on the pillow, and when you touched them, gray powder
came off on your hands. Out the window, it was black beyond
belief, because the nearest electricity was thirty miles away. That
my father was three thousand miles away was a meaningless reality.

His disappearance was caused not simply by the general outbreak
of war in Europe, but in particular by the siege of Britain by sea.
There was plenty of work for navy civil engineers in California,
and more on the Gulf and Atlantic coasts, but in one of those
capricious bureaucratic decisions, he was chosen for a program
intended, at the beginning, to succor beleaguered Britain.

The fall of France, Belgium, and Holland in September 1940
created an absolutely unique problem in the economic history of
Britain. For the first time, she was dependent on supplies from
North America. Although the United States had been an ally ever
since the unpleasantness of the Civil War, when Britain had abet-
ted its trading partner, the staple-exporting Confederacy, and even
though timber- and mineral-rich Canada was a member of the
British Empire, some 90 percent of Britain's imports in the 1930s
came from Europe. German aerial bombing of her ports and mining
of the North Sea and the Channel, German submarines operating
with impunity all about the British Isles, and the sorties of German
surface raiders—all these alone would not have created so great a
crisis, but the only supply line left, the one to North America,
took weeks longer than the customary shuttling of goods from the
Continent, and every day at sea was dangerous. The extra time
required to carry goods, and the "turnaround time" for empty ships
to return to North America, would have cut the real carrying
capacity of an unthreatened British merchant marine by 60 percent.

And the loss of ships was almost unbelievable, the efficiency of
the German submarine fleet being quite unanticipated. From the
British declaration of war after the invasion of Poland in September
1939 until May 1940, when the Blitzkrieg swept across Northern
Europe, German submarines sank 242 British and Allied mer-
chantmen, ships with a carrying capacity of 850,000 tons. With

Western Europe conquered or neutralized, Germany then turned all her raiders, submarines, and bombers loose on the Atlantic supply lines. In the last seven months of 1940, submarines sank another 1.75 million tons of shipping, while mines, aircraft, and surface raiders accounted for the destruction of nearly one million additional tons of carrying capacity. British imports of raw materials, food, and manufactured goods fell in 1940, from forty-five million tons annually to just over thirty million, a figure that was not to be exceeded during the war. This forced a subsistence diet upon the population and shortages in the factories of the British Isles that would last until well after the end of the war.

The first effort to break the stranglehold on Britain was an American provision of surplus war materiel, of which the public knew only of the transfer of fifty decommissioned destroyers to the British, in trade for American rights to build and use bases in British possessions in the Caribbean and South America. This destroyer/bases deal also included, but did not publicize, the supply of a dozen long-range seaplanes (Consolidated PBYs, known in Britain as Catalinas) for reconnaissance against submarines and surface raiders. Additionally, the British got several hundred thousand antiquated firearms, used to arm the Home Guard, a force of equally superannuated Britons and Scots who patrolled the coast against the then very real threat of German invaders.

With the implementation of the Lend-Lease program in the spring of 1941, an entirely unpublicized program caused my father to disappear in secrecy, and us to leave San Diego and go to Montana. As the Battle of Britain slowed the Luftwaffe's efforts to soften up Britain for invasion, and as the United States Congress continued to resist any effort by Roosevelt to engage the nation directly against Hitler, a very bold and unprecedented plan was afoot in the navy. It is not clear, even now, reading the declassified correspondence and memoranda of meetings, exactly what Roosevelt intended to do about the convoys to Britain. He apparently intended, until political opposition made it impossible, to undertake armed escort of all convoys, whether of American-flagged ships (a

tiny number, throughout the war) or British ships, all the way
from North America to the western ports of England and Scotland.
This proposed policy may have been meant to do more than merely
provide protection for the convoys; Roosevelt may have thought
that, if enough American lives and military ships were lost, Congress would be forced to declare war on Germany.

The navy's plan required support bases in Britain, and the navy
rarely operated bases on foreign soil, however friendly. Also, the
scarcity of building materials and labor in Britain required an
equally great revolution in building methods: the component buildings, including electrical systems and plumbing, and every scrap
of material for wharves, pipelines, and fuel-storage tanks, were to
be precut, packaged, and shipped in as complete and prefabricated
a state as possible.

This plan would have been undertaken sooner than the spring
of 1941, except that the Congress, which controlled the purse, was
in no bellicose mood, had no intention of sending Americans out
onto the Atlantic convoy lanes or, worse, to the threatened British
Isles. But passage of the Lend-Lease Act gave the program a legal,
if somewhat deceptive, method for beginning the overseas construction of bases. The American government would provide the
construction materials, purchased under a loosely defined authorization for "temporary aviation facilities" that justified the portable
buildings and all the other components of the bases. The British
would pay for the labor costs, as partial repayment for American
repairing and refitting of British merchant and military ships at
the North American end of the convoy line. This thin cloak of
legality and the slight odor of deception that hung over the program
required exceptional secrecy for the United States military personnel involved in the construction. The "cover" in this case was the
usual one in such circumstances: the dozens of navy civil engineers
assigned to build the bases were named as naval attachés at the
embassy in London.

The plan was not only audacious from an engineering viewpoint,
but further complicated by a fundamental navy principle: redun-

dancy. On April 5, 1941, the Senior Naval Observer in London was notified of the American plan to build two identical destroyer bases, "one at Londonderry, and the other at Gare Loch, Scotland." And there would also be duplicate seaplane bases for the Catalina aircraft—one at Loch Erne, in Northern Ireland, the second at Loch Ryan, on the coast southwest of Glasgow. The Northern Irish bases had the attraction of being the most distant sites from continental Europe and thus less likely to be bombed (the great blitz of London, Coventry, and Glasgow had befallen those cities in the winter of 1940–41). On the other hand, the Irish Republic was officially neutral, and suspected of genuine sympathy with the Axis powers; both Londonderry and Lower Loch Erne (or Lough Erne, in the Irish spelling) were on the very border between the Free State and British Northern Ireland. The Scottish bases, although thought to be more vulnerable to attack by the Germans, were surrounded by a trustworthy anti-Nazi local population.

The navy was eager to join in the North Atlantic war then under way, but only on its own terms. These would require full repair and fuel facilities for American convoy escorts and patrolling seaplanes. There would be no shared facilities, no dependence on British supply or foreign craftsmen. As the commander of the American convoy escorts already operating between the United States and Iceland wrote, this plan was unique: "The coordination, construction, and operation of advanced bases in the British Isles presents an entirely new departure in the history of our Navy, inasmuch as the construction of the bases is to be started in a belligerent country, while the United States is still at peace." The American escort ships, from destroyers on up to battleships, were intended to be independent of shore stations while in action, with their own tenders, repair ships, and oilers. But the concentration of German aircraft and submarines made tender vessels a most inappropriate support. Shore stations, however difficult to construct politically and physically, were the only answer.

My father's orders to proceed to Great Britain are quite complete in his personnel file, beginning with assignment to the Quonset

Point, Rhode Island, Naval Air Station, where the premanufactured components of Bases 1 and 2, A and B, as they were known, were being designed and fabricated. And there are several "temporary-duty" orders to New York City, where the primary contractors, Fuller Construction and Merritt-Chapman and Scott, had offices. Merritt-Chapman was New York's largest waterfront contractor, capable of building and repairing both docks and the ships that used them. The George A. Fuller Company (of which Fuller Construction is a subsidiary) was one of the larger general contractors in America, with its own office building at 57th Street and Madison Avenue. (The Fuller Building, a forty-story Art Deco skyscraper, virtually created the 57th Street art-gallery district when it opened its doors in 1928—the first five floors were designed as art dealers' gallery spaces.)

While my father was at Quonset Point, in addition to helping with the design and scheduling of the component parts of the bases, he became familiar with some of the emoluments of officer status, including paid travel for dependents between duty stations. At the same time that my mother was taking my sister and me back to Montana, fleeing from the unanswerable questions of her friends, my father remembered to put in for travel expenses for my family's theoretical movement from San Diego to Rhode Island and, when he left for England, for an equally theoretical movement back to California. My mother did travel east to say goodbye. My sister and I got parked with relatives. I like the phrasing of the telegram sent all the way from London to Washington to pay for the trip:

TO BUNAV DEPENDENTS LIEUT MAURICE R MONTGOMERY USNR
WIFE MARY E DAUGHTER MARY L AGE FIVE SON MAURICE R AGE
THREE TRAVELLED QUONSET POINT RI TO ALHAMBRA CALIF DEPART
ING . . . JUNE ARRIVING & JULY X REQUEST AUTHORITY PAYMENT
TRAVEL.

The payment was $136.48, each way.
But the order that must have thrilled him most arrived on June

3, 1941. Imagine if you, too, had anticipated a war in Europe for at least five years, and you, too, now thought that all the trust placed in you by the civil engineering faculty of Iowa State University and the President of the United States and everyone in between was now to be employed, that in a very real sense, you were about to be what life had shaped you for:

> When directed by the Officer in Charge of Construction, Naval Air Station, you will regard yourself detached from duty at the NAS, Quonset Point, R.I., and from such other duty as may have been assigned you; will proceed to New York, N.Y. and take passage to Lisbon, Portugal, via a Pan American Airways clipper, and thence proceed via commercial aircraft to London, England, and report to the Naval Attaché, American Embassy, for duty as Assistant Naval Attaché.

To neutral Lisbon, by flying boat, a city already packed with refugees, spies, diplomats, and People Who Did Not Speak English! To London, where the resolute British you had seen on the newsreels were battling the great fires of the blitz! To the American embassy, where you would have diplomatic status! From Chinook, for God's sake, to London!

And, better—if that is possible—on to Scotland! To someone growing up in Montana, the only two sports worth knowing about were fly-fishing and golf. And we Scots had invented both of them.

On July 8, 1941, my mother received a telegram addressed "care of Thomas Shore, Miles City, Montana":

> LIEUTENANT M R MONTGOMERY USNR ARRIVED LONDON JULY FIFTH

It would be two years before he came home.

What a small navy it was, even with the preparations for the possibility of war that consumed its energies in 1941. Chester Nimitz, who would become Commander in Chief of the Pacific fleet, was, as Chief of the Bureau of Navigation, sailing a desk that included personnel matters in its omnibus capacity. Ben Moreell, Chief of the Bureau of Yards and Docks, and thus commander of all civil engineers, had the time personally to sign orders and sit his new reserve officers down for a chat. One of the matters he apparently discussed with them was the possibility, when the going got tough and the bureaucracy was stifling them, that he would accept a personal letter from any of them, not to be sent up through the chain of command, if things got bad enough. My father never wrote him one, but long after the war he remembered that invitation, and did write to Moreell's successor. It was not a privilege to be exercised lightly.

More than the satisfaction of being a naval officer and practicing his profession, my father had a sense of being a key player in what he must have seen as the first move in a most audacious plan to come to the aid of Britain, to begin America's war against Hitler. These few dozen civil-engineering officers were an outward and visible sign that Roosevelt's America was really going to come to the aid of Churchill's embattled island. The two pairs of bases, one set for ships, the other for seaplanes, were to be raised on foreign soil, the navy was coming, and the engineers went before them in the wilderness to make a place for them.

That is what construction men always do, but never before had such a promise been made in such desperate times, so far from home. They were not just naval attachés, but proof that the Yanks were coming. As the construction work in Scotland and Northern Ireland got under way, they were promoted to the even more dignified category of Special Naval Observer. And each one of them acquired, for formal occasions, full dress uniforms with those wonderful fore-and-aft hats worn by everyone since John Paul Jones, and swords. My father was thirty-seven years old, and had not been so impressively attired since he attended Masonic Lodge meetings in Chinook.

10

An Orphan's Journey

Pearl Harbor, and the immediate entry of the United States into World War II, affected my father's work in Scotland, as I shall relate later. But the dislocations that his navy duty forced on him and our family were trivial compared with what happened to my wife's family. For they were ethnically Japanese, and they lived in California, a state of no grace at all on December 8, 1941.

Of the more than one hundred thousand "Japanese aliens and others of Japanese ancestry" residing in the Western Defense Command, only a few hundred escaped the assembly centers and concentration camps. The United States, after Pearl Harbor, did not

encourage Japanese to move about freely. My father-in-law managed to avoid going to "camp," as it is called in the Japanese community, and he kept his family with him for the duration of the
war. He also made a contribution to the war effort, as an employee
of the navy's Japanese-language school. I think this war effort
helped to reconcile my parents to their son's choice of a wife,
although it was only a small help, and slow to take effect.

My father-in-law was Lee Mitsuyoshi Watanabe, M.D. He was
born in a tiny fishing village on the west coast of Japan, in Matsue
Province, which is famous for growing buckwheat and for the
Izumo shrine, the oldest wooden building in the world and nearly
as important in Japanese history as the better-known Ise shrine,
over on the east coast, near Kyoto. His name was not really
Watanabe but Ueyoshi, and he was not originally named Lee—
that is his American name. His father died when he was a baby,
his mother when he was twelve. Much is made now of the Japanese
regard for education, as if it were some kind of postwar phenom-
enon, like Toyotas, but it was always so, and the Meiji reforms
had brought it to even small villages in distant provinces. It was
understood that my father-in-law was simply too intelligent a child
to be left an orphan—which is to say, to be purely a nobody—and
the village schoolteacher arranged for Mitsuyoshi Ueyoshi to be
adopted. My father-in-law wanted to emigrate to Brazil and become
an orange rancher (we Westerners "ranch" everything, including
citrus fruit and chickens), but that was not the plan of his teacher.
There was a family of good character from Matsue who lived in
Fresno, California, where they grew strawberries and table grapes,
and that is how as a teen-ager he became Lee M. Watanabe, of
the Watanabe family of Fresno. Technically speaking, he should
not have been allowed to emigrate to the United States, as the so-
called Gentleman's Agreement of 1908 had put an end to immi-
gration from Japan except for members of Japanese families already
resident in the United States. But his adoption, although it was
done by simply re-registering him on the village record of births
and deaths, was not in any sense fraudulent: the Japanese have

for centuries made a practice of adoption by registration, some-times to provide a son and heir to a childless family, and not infrequently, as in his case, to give a family to an orphan, and thus genuinely to integrate the child into the existing, family-centered, society.

Lee Watanabe was not only too intelligent to stay trapped in the depths of Japanese society but also too ambitious to want to grow up to be a grape rancher. He attended public school in Fresno, losing only a year to his age-mates, learning English with extreme rapidity. He worked his way through two years at Fresno City College and then transferred to Stanford University, where he completed premedicine in 1928, and became a lifelong fan of the rarely successful but always interesting Stanford football team. Students of Oriental ethnicity were lumped together in Stanford University's scheme of things, and a separate undergraduate house for the Chinese, Korean, and Japanese students, both American residents and foreign students, was provided for their communal life. It was segregation (black students were virtually unknown), a well-intentioned and paternalistic segregation. We have a few old photographs of Dr. Lee taken with his housemates, and there, with almost Biblical flowing white hair, is pictured Stanford's president-emeritus, David Starr Jordan. Both Jordan (an ichthyol-ogist by profession and the true author of the often-told anecdote about the absent-minded professor: "Every time I learn a student's name I forget a fish") and Ray Lyman Wilbur, a medical doctor and president of Stanford in the 1920s and 1930s, encouraged my father-in-law to be a doctor, the first resident Japanese to achieve that goal at Stanford.

In those years, Stanford's medical school was in San Francisco, where city hospitals could provide clinical experience for students. Dr. Lee completed his studies on time, graduating from the old Stanford-Lane Medical School in 1932. He managed to pay for all this by selling aluminum cookware as an undergraduate and, in medical school, by working as a houseboy for a San Francisco family (with whom, by the way, he did not later try to stay in touch). It was very good cookware; my mother-in-law still has a complete, well-used set, now fifty years and more after he brought one to his new wife.

He was one of only a handful of Western-trained Japanese physicians in all of California in 1932. After graduation, he was not able to get an internship in one of the great teaching hospitals, but only a specially endorsed internship at Fresno City Hospital, which had, fortunately, enough Japanese patients from the local farming community not to be disturbed by the idea of putting a Japanese doctor on staff. Within a month of his arrival, the small hospital's only full-time staff member quit, so my father-in-law spent a year of internship as *de facto* head of medicine and emergency surgery in Fresno. It was great training, apparently. In the 1930s, it was not unusual for a doctor to be all things to all patients, and for the next three decades, my father-in-law was a general physician and general surgeon, worked the emergency room when necessary, and delivered babies.

After his year in Fresno, he moved to San Jose, California, where there was a substantial Japanese population but no Japanese doctor. (Or, to be precise, no genuine Japanese doctor. There was, in the ghetto in North San Jose, a Japanese hospital owned by a Caucasian doctor and staffed by a Japanese herbalist. It was regarded by the residents of Nihon machi, Japantown, as a place you went to die. The building is still standing, on North 5th Street, across from the Methodist church; it is the Japanese community center now, and old men play Go and Japanese chess up on the second floor, where their relatives once went to die.) Dr. Watanabe's first contribution to the community was his acceptance at the San Jose public hospital, which meant that for the first time Japanese patients would have access to modern medicine, such as it was in 1933, when surgery was still a problematic event, with the ever-present threat of untreatable infection, when pneumonia still killed. In the next eight years, he built his practice, and his reputation in the medical community, almost without reference to his race.

By December 1941 he had three children, a thriving practice that included a large number of Caucasian patients, a new house on the fringe of Japantown, just a block out of the ghetto (bounded by North 3rd and 5th streets, along Taylor and Jackson), where the heart of Japantown still lingers today. He was also, in the fall of 1941, chief medical officer of the Santa Clara County Civil Defense Volunteer Medical Service—and, after December 7, in well-perceived peril. In addition to the general anti-Japanese feeling provoked by Pearl Harbor, there was a large Filipino population in the agricultural Santa Clara Valley, and the Japanese attack on the Philippines on December 8 provoked small riots and shootings in central California. He never talked much about the war, except, as usual, to tell a medical story. He recalled driving all the way to Gilroy, twenty miles south of San Jose, to patch up a Japanese farmer's wife who had been shot by one of the Filipino farm hands. He got the bullet out, operating on the kitchen table. As usual, he remembered details that make most sense to a fellow surgeon, in this case that she was "enormous, really fat," which made it hard to close the incision neatly. I wouldn't want you to think he was a classic cold-blooded surgical type; but it is in the nature of his profession to focus on the practical side of problems, just as my father remembered difficult soil conditions at construction sites across the world as vividly as though they were under his feet at that moment.

The real reason my father-in-law and his family did not end up in "camp" had more to do with his experiences as a Stanford undergraduate than with his profession. Although he had the income, and the potential of income, to move about more freely than the typical Japanese resident, most of the few Japanese doctors and dentists in the West ended up in the so-called Relocation Centers, sometimes under direct and considerable social pressure to "relocate" with their patients. The ones who might have left delayed too long, until curfews, travel restrictions, and finally the orders to report to the assembly centers were wrapped tightly about them.

What saved the Watanabes from going to "camp" was an item

in the local newspaper that said an army lawyer from Washington was coming to California to deal with the problem of the Japanese. He was Karl R. Bendetsen, from the Alien Control Division of the Provost Marshal's office, a Stanford graduate from the class of 1928. My father-in-law called his classmate up at his hotel in San Francisco and said: "What are these rumors about sending us to camps and things like that?" I remembered him telling the story, so, forty years after the telephone call, I called up Karl Bendetsen, who by then was the retired president of the Champion Corporation, and I asked him if the story was accurate.

Bendetsen remembered it very well, and he remembered this:

"I said, 'Lee, you'd better get out of town.' "

And he did.

11

For the Sake of the Children

What provoked my father-in-law to ask the question of his Stanford classmate was more than vague apprehension. Public outcry against Japan was quickly, perhaps understandably, extended to ethnic Japanese in America. It was only a generation since World War I, when the fight against the Kaiser had extended into every village and city in the United States, had become an attack, often physical and always psychological, on Americans of German ancestry. The Japanese in the United States lived in narrow and tightly held communities—in part by choice, as in the small farming towns, elsewhere by deliberate discrimination. They were identifiable, always the first step in racial hatred, and they were also somewhat mysterious, and lent themselves to the worst fantasies of their Caucasian neighbors.

Fears of Japanese subversion and sabotage actually preceded Pearl Harbor, which was the reason that the Army Air Corps fighter planes were parked in the middle of the island's air bases, wingtip to wingtip, such perfect targets for the Japanese fighter-bombers. American fears centered on sabotage itself, not on something so audacious as a thousand-mile aircraft-carrier strike.

The Western Defense Command, consisting geographically of those portions of the three Pacific states lying west of the Sierra Nevada and Cascade mountains, was under the command of a General John Lesense DeWitt, and he was convinced, on December 7, that the next Japanese strike would fall on his coast. His first, not entirely unreasonable, plan was to put a curfew on all enemy aliens—German, Italian, and Japanese. In addition, military authorities had already defined strategic areas around aircraft plants, navy yards and bases, and airfields, from which all enemy aliens would be prohibited. And the Federal Bureau of Investigation, which had the legal authority and responsibility for domestic intelligence and anti-sabotage arrests, moved to round up known or suspected enemy agents on the day after Pearl Harbor. In the Japanese communities, most of the senior business and community leaders spent at least a night in jail, and some spent the entire duration of the war in high-security camps.

But Pearl Harbor put a special onus on Japanese-American citizens and their immigrant parents that did not bear on Italians and Germans. Patriotic vows and the lack of any proof of sabotage or spying were no assurance. Rumors circulated instantly and endlessly. Every Japanese farmer who was renting crop land under the flight paths of airports and airfields seemed to have positioned himself deliberately for a strike at our evidently pitiful defenses. Wild talk abounded of airfield-identifying tomato hot caps, burning arrows in cane fields, mysterious lights in the night. Naval intelligence spent the weeks after Pearl Harbor sorting through assertions from Army Intelligence about Japanese saboteurs and spies. Farmers carrying lanterns while going to the outhouse (and it was not peculiar to Japanese farmers to lack indoor plumbing in 1941) were thought to be signaling submarines if on the coast, or airplanes if inland. Army radio technicians picking up Tokyo radio broadcasts swore they were coming from secret transmitters in Little Tokyo, near City Hall in Los Angeles.

The war hysteria was also manipulated by Californians who had economic scores to settle with the Japanese community. Although state law prohibited Asian aliens from owning land, Japanese farmers had managed to buy property in the names of their American-born children, and had, by sheer hard work, captured some small segments of California's agricultural industry. They specialized in difficult, hand-work products like strawberries and other specialty fruits. Nativist groups, particularly the Native Sons of the Golden West, found in Pearl Harbor the ultimate argument for the pattern of discrimination they had preached since the turn of the century, and it did not fall on deaf ears, either at the Western Defense Command or in Washington, D.C.

Across the continent, in Washington, a special assistant to the Secretary of War, one John J. McCloy, was the prime mover for a plan to remove all Japanese, regardless of citizenship, regardless of any evidence of loyalty, from the Western Defense Command. A Wall Street lawyer, McCloy had worked first as a volunteer, then as an official assistant to Secretary of War Henry Stimson, and he peppered his boss with long memoranda about various threats to the national defense. One memorandum, preserved in the Stimson papers, imagined a Nazi conspiracy to infiltrate the aircraft workers' unions. American factories were fully gearing up by the summer of 1941, in part to build aircraft for Britain, and it was clear, McCloy thought, that the unwillingness of peacetime union members to work on Saturday afternoons and Sundays was due to Nazi influence; he proposed a series of black-bag breaking-and-entering jobs to catch out the Nazis who were crippling the defense effort. Stimson, to his credit, mildly responded that he

thought the aircraft workers were probably just like the rest of us
and only wanted to spend some weekend time with their families.
And the FBI, after some initial enthusiasm for "second story" operations, refused to have anything to do with McCloy's plans for illegal
search and seizure. That scheme died easily, but when it came to
uprooting the Japanese, McCloy, and Stimson, had more success.

The plan to move alien Japanese encountered little resistance,
for the rights of enemy aliens in wartime are limited at best. But
U.S. Attorney General Francis Biddle was shocked at the idea of
violating the civil rights of the citizen Japanese. Herbert Hoover
thought it a mad scheme, and most unprofessional. His FBI, after
all, had already rounded up every known and seriously suspected
enemy alien in the entire United States. But McCloy won the
argument, with help from the attorney general of California, who
managed to press his argument not only politically but also through
the words of the most influential egghead columnist in the country,
Walter Lippmann. Attorney General Earl Warren's special contribution, as Lippmann's syndicated column for February 12, 1941,
retold it, was the assertion that proof of Japanese disloyalty lay in
the very fact that there had been no sabotage to date. This was
not, Lippmann wrote, echoing Warren, whom he had interviewed,
"a sign that there is nothing to be feared. It is a sign that the blow
is well organized and that it is held back until it can be struck
with maximum effect."

McCloy and Stimson won over President Roosevelt. Indeed, FDR
may have thought of the idea himself. His personal secretary, Missy
Hand, recalled much later that, on the eve of Pearl Harbor, Roosevelt asked whether the Census Bureau could sort its IBM cards
and come up with the names of all Japanese residing in the United
States. Several authors who specialize in conspiracy theories about
why we were so undefended at Pearl Harbor, including John To-
land, retell Missy Hand's story, though they have been unable to
find the memorandum that set the Census Bureau in motion, which
they regard as an important scrap of evidence in their case against
Roosevelt. But it would be more interesting, today, as an example

of how feared were the resident Japanese, citizens and aliens alike. On February 19, 1942, Roosevelt signed Executive Order 9066, which empowered General DeWitt to remove "any person" from his Western Defense Command on his own authority. What was meant was not any person, but persons of Japanese descent. The Americans used the same basis for the definition of Japaneseness as Hitler used for Jewishness and Southern segregationists for Negritude: one-eighth part, one great-grandparent, would suffice. There were virtually no mixed-blood Japanese, but those few, small children mostly, had to go to "camp." During the week after Roosevelt signed Executive Order 9066, Karl Bendetsen told my father-in-law to get out of town.

It was not easy for Dr. Watanabe to leave his patients behind. The Caucasian ones would do well enough, he knew that. As chief of medicine at San Jose Hospital, he worked with and had confidence in the local physicians. But many of the older patients were *issei*, first-generation Japanese immigrants, most of whom did not speak enough English to describe their symptoms.

And it was more than mere language. He had become one of the community's leaders. He was a *sensei*, an all-purpose honorific that means both "doctor" and "teacher." He was a living example of what Japanese-American children could become, and now he was choosing to leave them behind. My mother-in-law remembers the night after he talked to Bendetsen, the night he told her that the family would have to leave. It was, she said, the only time she ever saw him cry.

It was not easy for her. I asked her once, how she felt about it all, and she said she had worried about the children. "Most people are really very good," she said, as she often does. And she never talked about it with the children, never told them how it felt. She told me in part because I had asked, and in part because I was old enough not to be hurt (though she understood that I *could* be hurt, for she knows that when I call her "Mom" it's not just a funny American shorthand for "mother-in-law").

When I asked her, "What were people like, when you had to

leave?" she knew I didn't mean her good friends, who looked after the house while they were gone, sent them letters, made sure the rent was paid, and welcomed them back; she knew I meant the other ones. Well, she said, there was one woman who lived down the street, and she had a child too (this child was mildly notorious for cheating at children's card games, but otherwise regarded as a neighbor), and that child and her children played together, before and after the war. "You remember her," she said, speaking to my wife. "She came down when we heard we were leaving and asked if we wanted to sell the lawn furniture."

My wife did not know this part of the story, and asked: "She didn't say she was sorry or anything?"

"No," she said. And then again, "Most people are very nice." My mother-in-law has a pretty good idea when my wife is going to ask another question, so, before my wife could ask it, she added, "I didn't say anything, because I didn't want the children to have a bad feeling." And then she said something in Japanese—which she translated right away, because she does that for me whenever she speaks in Japanese—"*Kodomo no tame ni.* For the sake of the children."

My father-in-law did not expect this foolishness with Executive Order 9066 to last. He maintained a faith in the country's ability to come to its senses, and so he planned to make use of the time. A phrase in Japanese sums it up: *shikata ganai.* This translates rather badly into English as "It can't be helped," or "It must be borne." But it connotes more than stoicism; it implies that you will do your best with what you have to work with. And he wanted to make good use of this temporary break in his practice.

He applied to do postdoctoral work at the Cook County, Illinois, Graduate School of Medicine, one of the few such institutions in the United States in 1942 where practitioners could brush up, see and participate in the newest kinds of surgery. And so the Watanabes did not just "get out of town"; he packed up his wife, three children, and a baby sitter in his Lincoln Zephyr and headed for Chicago.

That didn't work. The documents that would explain exactly
what happened have disappeared over time. But this is what he
told me: When he showed up at Cook County Hospital ready to
learn, the staff refused to allow him, as an enemy alien, to treat
patients, to touch them, to operate on them. And since that was
the nature of the training in this postgraduate program, there was
nothing for him to do. In the summer of 1942, he found himself
trapped in the Middle West without a practice. He tried the Mayo
Clinic, an institution gracious enough to allow him to attend it as
an observer, and for a few months the family lived in a motel in
Rochester, Minnesota, while he sat in the theater of the Mayo's
operating room; then that, too, came to an end.

My wife's uncle Ariake Inouye, by that time, had moved to
Boulder, Colorado, where his family lived in a rented house and
he taught advanced Japanese to what was by then the second full
class of naval students. Eventually my father-in-law joined him on
the staff of contract instructors at the Naval School of Oriental
Languages.

"I think Dr. Lee had run out of choices," Uncle Ari would say,
much later.

The Watanabes spent two years in Boulder. Dr. Lee taught the
advanced students, having as much proficiency in Japanese as any
man on the campus and a better-than-average facility with English.
My mother-in-law taught a little conversational Japanese to the
young men, and spent more time with the association of students'
wives, also teaching conversation and Japanese customs. It was not
an unhappy time, and although Dr. Lee had enough patriotism left
to teach with enthusiasm, he was unhappy at being away from the
practice of medicine. In the spring of 1944, toward the end of a
class cycle, he traveled to Salt Lake City, where a substantial
Japanese community had grown up, composed mostly of California
farmers who had managed to get out before the relocation order
trapped them.

In Salt Lake City, they were quite happy to get a board-certified
doctor, regardless of race. Dr. Lee was accredited to the city hos-

pital and then went down to Japantown, as one old acquaintance of his told me, "and cadged enough gasoline ration coupons to go back to Boulder and get his family." As farmers, the Japanese-Americans in Salt Lake had better access to ration coupons than other residents.

The Church of Latter-day Saints has had a mixed record in dealing with people of color, but that was on religious matters, including the possibility of rising to certain levels of membership in the temporal church or going to Mormon heaven. To this way-faring stranger and his family, they were both kind and neighborly, and included the Watanabes in their monthly survey, asking my mother-in-law if she had enough food, clothing, and heat. Of course they had all these things, but, as Mom would say, "It's nice to be asked."

If for some reason I had to prove to you by producing a piece of paper from some official archive that my father-in-law did indeed teach at the Naval School of Oriental Languages, it would be impossible. During the better part of a year, I made a number of trips to many archives, but never turned up a single list of faculty (beyond the earliest list, found in correspondence between the navy and the army authorities, when the school was at Berkeley). In large part, this is simply because the navy did not, does not, care. The need to depend so completely on men and women of Japanese ancestry to train Caucasian Americans who would go forth into the Pacific Theater was, from the navy's point of view, an unfor-tunate wartime exigency. There is just a single piece of semi-official paper in a family scrapbook, a Proclamation of Appreciation from the naval officer in charge of the school, printed in red, white, and blue, thanking the faculty, on the Fourth of July, 1943, for their loyalty, patriotism, and contribution to the war effort. On the bottom of it is written in ink, in an unfamiliar hand, "Dr. Lee Watanabe." If someone had not taken that small trouble, there would be no evidence at all.

12

A Right Way, a Wrong Way, and the Harvard Way

In the summer of 1941, as the U.S. Navy was making its plans to build the four bases in the British Isles to confront German aggression, it was also preparing for what seemed an inevitable war with Japan. Amid the construction of ships and bases and the development of new naval aircraft, a smaller program centered on schools to prepare Japanese-language intelligence officers, a program which the following summer was to provide my father-in-law with his chance to make a patriotic contribution.

At the onset, there were supposed to be

two redundant Naval Schools of Oriental Languages. Just as this
was a rich and fearful enough country to build duplicate bases for
the proposed convoy escort force, so there was enough money for
fail-safe language schools.

The story of the origin of the navy's Japanese language-school
program is complicated, instructive, sometimes amusing. The ris-
ible matters have mostly to do with Harvard, an educational institution that seems to sail on through any waters, even those
temporarily roiled by world wars and other distractions. I think of
this part of the story as: How my father-in-law almost ended up
teaching at Harvard.

By the time Dr. Watanabe signed on with the navy to teach
Japanese, it had only the single school located at the University of
Colorado in Boulder. The original, grand scheme for a pair of
mirror-image schools, one on the West Coast, at Berkeley, one on
the East Coast, at Harvard, had fallen to various exigencies. Neither one was bombed out of existence—which was the logic behind
having two schools, in case San Francisco Bay turned out to be
Pearl Harbor, or the German blitz moved from London to Cambridge, Massachusetts. (There was no other excuse for doubling
up the schools; the number of professional teachers in the United
States qualified to instruct navy officers in Japanese was no greater
than two dozen, from coast to coast.)

However, the choices of Berkeley and Harvard were not capricious. The presidents of the two universities, Robert Gordon Sproul
in California, James Bryant Conant in Cambridge, were activists
in the national defense. Conant, in particular, was the designated
academic spokesman, giving interviews to the press and speaking
on national radio for the anti-isolationist "Committee to Defend
America by Aiding the Allies." He was a charter member of the
secret, or at least discreet, "Century Group," who met at the
Century Association clubhouse in New York City to devise schemes
for war preparation. It had been the Century Group's particular
contribution to think up the quasi-legal scheme to trade surplus
American destroyers for British bases in the Caribbean and Central

America. And Conant and Sproul were the two university leaders who put together the academic team that would create the world's first atomic bombs. Conant's house was picketed in June 1941, during graduation week.

In addition to his work for the Committee to Defend America, Conant chose, with the support of the Harvard Corporation's pro-war members, to give honorary doctorates to the British ambassador, Lord Halifax, and, even more annoying to the students, to Clarence A. Dykstra, who was both the president of the University of Wisconsin and the director of the newly formed Selective Service. Even the yet-unimagined atomic bomb was foreshadowed at that commencement: Ernest O. Lawrence of the Berkeley radiation laboratory and Vannevar Bush, head of the National Defense Research Committee, were also honored, although their names were not chanted by the protestors gathered on Quincy Street in front of Conant's home. In a rare public statement about internal matters, the Boston office of the Federal Bureau of Investigation announced an immediate investigation of the student protest, citing the probable involvement of subversives and foreign agents in the demonstration.

Ever since the end of World War I, in which the Japanese had been our allies, the navy had prepared a few junior officers for duty in intelligence, liaison, and observation with the Japanese Navy. A bright young Academy graduate would be assigned, sometimes over his protest, to the Tokyo embassy as a naval attaché; his real duty would be to attend, five days a week, language classes at the Naganuma School, one of dozens of Japanese-language schools in Tokyo, but the best connected; most of the years between the wars, it held its classes in the American embassy. But by the winter of 1940, only a dozen American officers had managed to learn and retain their Japanese-language skills, certainly too few to handle even peacetime decryption and translation, or to serve as intelligence officers at the legation in Japan.

The Naganuma program (which is still taught in Tokyo, and whose texts are still used in some American colleges) was a three-year course. The navy, however, intended to turn it into a one-year program by a very simple expedient. The Naganuma texts were in chapters, and in Tokyo each chapter took one week to master. The navy—and this is only a slight oversimplification—would simply require that students in the two university-based Japanese-language schools in the United States learn one chapter a day. This would get them through the basic course in thirty five-day weeks, and leave time enough for additional technical terms and greater fluency. (The Naganuma texts were useless for either describing or deciphering military events and military hardware.) Faced with the problem of creating several hundred proficient language specialists in short order, the navy knew exactly how to go about it: do what they had been doing for twenty years, but do it faster. Navy veterans will recognize this attitude, which is summed up in the commonplace wisdom that "There is a right way, a wrong way, and the navy way."

The two schools began instruction in the fall term of 1941 under the general supervision of Lieutenant A. E. Hindmarsh, who had joined the Office of Naval Intelligence after a brief stint as an assistant dean in Harvard's Graduate School of Arts and Sciences. Such minor administrators were known then, and still are, with the appropriate sniff from a professor when he says it, as "baby deans." It was Hindmarsh's decision, and one calculated to meet with approval within the navy, to build the new schools on the tried-and-true Naganuma program.

The United States Army was simultaneously gearing up to teach Japanese, and the contrast is instructive. The army school was established on the grounds of the Presidio of San Francisco, also in the fall of 1941, but without redundancy, and the instructors were civilian employees of the Department of the Army, plus a few Japanese-American enlisted men. This Fourth Army Intelligence School began on October 15, 1941, with twenty-five students and twenty-five instructors, all of them, except for the director, an ethnic Japanese. Before the war was over, the army had trained almost six thousand Japanese-Americans in radio intelligence, interrogation, and combat intelligence. Hundreds became commissioned officers, serving in back offices and front lines from Pearl Harbor to Burma. The army also trained Caucasian officers in Japanese at the University of Minnesota, to provide white officers for the not wholly trusted Japanese specialists.

The navy's system was quite different. Instead of hiring its own faculty, the navy contracted with the universities, and the instructors were thus kept at arm's length from the navy itself. This was in large part because the navy had no persons of color serving in any capacity whatsoever except as mess stewards. The perhaps unintended result was to prevent the navy instructors from enjoying any of the benefits of direct employment either by the universities or by the U.S. government. Sadly, and perhaps deliberately, this is why there is virtually no paper record at all, in any archive, that even lists them by name. There is nothing quite so ephemeral as a university contract, except its pay records.

Although the fear of a blitz's striking Harvard and destroying the East Coast Japanese-language school was unfounded, the principle of redundant duplication turned out to be the salvation of the navy's program, for the Harvard school managed to self-destruct within months of its establishment. The nominal head of the school was a White Russian émigré who had passed through Japan on his way from the Bolshevik revolution to Harvard University, a most mercurial man by the name of Serge Elisseeff. The actual director of the Harvard program was a junior faculty member with a now more memorable name, and career, Edwin O. Reischauer. At Berkeley, a Miss Florence Walne, who was just finishing her Harvard Ph.D. while teaching at Berkeley, was chosen as the West Coast school's director. The navy entered into straightforward contracts: the universities would be paid a lump-sum tuition for each student, and the schools would teach them Japanese, beginning with the Naganuma books, eight hours a day, five days a week. The University of California at Berkeley accepted the navy's offer of six hundred dollars per student. Harvard refused, however, and finally squeezed nine hundred dollars out of the navy, arguing that faculty and instructors could not be found who would meet Harvard's high standards at the lower price.

Lieutenant Hindmarsh selected forty-five students for the fall term, twenty for Berkeley, twenty-five for Harvard. They included recent college graduates who had done coursework in Japanese, naval agents (civilian employees of Naval Intelligence) who had college degrees with honors, and a few regular-navy officers with either some Japanese or very high academic records. None of them, remember, was an ethnic Japanese. That would be quite beyond the realm of possibility in the navy until long after World War II.

Because of the impending sense of doom about relations with Japan, a larger number of Harvard students than usual enrolled in the department's courses, and Elisseeff and Reischauer regarded the navy contract as a mere extension of their general intensive course in Japanese. The navy students were mingled, as the dollars were also mingled, into the general courses, much to the dismay of Lieutenant Hindmarsh.

He planned to visit Harvard in early November 1941, just as other supervisors of navy contracts would visit a shipyard or an aircraft factory, to inspect the progress of the manufacture of naval language personnel. Harvard frantically tried to delay the inspection, in part by pointing out that the twenty-five navy students were not quite ready for testing.

Hindmarsh's letter to Elisseeff is worth quoting at length; although it is entirely from the navy's point of view, it paints a perfectly believable picture of Harvard as it was, and for that matter Harvard as it always will be:

You say that eight of the twenty-five students enrolled in the Navy course have not been held to the schedule which we agreed upon in the appendix to our contract and which was emphasized as vital to our program in my letter of September 30 to Dr. Reischauer; this schedule calls for the completion by every student of a minimum of one lesson per day out of the basic Navy course (Naganuma). . . . Our plan to inspect the course and examine the students on November 4 was based on the assumption that the students would have completed on that day (which will be the thirty-fifth day since the course began) the first thirty lessons. . . .

I am sure you will appreciate our point of view; we have, at considerable expense, prepared and proved [provided?] a basic course for Naval students; the University has agreed to teach that course according to a written schedule. . . .

Will you, therefore, inform the entire student body that the examinations on November 4 and 5 will cover the first thirty lessons and that all are expected to be prepared. . . . We insist that such action be taken. We . . . accept full responsibility—financial and otherwise—for our choice of materials, methods and realization of results.

The results of the examination were disastrous. Only the students who were formerly undergraduate majors in Japanese had succeeded in mastering Naganuma or the equivalent. Even the students who failed completely were allowed to continue, however, for the blame, in the navy's view, was entirely Harvard's. Part of the problem was that Professor Elisseeff and Reischauer had just compiled their own textbook of Japanese, which they sold to the students, including the navy students, and used in the course. Elisseeff claimed the use of this text was necessary because the Naganuma texts were inadequate in "grammar notes." That the navy was uninterested in the fine points of Japanese grammar was not something that Harvard ever quite understood.

Professor Reischauer, years later, recalled the difficulties of working with the navy and in particular with the former Harvard assistant dean, Lieutenant Hindmarsh: "There was friction right from the start. Hindmarsh had an unpleasant personality. Our feeling was very keenly that they had come to us for aid and expertise." This *was* exactly what they felt in 1941, as Elisseeff wrote to the navy:

We have naturally assumed that the Navy Department, in asking our aid in the project to train Japanese language officers quickly, had confidence in my ability and judgement in such work and in the ability and competence of my colleagues. . . . We have attempted to be as cooperative as possible . . . acquiescing to the suggestions made by the representatives of the Navy Department, who themselves have had little or no experience with the teaching of Japanese. We naturally expect to receive comparable cooperation on a basis of mutual respect and confidence from the representatives of the Navy Department.

What was particularly infuriating to the Harvard faculty was that the navy insisted on assuming that there was some entity called the Harvard University Graduate School of Arts and Sciences that had signed a contract and was responsible for performance of the contract. Here are Elisseeff's last words on the subject:

> We naturally shall welcome all criticisms and suggestions founded upon a clear knowledge of the actual situation. . . . I also should like to suggest that it would facilitate matters if communications concerning the course are addressed to me or to my administrative assistant, Dr. Reischauer, *rather than to other officers of the university who have no direct connection with, or any supervisory powers over, the course.* [my italics]

Seldom has a single paragraph in a letter summed up so clearly the difference between being a Harvard professor and being an ordinary mortal, and I say that with some insider's knowledge.

The admonitions of the navy were unavailing. In February 1942 Harvard was still mingling funds and students, and not providing a sufficiency of instructors. The navy discovered the reason for the shortfall in instructors through the routine process of certifying the loyalty and patriotism of potential instructors for the schools. The chief of the Office of Naval Intelligence was obliged to write to Reischauer on the last day of February 1942:

> Several Federal investigative agencies have informed us as a matter of domestic intelligence that persons who have been approached by you as prospective teachers in Japanese in the Navy language

course at Harvard have been led to believe that the Navy determined and controlled the salaries paid to such teachers. More specifically, within the past few weeks one competent Japanese linguist was allegedly informed that a salary of Two Hundred Dollars ($200) a month, which was offered him to teach in the language course at Harvard, was the maximum because of the fact that the Navy was not providing funds sufficient to allow the salary more commensurate with the instructor's obvious qualifications and experience.

. . . I recall that the tuition fee of Nine Hundred Dollars ($900) . . . was predicated upon the assumption that it was ample to enable the University to meet the financial obligations of this course without loss to itself and with the continuing ability to pay reasonable salaries to the instructors.

The Harvard course continued without much benefit, and was formally terminated in September 1942. The few navy students who survived, or who had arrived in Cambridge with a basic knowledge of Japanese, were transferred to the West Coast school. (My wife's uncle Ari Inouye, a Berkeley graduate and one of the ten original instructors there, remembers them arriving in Boulder "carrying those funny green book bags.") The navy was decent enough about the problem with Harvard, and explained to the West Coast faculty that the Harvard course had been an "experiment which did not work," not that it was a contract that had to be canceled.

Although, in retrospect, establishing duplicate Naval Schools of Oriental Languages seems excessive, it could well have been the case that the Berkeley school, surrounded by the panicking citizens and army personnel of California, would have been the one to fall—either to a lynch mob or to even more rigid anti-Japanese action by the Western Defense Command. And if Reischauer did not succeed as a navy employee, he did go on to a very important role with the army—establishing the Japanese-language program for cryptanalysts (code breakers) at the Army Signal Corps installation at Arlington Hall, in Washington, D.C.

The navy's widely scattered archives on the Japanese-language schools resemble in some important and disappointing ways the records of all old, disbanded communities. There is, for example, no complete record, anywhere, of all the graduates. (The only lists of successful students are annual short lists of graduates who chose to transfer from the navy proper to the marines: these survived because they required personnel action in Washington.) But the Bureau of Navigation's personnel section, and its successor, the Bureau of Personnel, retained lists of everyone who *failed* the course, embarrassingly available to any researcher in the National Archives in Washington, D.C. This was because flunking out required personnel action and reassignment. In that sense the navy records resemble the early archives of Plymouth Plantation, in which the settlers are most thoroughly accounted for in case of testamented death, or accusations of fornication, buggery, bestiality, or nonpayment of taxes.

The West Coast school suffered not at all from internal university mismanagement, only from the dislocations of war itself. The school at Berkeley had a class of twenty naval agents in the winter of 1941–42, with a faculty of ten. The director, Florence Walne, had no particular difficulty living with the navy's prescribed curriculum. (Professor Reischauer remarked to me a few years ago that she was "just a woman" and thus easily browbeaten by the navy.) The other nine faculty were ethnic Japanese, including two aliens and seven American-born citizens. The contract with the University of California, Berkeley, served as a screen between the navy and the people of color who staffed the school. They received no benefits, got no credit for government service, and were dismissed at the end of the war without notice. The official navy history of the School of Oriental Languages lists not one of them by name. If it had not been for the hysteria in California after Pearl Harbor, there would be no official record at all, but the events of early 1942 created paperwork—correspondence between the navy and the army.

Very shortly after Pearl Harbor, General DeWitt became convinced that the hundred thousand resident ethnic Japanese, about half alien and half citizens, constituted a great and imminent threat to his command area. The immediate solution was to enforce a curfew on all Japanese and then, in February 1942, the incarceration of all ethnic Japanese in what were called "Assembly Centers." Horse-racing tracks and fair grounds were preferred as Assembly Centers, because the horse stalls and animal pens could be used for housing. It was that kind of a winter in California in 1942.

The instructors at Berkeley were given passes that allowed them to leave their homes to teach evening and weekend classes. The navy corresponded regularly with the army on the subject of its Japanese instructors (thus creating a record). As the roundup and incarceration progressed, and as plans were made for moving the Japanese to concentration camps (which is what they were called originally in the official correspondence, until the authorities came up with the more pleasant name of "Relocation Centers"), additional passes and permissions were required to keep them on the Berkeley campus. I list them, in their honor:

> Susumu Nakamura (chief assistant to Miss Walne)
> Ensho Ashikaga (also a member of the Berkeley faculty)
> Chitoshi Yanaga (likewise a university instructor)

And the contract-only employees:

> Grace Fujii (Susumu Nakamura's sister)
> Hidekazu Hayashi
> Yuji Imai
> Ariake Inouye (my wife's uncle)
> Kozo Takemoto
> Kiyoshi Tomizawa

These names appear in correspondence between the District Intelligence Officer, 12th Naval District (San Francisco), and the Provost Marshal, Western Defense Command (The Presidio, San Francisco). The complete archival records of the DIO 12th are in the regional office of the National Archives in San Bruno, California: seventy cubic feet of everything from investigations into price gouging to preliminary investigations for courts-martial. The last scrap of information on the School of Oriental Languages is dated June 1942.

It became clear to the Japanese language school faculty, after weeks of negotiating with the army, that not even a handful of them would be allowed to live within the confines of the Western Defense Command, and the school was picked up bodily and transferred to the University of Colorado, Boulder. Colorado was in the 9th Naval District (Chicago) then, although it would later be returned to the 12th (San Francisco), and that district's files suffered a not-uncommon fate. When the navy decides to save something, it does a good job. When it decides to throw things away, it is equally impressive. All matters relating to the School of Oriental Languages were technically personnel matters, and the correspondence was therefore filed, no matter who had received it for whatever purpose, in a file folder with an alpha-numeric code beginning with the letter "P," as prescribed in the United States Navy Filing Manual, 1941 edition. The prefix for the Japanese-language school is "P11-5" for (P) personnel, (11) officer training, (5) foreign languages. The filing suffix is either "EF37" for Japan or, after the school was established in Boulder, NC155, since the school was the navy's 155th college-based school. At some point in history, apparently in the early 1970s, the custodian of the Naval District records realized that in the mass of personnel files he was holding there was probably—in some cases, certainly—embarrassing material. After all, about the only way you get a personnel file generated on you at headquarters is to screw up royally and deliberately. A ukase was issued to destroy all personnel correspondence files because public access to them constituted potential invasions of privacy, and they were all chucked, including the general personnel subject files like P11-5/NC155, thus destroying the only consolidated archive on the Naval School of Oriental Languages. So it goes.

When negotiating with the army over keeping the school's instructors at Berkeley, the navy exaggerated its close ties with the

Japanese instructors. My uncle-in-law's pass, which he needed to walk from his parents' home to the Berkeley campus, where he was going to teach the officers who would win the war, reads thusly:

To Whom It May Concern:

The bearer, Ariake Inouye, University of California, Berkeley, Calif., is an employee of the United States Government and is hereby authorized to reside within Military Areas and Zones as prescribed in public proclamations issued by this headquarters. The bearer is further authorized to travel within military areas and zones without restriction as to curfew regulations as applied to Japanese aliens and others of Japanese ancestry.

By command of Lieutenant General DewITT:
/s/ R. P. Bronson,
1st Lieut., A.G.D.
Assistant Adjutant General

Contract employees were allowed to keep their immediate families with them, meaning spouses and children. My wife's maternal grandparents were sent to live in a horse stall at Tanforan Race Track, and then they were sent to camp in the desert. The navy was not interested in parents.

13

Fragments of Memory

As hard as all this was for my wife's family, they were lucky inasmuch as they were able to stay together. They have a complete, mutual, seamless history. There is no place they were not together; all of them remembered the hollyhocks in Boulder and the cows outside the motel in Rochester and the neighbors in Salt Lake City. They don't have to go back to see these places again, so complete is their collective memory.

For our family, it is different—not worse, just not the same. If I had been able to tell my father stories, to hold his attention, more than anything else I would have told him what happened to his family while he was in Scotland.

There is this thing that happens with children: if no one is watching them, nothing is really happening to them. It is not some philosophical conundrum like the one about the tree falling in the forest and no one hearing it; that is a puzzler for college freshmen. No. If you are very small, you actually understand that there is no point in jumping into the swimming pool unless *they* see you do it. The child crying, "Watch me, watch me," is not begging for attention; he is pleading for existence itself. *They* will remember. *They* will hold it, keep it, make it true. Everything else is dreams, not memories.

This is what I would have told my father, about 1942 and 1943, when he was gone.

I was afraid of nothing, Father. You would have liked me then, particularly. By the time you came home, I was old enough to be a little bit afraid. You should have seen me the day I ran across the street. It must have been in Tujunga, California. I think we were walking to the grocery store, and I was allowed to run ahead once we got close to the curb on the other side of the street; one more time I tripped and fell down, and this time managed to hit my head on the curb. I did not cry. There is one way to make children stop crying if you must, and that is to surprise them greatly—it is the same thing that stops hiccups—and I was astonished at the blood. Today, forty-five years later, I have a habit of rubbing the scar that hides high on my brow, just under the hairline. Oh, how I bled; you would not have thought the young man had so much blood in him, Father.

The taxicab man was very nice. First I bled all over his taxi seat, and when we got to the hospital he insisted—I have the clearest memory of this part of it—he absolutely insisted on carrying me inside; when they put me on the gurney in the emergency room, I sat there not crying at all, and stared at the taxi man because he was solid blood from his necktie on down. He wore a black necktie on a brown shirt—I believe it was some kind of a uniform for taxi drivers—and from just below the knot of his tie to his waist he was bright blood-red. Everyone was very concerned and very nice, and they did a fair job of sewing up my cut. It is the only really noticeable scar I ever got, and sometimes I am glad of its palpability, which reminds me that it was true that I was brave and did not cry, or perhaps I was not brave at all, only terribly surprised, but it would have been the same thing if you were watching.

And you missed the day I drowned. That was in Montana, in the summer of 1943, and if you took me there right now, I could find the place again. I was very brave, like most five-year-olds, and did not know I could not swim—it hadn't really been made clear to me, because we didn't spend much time around water and no one had swimming pools—that was not one of the things you had then. There was a small floating dock, and the smell that is still perhaps the finest of all smells in North America, which is grass and pine trees and, very faintly, almost unnoticeably, gasoline mixed with outboard-engine oil, what remains in the air at the dock ten or fifteen minutes after someone has started an outboard engine and it has smoked and coughed once or twice before the person pushed in the choke lever and leaned the mixture—this is the perfume of lakes. I just went in the water, by myself, off the floating dock, and surprised myself very much by coming up underneath it. I wish I had told you about this. You see, I thought of you. You were in the navy and you wore a blue uniform, I knew that from the pictures we had, and you would know about water and boats and floating docks, and you would know I was there, under the dock, and it was all quite peaceful, perhaps because I thought you knew I was there, perhaps because I was so foolishly brave that I did not know I was going to sink slowly down in the water. I could see the dock and the bottoms of boats tied to the dock. They were looking for me by then, and when I sank enough so that they could see me in the sunlight in the water, someone saved me, and I suppose they thumped me on the back or pushed on my stomach and all the water came out and there I was. On the way back to the car, barefoot, I stepped on a bee, which was the worst thing that happened to me that day.

And you should have been there when we went out to see the

train wreck. This was in Montana, too. It was a freight train with cars filled with wheat, and now the wheat was piled up along the railroad tracks and people were scooping it into paper bags and even putting it in their pockets. People had chickens, in Miles City, and they were going to take the wheat home and feed the chickens. I knew that. We did not have chickens at the house we lived in. There were no pets at all in that house. If you had been there, we would have had chickens, or maybe even a turkey, which was something other people had. You should have seen the train wreck, and you should have come with us when we went out to the pine woods to get mushrooms, which were perfectly safe because Auntie Boo had gone out to get mushrooms at the same place for years, and no one ever got sick, did they?

And you would have liked the day they killed the pig. We had to have ration stamps for meat, but if you knew someone who lived way out in the country, you could drive out and buy meat, and the day we went, when we got there they were killing a pig, and I had never known that meat could be quite so interesting. I think I got to be kind of bloody-minded in Miles City, Montana, because of the pig. Also, I got to be a comedian. We drove a long way into the country, most of it on dirt roads, and I rode backward, looking out the back window of the car with my elbows resting on the shelf under the rear window, watching the dust swirl up behind the car. I think the pig was strung up when we got there; in any case, it was almost ready to die, and they had pulled it up by its hind legs, and nobody said I couldn't watch, and then they cut it open and all these long, ropy, things came out of the pig, and I said, "Look, there's the sausages," and Auntie Boo laughed and maybe Mother laughed, too. It was just about the funniest thing I ever did say, they said. I was serious, but when a child makes people laugh, he has more sense than to argue, and he revels in the laughter. On the way home, in the car, someone asked me what I wanted to do the most, and I said: "I want to go to a zoo and see the brassieres." They practically drove off the road, everyone was laughing so hard. What I meant to say was "zebras," but it didn't

come out right. I had a book with pictures of zebras in it. And I
knew what a brassiere was, although I had no idea—or maybe I
should say, no memory—of what was inside a brassiere. It was a
long time before I found out. If you had been there, you might
have understood that I didn't always try to make people laugh; it
was just something that happened. Later, when you were home,
I would use too big a word for the occasion or make some mistake
like thinking pig guts were sausages, and you thought I was being
a wise guy. Sometimes I was, Father, but sometimes it just happened, and I think, because you missed some of the first times it
happened, you didn't quite understand.

Also, you should have been there when Mom threw away my
teddy bear. This is what happened. I had a bear, which was the
closest thing to a pet we could have in that house in Montana, and
I left it outside in the early winter and it got covered up with snow.
That was the year I went to kindergarten, which is probably about
the time you are not supposed to have a teddy bear any more, but
I didn't know where it was and I worried about it. In school, you
had to color oranges with the orange crayon and apples with the
red and grapes with the purple. Now I understand that the idea
is to get used to counting things—call it "math readiness" or something like that. But I had an awful time keeping the orange inside
the dittograph-blue outline of the orange. The apples and the grapes
were even harder, because the apples were a funny shape and the
grapes were so small. I think I spent all the math-readiness time
worrying about keeping the crayon marks inside the blue lines on
the paper. When it came time to take a paper home, the teacher
would do the edges of the fruit for me, and I would keep most of
the crayon inside. When school was almost over, I found the teddy
bear, which was gray where it used to be brown, which is what
happens to bears left out in the rain and buried under the snow.
And it was thrown away.

We used to talk about what we would do when you got home,
and I honestly cannot remember a single thing we were going to
do, because that wasn't the point, really. The point was that better

things would happen, and I was quite sure that three things would
have happened if you were there: first, it would not be so cold,
going to school; second, it would be easier to color the oranges;
third, I would not be too old to have a teddy bear and no one would
throw it away. Such was the universe of things that would happen
when you came home.

Also, I could go to the boys' room. I never told you about that.
We didn't have much bathroom talk, which is fine by me—I don't
have much interest in extremely progressive parents and leaving
the bathroom doors open and frank talk about things like that—
but I would surely have liked to be able to go to the men's room
at least one time between 1941 and 1945. For one thing, it is hard
enough to go to the bathroom in a room full of strangers without
women telling you how cute you are. One thing at a time, that's
what I wanted.

And you would have been proud of us, the day Penny and I
finally did something to contribute to the war effort. That was
when we gave water to the marines. We were good about all the
other things kids did. We washed out empty tin cans, cut both
ends out, stamped them flat, and took them back to the store
for the tin-can drives that were going to make sure everyone had
enough ammunition. We saved bacon fat, although we were not
big enough to pour it when it was still hot in the pan, but we
were old enough not to think it was garbage and throw it away.
And we were pretty good about the meat-rationing stamps. It's just
that there really wasn't any meat as good as hot dogs, and we wanted
to have a wienie roast in the back yard. We did fib about that. I
think it was my idea. Here's what we did. We'd go to one mother
on the block and tell her that we were going to have a wienie roast,
if it was all right with her, because it was all right with our mother,
and she'd say, Well, o.k., if it's all right with Mrs. Montgomery
I guess it's all right with me. So we'd have one mother who was
going to use her meat coupons for wienies, and we'd tell Mom, or
maybe another mother, that it was all right with this lady, and did
she want to get wienies and come to the roast? And if it was all

right with her, then we had two mothers, and the rest was easy. Finally, one of the mothers called up Mom and said she was sick and tired of spending her good meat-ration coupons on these probably not very nutritious wienie roasts, and would Mom stop encouraging us? And that was the end of wienie roasts, although I got away with it without a spanking because it was, well, kind of a cute trick. We got away with a lot, because moms couldn't say: "Just wait until your father gets home."

But I meant to tell you about the marines who didn't have any water. I don't know where we were going, back to California or back to Montana—it was one of those moves we kept making because you weren't there—and we were staying in a motel. I think we were coming back to California to meet you because you were coming home from Scotland. It was one of those old cabin-style motels. This is what happened. Penny and I were sitting on the front stoop of the cabin, and all of a sudden a whole armored column of marines came down the street in tanks and half-tracks and armored personnel carriers and antitank vehicles. (We knew what these vehicles were, because they were like the ones on the posters at school for the war-bond drive. There was a place on the posters to mark down how many war-bond stamps your class bought, so you could say that your first-grade class bought a gun for a tank or an engine for a half-track.) And we walked out onto the street and stood almost right next to the tanks as they went by, the treads making a deep scraping sound on the asphalt paving. One of the marines waved down at us and yelled something we couldn't really hear, and so we just waved back. I probably saluted, too. I did a lot of saluting. The next personnel carrier came by, and another marine yelled and waved at us, and we heard him, and he was yelling "Water!" So we ran over to the cabin—there was a hose outside—and we turned the water on and found some empty soda bottles and milk bottles and filled up the bottles, and then we ran out to the street, and the marines would take the bottles, drink them down, and hand the bottles back, and we'd run over to the cabin and fill them up and run back out into the street and hand the water to the next marines going by. If you just walked fast, you could keep up. It seemed as if we did it all afternoon, I guess maybe for an hour. I tripped once or twice and spilled some water but never broke a bottle. Mom wasn't there; I think she was house-hunting. This was probably somewhere near Port Hueneme—that would make sense, the marines running their vehicles overland, headed for the ships—and it was perfectly flat country, as it is around Port Hueneme.

I don't think we told her what we'd been doing, when she came back to the cabin court. It was too important to talk about. We'd saved all these marines from dying of thirst, and we were very tired and very proud of ourselves. We were also not supposed to talk to strangers, even marines, and we certainly were never supposed to run out in the street, and never, ever run while carrying a glass or a bottle, because we could fall down and break it and cut our-selves. We knew the rules. But if you had been there, we would have told you; it would have been too important to the war effort for us to get in trouble for doing it. We knew, somehow, that fathers understood the war effort better than mothers did.

You did come home for the first time, in the middle of the war, and I never said I was sorry for the things I said at the airport. We went to the airport to meet you, and I guess I probably em-barrassed everybody. This is what happened, and I bet you forgot—one more reason I really do regret not talking about it, because if you did forget it's as though it never happened. I was only five, and you had left for the first time when I was three. We went to the airport to meet you and all these men got off the airplane and people were hugging them and things like that, and this stranger got off and started kissing Mother. An imposter. An army man. Navy men wore blue. I knew that. I had pictures of you in a blue uniform. For heaven's sake, I had a blue uniform with gold buttons, just like yours. There's a picture of me wearing it, saluting Mom—she's sitting on a front porch somewhere, and I'm saluting her. In my blue uniform just like yours. I think it was three days before I believed you were my daddy. I'm sorry about screaming at the airport. I suppose I wasn't the only kid who ever went to the airport in World War II and yelled, "That's not my daddy, my daddy's in the navy," when some man hugged their mommy. I hope somebody thought it was cute, I hope you had somebody grin at you. I hope somebody understood that this little kid had never seen a navy officer in summer khakis. I hope all of those things, but most of all I hope you understood that I had not forgotten you. I was just mixed up by the uniform.

There's one more thing. You were home when it happened, but I never did tell you, because I was ashamed. I think it started with the pig, when I was more interested in the possibility of sausages than the squeal the pig made as they killed it. I did, I think, really get bloody-minded, because we had not only the day with the pig but more than one day with chickens, both in Montana and in California, and when we went to get a chicken without meat-rationing stamps, boy, did we get a chicken, plus a lesson in how it got caught and got its head wrung off by swinging it around and after its head was gone it ran for a long time making blood on the grass. It didn't bother me a bit and still doesn't. That's just the way it was if we wanted a chicken, and we did.

Anyway, when you came home from Scotland you had that shotgun, the one in the leather case that smelled wonderful even before you opened it, and smelled spectacularly good when you did open it and showed the gun to me. It was the special oil on it, from the brass can labeled—and by the time you came home from Scotland I could read—"Rangoon Oil." I still have the gun and the oil can. I don't use the Rangoon Oil, but sometimes I go down in the basement and unscrew the cap and just smell the Rangoon smell, and it reminds me of you and the night you didn't shoot the deer.

The deer came down when it was time for us to go to bed, and ate the flowers in the yard. This was the house at the Old Hearst Ranch, by Camp Shoemaker, in Pleasanton, California, when you were home for a few months. And Mother said those pesky deer were going to eat all her fuchsias, and you said, "Well, I guess I'll just have to take the shotgun and shoot one."

I liked that idea. It was going to be like the pig, only better. It was going to beat getting a chicken from the chicken lady all to pieces. So, when I was supposed to be in bed, I got right out of bed again and stood by the window, looking out toward the flowers, and Penny said: "What are you doing, you're supposed to be in bed." I explained that you were going to shoot a deer any minute now.

And she said: "No, he's not." And I came apart. I mean hysterical. I ended up lying on the floor screaming in rage and kicking the furniture and starting to sob, and yelling, "Daddy's going to shoot a deer. He is, too; he is, too." I mean, I wanted to see the hide come off and everything. I wanted to help skin that deer. I wanted deer meat, whatever it tasted like—nothing would taste better than meat you killed and cut up right there in the back yard, I knew that.

Mom came in and was really concerned, because I was probably red in the face and everything, and usually I didn't cry much (the day at the airport when you came home had been an exception). And she said "What's wrong?" or words of that sort, and I could hardly talk I was so choked up, and I sobbed something like, "Daddy's not going to shoot a deer," or maybe I said you *were, too*, going to shoot one, and she thought I felt sorry for the deer.

Mom tried to soothe me: "Don't worry, dear, Daddy's not going to shoot a deer. That's all right, that's all right." And then I really, completely lost control. After a long time, I cried myself to sleep. How I wanted you to shoot one of those pesky deer! And the other reason I cried was this: I had finally figured out that parents didn't always understand. They tried, and they said things like, "I understand, dear," but they didn't.

If I'd told you the story about the deer, maybe you would have laughed. When I'm in the mood, I can make perfect strangers laugh, telling that story.

14

An Official History of the British Bases

What, then, was this great wartime emergency that took my father away? It is not much mentioned in the published histories, in part because building bases is not very romantic stuff, and in part, I fear, because the civil-works project in Scotland quickly became a bit of a humbug. That is the nature of war, to be a mixture of great purposes and humbugs. The Scotland business was ill-planned, or else it was a well-planned part of the vast and inevitable waste that war creates.

But that is not how it was at the start. In the beginning, it was wonderful.

Three events in America made it clear that the United States was committed to resisting, some day, somewhere, the Nazi regime. The re-election of Roosevelt in 1940 to an unprecedented third term, swamping the isolationist sentiments of the Republican party, was the first sign. The subsequent trade of fifty superannuated World War I destroyers to the British in return for Caribbean naval bases was a second indication that we would do anything short of war—but nothing clearly preparatory to war—to assist England in her truly dark hour. And in the spring of 1941, after the winter blitz in England and Scotland, the passage of the Lend-Lease bill indicated that we were to become the arsenal of Great Britain, if not of democracy itself.

Lend-Lease was a remarkable program that could only have been invented by Americans already practiced in the deficit financing that characterized Roosevelt's great public-works programs of the Depression. Just as you might build great dams, anticipating some unspecific benefits and therefore revenues in the distant future, so America agreed to a massive loan, not of money, but of material, to the British government. (After Germany attacked Russia in the summer of 1941, even the Soviets would benefit from Lend-Lease supplies.) Everything was to be lent: food, munitions, aircraft, warships. Everything was to be done to assure the supplies' arrival in Britain, including convoy protection from the United States to the British Isles.

This had been established in the war plans of the United States, in particular in a document known as Rainbow 5, which detailed the defensive and offensive strategy that would begin as soon as "M-Day" arrived, the day we declared war on Germany and her allies.

The execution of Rainbow 5, which was to conclude with an invasion of the European continent, though not necessarily by American troops transported to the British Isles, implied American responsibility for the convoys that would bring war materiel to Britain, and American participation in a full blockade of Nazi-occupied Europe. The solution to the problem of convoy duty that spanned the Atlantic was the creation of "Advance bases," and the very first to be built in Europe were to be the destroyer repair-and-refueling bases at Londonderry, Northern Ireland, and Rosneath, Scotland. Further convoy protection and patrol would come from two seaplane bases, where PBYs (known as Catalinas, in Britain) would operate long-range patrol and harassment against the German submarine fleet.

To build these bases in 1941 was to violate even the pretense of American neutrality. A planning team arrived in Britain in January 1941, and within a month had selected the sites. But there was no legal mechanism, no cloak of deception, that might allow their construction until the passage of Lend-Lease on March 11, which made it possible to slip the authorization—fifty million dollars in the first phase—past a Congress still wary of sending *our* boys over *there*. The Advance bases had no function other than to support navy convoy escorts and antisubmarine aircraft. If they were completed before "M-Day" arrived or if, for some unforeseen reason, the United States never entered the war, they were simply to be turned over quietly to the British and billed against Lend-Lease.

Within a month of the enactment of Lend-Lease, the orders came detaching my father from his assignment as assistant to the Officer in Charge of Construction at North Island Naval Air Station, San Diego, sending him to Washington, D.C., and on to Quonset Point, Rhode Island, where he began planning the shipment of prefabricated housing units and shiploads of construction materials and equipment. The housing units were, of course, the ubiquitous Quonset huts of World War II, although the first ones, properly speaking, were copies of the British Nissen hut. It was all, for political as well as military reasons, a very dark secret. Yet the prewar navy was not so clandestine a service as it would become after Pearl Harbor, and junior civil-engineering officers usually didn't operate under cover of darkness, which is why my mother found it impossible to explain to her friends where her handsome young husband had disappeared to.

From Roosevelt's perspective, the grand alliance he was forging with Britain was a naval alliance. Churchill's coy reference to himself as the "former naval person" played on Roosevelt's own history as Undersecretary of the Navy in World War I. This pair of leaders with self-images as old sea dogs were solidly behind the navy's Advance base program, and every officer employed on the project could rightfully see himself, even if a clandestine operative, as one of the first emissaries of American might.

There are two unpublished, mimeographed, filed, and forgotten histories of the British Advance bases, typical dour documents of naval administration that clog the shelves of the Naval History Department at the Old Navy Yard in Washington, D.C. One is included in E. E. Morison's preliminary study for his administrative history of the navy in World War II, and the other is a specialized history of the Bureau of Yards and Docks in the European Theater by another naval reservist, Commander R. E. Swarthout. The only published record, of the sort you can find in a substantial public or university library, is the appropriate chapter in the official history of the Bureau and the Civil Engineer Corps: *Building the Navy's Bases in World War II*. It is where you begin, trying to figure out why you were in Montana and your father was not.

Base II, Rosneath—On the rugged western coast of Scotland, the Rosneath peninsula, 2 miles wide and 7 miles long, is bounded by Loch Long, Gare Loch and the Firth of Clyde. . . . The original intention was to provide facilities for the operation and repair of destroyer squadrons and submarines, with accompanying fleet-supply facilities, ammunition and fuel storage installations, plus personnel accommodations for 4,500 men and hospital facilities for 600 men.

A detachment of Royal Engineers was already engaged in building a shallow-water unloading jetty for barges . . . when the naval forces [naval forces!!] arrived in July 1941.

The arriving American navy at Rosneath consisted of Lieutenant Commander Harry Bolles, (CEC) USN, as Resident Officer in Charge of Construction, and four junior officers, including Lieutenant M. R. Montgomery, (CEC) USNR. (The letters R.O. in

C.C. are pronounced "Roink." The supervising officer for all four British bases was Commander H. P. Needham, O. in C.C., pronounced "Oink." These are not regarded as humorous pronunciations in the Civil Engineer Corps.)

Harry Bolles, who would be killed in a plane crash in Alaska in 1943, was the only regular navy officer at Rosneath, an Academy graduate, boxer, oarsman, golfer, and spirited leader who had been, as they still like to say in the navy of first assignments, "destroyer-trained." Unlike the army, which trains civil engineers at West Point, the navy made civil engineering a postgraduate program, assigning willing or able lieutenants to Rensselaer Polytechnic Institute in upstate New York for a two-year course. A firm distinction in the peacetime navy, even when gearing up for war, was made between Academy engineers, who were regarded as natural leaders of men in difficult conditions, and reserve engineers, who were expected to provide engineering and planning expertise, if not active leadership.

An official history tends to avoid personalities as if they would sully the institution's grandeur. But its dry account was a necessary first step in my historical process, and had a certain peculiar charm. An official narrative has an effect like a view from an airplane. Anonymity is preserved by the distance, but the scope of something—a city, a construction project—becomes clear. For that reason, a young Henry Thoreau climbed Mount Wachusett, the southernmost of the Monadnock range, to see how Concord lay in the landscape. When a neighbor chided him, saying he should have taken a telescope so that he could see Concord close up through the glass, Henry responded, "But I know Concord, close up."

We will do it the way Thoreau did it, taking the most distant, Olympian, official view. This is the story as it was retold in *Building the Navy's Bases Overseas*:

> The contractors began work with 150 Irish workmen in August. Considerable delay on major projects was caused by lack of a rock crusher which was needed for road construction.

Pile-driving for the pier, and construction of personnel buildings, hospital, roads, reservoirs, and a water-filtering and purification plant were under way when the United States entered the war in December, 1941.

The scope of the proposed work [at Rosneath] was reduced one-third at that time. It was decided to provide the submarine facilities and the repair shops as planned, but to delete destroyer facilities, especially as the critical machine tools were required elsewhere. [The destroyer repair squadron, with its equipment, was sent to Pearl Harbor] . . . Waterfront work for destroyers, which had not been started, was cancelled, and a substantial reduction was made in the size of supporting activities, the tank farm, hospital, and others.

In April 1942, all projects except the tank farm, materials for which had been delayed, were well under way, and the British were progressively occupying the base. Shortly thereafter, in June, the contractor's crew was shifted to the Dunbartonshire pipe line.

Facilities at Rosneath included a large wooden wharf which provided 4,750 lineal feet of deep-water berthing space and 1,500 lineal feet of shallow water, including four submarine slips . . . an ammunition dump; 21 storage warehouses, a 200-bed hospital; eleven 10,000-barrel fuel-oil tanks and ten 14,400-gallon gasoline tanks with a distribution system to the waterfront; 153 air-raid shelters; housing and messing facilities for 4,500 officers and men (over 500 standard Quonset huts) [in 1944 Rosneath subsisted more than 6,300 officers and men]; and 10 miles of water-bound [that is, without asphalt cement] roadway. . . . At the height of the work of preparing for British occupation in April and May 1942, there were 325 Americans, 1000 Irishmen, and 250 British working on the project.

The Rosneath facility was turned over to the British briefly, then reacquired by the United States in preparation for the first amphibious operation of World War II, the landing at Oran, northern Africa, in November 1942. It was then handed back to the British, reserving only the submarine base and associated repair facilities. Again, in August 1943, it was reacquired as a U.S. Naval Station, and used as a debarkation point for Army and Navy troops arriving

from the United States. After the Normandy invasion, it was returned to the British. Its peak population, more than 6,000 men,
turned over almost weekly, as they were transferred by ferry from
Rosneath to Helensburgh and then by train to Glasgow and on
southward to England. For more than 200,000 Americans, their
first footfall in Great Britain was at Rosneath.

The original contract for Rosneath naval base was well near
completion when a second project was added: a 25-mile pipe line
from Loch Long (lying just to the west, separated from Gare Loch
by the Rosneath peninsula) to Old Kilpatrick, below Loch Lomond.
There, it would tie into an existing petroleum system that served
both Glasgow and Edinburgh. This was meant to solve the problem
in approaching the Old Kilpatrick terminus—the incredible conges-
tion of the Clyde Estuary, where more than 90 percent of the
incoming military and civilian cargo had to be unloaded by lighters
and barges; also, Loch Long is so deep that sunken ships, still a
distinct possibility given German aerial and submarine attacks,
would not block navigation to the terminal. Again, from the published official history:

> The system was designed for high-pressure operation (the first
> in the British Isles) without intermediate pumping stations, and it
> was to have a capacity of 42,000 barrels per day through the 12-
> inch line and 30,000 barrels through the 8-inch [diesel-oil] line.
> The 25-mile route ascended from near sea-level at both ends to an
> elevation of more than 600 feet at the summit.
>
> Installation began in May [1942]. As work on higher-priority
> projects was "topping out," more materials became available for
> this project, and it was possible to build the force up to 1,800
> men. . . .
>
> Though every effort had been made to get as much accomplished
> as possible during the favorable weather and long summer days, the
> task was not easy on the main lines. A more difficult terrain for
> pipeline construction could scarcely be imagined than this route
> through the southern highlands of Scotland. Sparsity of adequate
> highways necessitated the building of construction roads, a task

which was made especially difficult by rugged country, peat bogs and subsoil [agricultural] drains. These drains, which were spaced 25 feet apart, presented a dual problem. Not only did they have to be replaced in workable order, but also, when cut by the ditchers, they had to be repaired immediately because they poured water into trenches dug for the line. The incessant rainfall, 5 to 10 inches per month, kept the earth perpetually saturated.

The installation was 70-percent complete by February 1943, but pumps and special equipment had not yet arrived from the United States when the contract was terminated for the civilian forces on March 31, 1943. In April, the Rosneath detachment of the 29th seabees . . . set out to finish the project. Shipments of material arrived. By July, both lines had been completed and tested, and the installations were turned over to the British Petroleum Board for maintenance and operation.

That is the overview in the grand scheme of things, and the more specialized official histories add their own peculiar dimensions to the flat narrative. The function of an official military history is not to celebrate, or even explain, but to justify and to draw lessons that may be applicable in the next military operation.

E. E. Morison's administrative history of the navy in World War II sees the importance of the four initial British bases as a rehearsal for the navy's vast program of overseas expansion. They were "the nuclear core of subsequent Advance base development," and created an "organization which was destined to direct the procurement, distribution and construction of several hundred shore facilities in all parts of the world." The British bases, in both scale and speed of construction, "dwarfed all previous advance base undertakings. . . . Established procedures would not suffice. . . . Since the facilities had to be constructed in minimum time from materials exported from the United States, it was essential that they be composed, so far as possible, of prepared units capable of speedy erection. In this requirement, mobility was born."

The classic mobile building, erected by Americans from Britain to Borneo, was the Quonset hut, which takes advantage of the principle of the arch, both in its half-round shape and in the corrugations of its individual panels, which are bolted together in a building that is either all roof or all wall, depending on your point of view. Galvanized-steel culverts used to carry water under roadways were the inspiration for the British Nissen and American Quonset huts, both in their round cross-section and in their corrugation. The manufacture of these free-standing and self-supporting buildings began at Quonset Point, Rhode Island, where contractors built a factory dedicated to the huts and to standard-plan rectangular cubes more suitable for aviation maintenance and warehousing.

The most curious aspect of the Advance base construction in Britain was caused by the ostensible neutrality of the United States. Whereas private contractors provided material all through the war and performed the actual construction of Stateside bases, under the supervision of Roinks and Oinks, the prewar navy had neither the manpower nor, in the case of the British bases, the legal authority actually to construct the facilities. American contract labor, mostly skilled tradesmen but including general laborers, was hired and transported across the submarined North Atlantic. A few similar Advance bases, particularly at Wake Island in the Pacific, would find civilian employees trapped by the Japanese attack on December 7, 1941. A classically inaccurate and romantic movie about the civilian workers in the Pacific stars John Wayne in *The Fighting Seabees*. There is no movie about the British bases, probably all for the best.

"Seabee," by the way, is the spelled-out acronym "CB," meaning "Construction Battalion," composed of enlisted men and officers who actually undertook the wartime Advance base construction. These were "line" positions for the officers (as opposed to staff positions such as my father's, when he was administering projects rather than commanding troops). The emblem of the Seabees is a banded yellow-and-black insect carrying five different construction tools and a tommy gun in its six legs. When I was a boy, I had several of them sewn onto various articles of war-surplus clothing.

Morison notes that, "since the contractors supplied all the equipment," it made sense that they construct the British bases,

> because of the technical neutrality of the United States but even more because other Public Works programs already taxed the limited personnel of the Civil Engineer Corps and authority to recruit such enlisted construction personnel as the CB's did not yet exist [in 1941]. Since Lend-Lease funds could not be allocated for a project of this nature [that is, congressionally appropriated U.S. dollars] and Navy appropriations were manifestly not available, the British government assumed the financial burden of actual construction.

While true enough, the point is more complicated: in fact, the fifty million dollars for the material components of the British bases was funded by a sleight-of-hand transfer of funds from Lend-Lease to navy accounts. The costs of actual construction, including loading the British ships that carried the base materials, unloading, and paying the wages of the civilians, were paid directly by the British government, an expenditure credited against their obligations to, for example, U.S. manufacturers of airplanes and ammunition that were being Lend-Leased to the British military. In any case, the navy had formal contractual obligations, on a cost-plus-fixed-fee basis, with Fuller and Merritt-Chapman and Scott, and were under the usual constraints of assuring that the money be spent wisely and legally. "The Navy's interests were safeguarded since it . . . detailed officers, headed by Commander K. V. Bragg, to oversee and to direct the work in the capacity of special naval observers." Thus did the fiction of neutrality cloak an American preparation for war:

> The United Kingdom bases [Morison continued] were of great importance as the major, almost the sole, means through which the Navy made pre-war preparations for Advance bases.
> The subsequent history of the United Kingdom bases was not that which had been anticipated. Although all four were put to good use and turned out to be the forerunners of many more American

bases in the British Isles, only from Base One at Londonderry did United States forces undertake promptly after Pearl Harbor the protection of North Atlantic shipping. [And little of that, compared with the Royal Navy and Royal Canadian Navy destroyers and corvettes based at Londonderry. With few exceptions, most notably the convoys to Murmansk, American forces remained based at Argentia, Newfoundland, and in Iceland, and turned over convoys regularly at a line seven hundred miles west of Londonderry.] Much of the special personnel also had an unexpected fate. Most of the members of the two Destroyer Repair Units were ordered to Pearl Harbor in mid-December 1941 to fill a need far greater than that for which they had been trained.

Nonetheless, the British bases were the true origin of the tremendous Advance base activity of the war. There were evolved and proven the organization, methods, and materiel without which the war against Germany and Japan could never have been won. The men who conceived and executed the United Kingdom programs built far better than they knew.

R. E. Swarthout sums up the British base program with less of an eye on the organizational result and more clarity about the simple enormousness of the task:

The combined area of the over four thousand separate buildings which had been erected was almost 60 acres—about the same as that of the famed Willow Run bomber factory. In and around these structures had been installed the facilities for 20,000 people to live and to work, and more than fifty miles of road construction had been required. Including the Pipe Line in Scotland and the Tank Farms, over 110 miles of pipe had been laid . . . and the tanks installed for all purposes had the tremendous total capacity of over 25 million gallons. . . . Not only had this construction been accomplished, principally, in the short daylight hours of the rainy winter months of far northern latitudes, and in the rural, undeveloped, and rugged countryside of a strange land at war, but the materials with which it had been accomplished, and which required a staggering number of merchant vessels for their shipment, had been procured thousands of miles away and transported across the At-

lantic at the zenith of the German submarine blockade. Truly, the
United States Navy and the more than 1200 civilians of the contract
forces who had left their homes to reverse the tide of [the German]
empire had much to be proud of in the magnificent accomplishment.

The curious sentence in Swarthout's history, echoing a similar
idea in E. E. Morison's, is the statement that "the subsequent
history of the United Kingdom bases was not that which had
been anticipated." Base 1, Londonderry, of use as a turnaround
for the limited number of U.S. Navy ships that worked convoys
all the way to Northern Ireland became an administrative area and
the navy's major radio facility for the eastern North Atlantic. Base
B, the isolated flying-boat base in Scotland, was never occupied by
U.S. forces. Base A, the flying-boat squadron facility on Lough
Erne in Northern Ireland, was turned over to the U.S. Army as
a replacement depot and training base, while the British Coastal
Command continued to use an immediately adjacent base for their
Lend-Leased PBY Catalinas. Base 2, Rosneath on the Gare Loch,
as we have seen, was turned over to the British on three separate
occasions, and reclaimed by the United States in two intermediary
phases.

Another curious sentence occurs in the semiofficial (subsidized
but not controlled) multivolume history of the navy in World
War II directed, and largely written, by Samuel Eliot Morison of
Harvard University. In the official accounts by Swarthout and
E. E. Morison, the change in plans—the abandonment, really—
of the British bases is accounted for by the unexpected outbreak
of war in the Pacific; the events of December 7–8, 1941, made the
British bases superfluous. But Sam Morison's brief account has a
flat and chilling summary:

> Around mid-June [1941], however, this plan for the Support
> Force to convoy shipping all the way across was given up in favor
> of the Support Force concentrating on the Argentia-Iceland sector
> of the transatlantic convoy route. That was the way the [British]
> Admiralty and the Navy Department wanted it from the first. Such

an arrangement would make for economy in administration and operation.

If Sam Morison is right, the bases were wholly redundant before the first shipload of Advance base materials ever arrived; they were off the program just as the first CEC officers, filled with enthusiasm for joining Britain in her struggle against the Nazis, reported for duty as attachés and observers to the London embassy. It would not be the first time in the history of warfare that plans developed their own momentum.

Sam Morison's version relied, according to the brief historiographical notes in his volume covering the Battle of the North Atlantic, on conversations with the commander of the Support Force for which these four bases were built, the same support force that remained based at Argentia, rather than at either Londonderry or Rosneath. It is difficult to believe that such a decision, which amounted to misappropriating fifty million dollars of Britain's scarce Lend-Lease credit and her own real pounds and shillings used for construction workers' salaries, would not leave a paper trail somewhere. But it is, as we shall see, a very lightly blazed trail. The birds of time have eaten the crumbs left on the forest floor, and it is almost impossible to find the way back.

15

More Detailed Records

At Port Hueneme, California, the old Pacific Theater Advance Base center is still in operation, now as the Naval Construction Battalion Center, a subset of the Naval Facilities Command. Visitors may bypass the usual military-security system and enter the base if their destination is the Seabee Museum or the Operational History Section. The wings of the Seabee Museum, set about a concrete central core, are the last Quonset huts at Port Hueneme; the operational-history archive, housed until a few years ago in a Quonset, has found more comfortable quarters in a flat-roofed military building of no architectural or historical interest.

The few old Quonsets you are likely to see these days are left-over Reserve Officer Training Corps buildings on university campuses, now possessed by Buildings and Grounds and housing lawnmowers, small tools, and offices. Here and there across the Midwest and the South, a few have been lovingly preserved by former navy pilots who use them as outbuildings on the small private airports that serve crop dusters and weekend pilots. And there are at least a half-dozen Quonset-hut barrooms in southern California, and perhaps as many more in some countryside I am less familiar with, built and operated by navy retirees. The decor always includes navy memorabilia, and, until death reaped so many of them, the bartender was usually called Chief.

The museum is predictable: wall maps of the great Pacific invasions, collections of native artifacts from New Guinea to Borneo (the first and last Seabee actions before the Japanese surrender), uniforms, equipment, and dozens of oil portraits of chiefs of the Bureau of Yards and Docks, commanders of Port Hueneme, and other famous civil-engineering officers, including Harry Bolles, handsome as in life, or slightly more so. His boxing-broken nose had been repaired rather better by the painter than by the doctor.

The operational archive was more of a surprise. It holds detailed records of the various Construction Battalions. Depending on decisions made long ago at distant headquarters at the end of the war, some are complete down to lists of every piece of equipment, some as skimpy as a few pay, medical, and court-martial records. What I had come for, without being assured that I would find them, were documents of navy contracts with civilian companies. Stirring the two-person staff into action, I was aware only that there were "some materials" relating to NOy4850, the overall Navy contract for the British bases.

On arrival, I was shown the correspondence files of the Chief of the Bureau of Yards and Docks, Admiral Ben Moreell. Moreell was something of a compulsive letter writer and, even better and even more unusual for a military officer, a compulsive letter saver. Although the perfect model of a modern admiral (the first member of the Civil Engineer Corps to reach that elevated title), Moreell had some civilian tendencies. He was civilian-trained, at Washington University in Saint Louis and not at the Academy at Annapolis. And from all indications gleaned by leafing through the papers, he regularly committed two sins against the military method: he not only encouraged subordinates to write him directly, outside of the chain of command and over the heads of their commanding officers, but also saved all unofficial letters that came into his possession. Many of these could not be sorted and pigeonholed according to the *Navy Filing Manual of 1941 as Revised*. Moreell's personal secretary filed his letters in a most unauthorized manner— by the name of the sender, or, if the subject of the letter was another civil-engineering officer, under *his* name.

Port Hueneme is located in the town of Oxnard, adjacent to the city of Ventura, about forty miles north of Los Angeles, past the rugged Santa Monica mountains. Just offshore lie the southern Channel Islands, which stretch from Santa Barbara at the north end of the chain to Santa Catalina, the Isle of Love, off Long Beach. The port itself is an artificial harbor in two distinct parts: a series of marina developments, with attendant condominiums, restaurants, and motels, make up the largest part; the navy and the civilian cargo port share the deep-water berthing. A spur line of the Southern Pacific Railroad serves Port Hueneme, as it has since World War II, and crosses the navy base as it moves cargo from Port Hueneme to the Oxnard rail yards. The first day I worked in the Construction Battalion history archives, I left the office after 6:00 p.m. (one of the staff members was working on a historical paper and we kept the office open late, together) and waited nearly forty-five minutes to get off the base, trapped on the wrong side of a slow-moving freight train. A full four-engine trainload of Mazda automobiles and trucks was coming out of Port Hueneme, crossing the very ground from which the facilities of the Pacific campaign had been shipped. Mazda is the American brand name for vehicles built in Hiroshima, Japan, by the Toyo Kogyo Company. In World War II, Toyo Kogyo manufactured many things requiring high-quality steel milled to fine dimensions, including naval cannons.

As very small children, for a few months when we lived in Ventura, my sister and I were taken to the beach and always came home with tarry oil stuck to our feet. This was removed by standing us up in one side of the double laundry sink and scrubbing us with lighter fluid. No one had invented something like Lestoil, that remarkable cleaner which hotels in Bermuda provide their guests so they will not track mid-ocean tar back into the rooms. The wartime Ventura oil was due in part to natural seepage from the Santa Barbara oil fields, and in part to discharged bunker oil left behind by the repetitive convoys of navy shipping that left Port Hueneme freighted with everything from Quonset huts to bulldozers. The sea has an odd capacity to dispose of oil, and only constant replenishment will keep a beach littered with tar balls. The beaches are fairly clean at Port Hueneme, except for the usual jetsam of pleasure boats: cigarette filters, plastic highball glasses, and snack wrappers. Much more than at Fort Peck, where the world has simply retreated from the old construction site, I felt here that the naval records were as ancient as pottery shards. At Hueneme, the bustle was all outside the torpid base; even the debris on the beaches was civilian and recreational.

Inside the operational archive, the world essentially stops in August 1945. A staff of two is in the process of cleaning, clarifying, and refiling the era of 1941–45 into the narrow upright one-half-cubic-foot gray paperboard boxes used for that purpose by most libraries, the ones known as Hollinger boxes. The cleaning-up work will take them into the twenty-first century, even if they merely succeed in removing the paper clips and press-down metal tabs that are slowly rusting through the carbon copies and original materials. More could be done, of course, including sanitizing the records. The only serious problem is raised in papers dealing with pay, promotion and demotion, and battalion-strength reports. This is because the major cause of manpower shortages, particularly in the better-populated islands in the Pacific, was venereal disease, noted in medical records and reports of summary courts-martial and, for repeated derelictions, in reductions in pay and grade. It is an unfortunate fact that you can get more detail on the clap than on any other aspect of a unit's military history. While concern for venereal disease and mosquito-borne infections occupies most of the medical effort, some few units, whose supply and finance officers were particularly meticulous or paranoid, will have complete inventories of every piece of equipment, down to Phillips screwdrivers, in their possession.

The records for the Rosneath naval base were contained in two easily found files. A final report on the contract, dated March 1943, summarizes the scope and chronology of the construction and, in unusual detail, indicates the changes in supervisory personnel in the "Log of Events." A second file, simply labeled "Base 2," includes miscellaneous letters, photocopies of telegrams, orders, memoranda, and handwritten notes apparently collected in Ben Moreell's office and lumped together for posterity's interest.

In the "naval forces" that arrived on British soil as the spearhead of the American forces, my father is listed as "Lieut. M. R. Montgomery, C.E.C., U.S.N.R.," ahead of three lieutenants junior-grade. One can overread a document, but the point here is that this one proves my father's plan had already borne fruit: by taking a commission as a naval reservist in 1936, he had already managed to steal a promotion on his peers; Lieutenants (junior-grade) Pritchard and Jenkins had gone on active duty in late 1939, a year before my father was called to active duty, but my father had, so to speak, time in grade, and therefore one more shoulder bar and sleeve stripe than his fellow assistant engineers.

27 January, 1942:

R.O. in C.C., Commander H. A. Bolles, C.E.C., U.S.N. was detached and Lieut. M. R. Montgomery, C.E.C., U.S.N.R., 1st Assistant, assumed command.

As all four of the British bases neared completion, the bulk of remaining work was then in Scotland: both the base itself at Rosneath, and the additional task of completing the twenty-five-mile pipeline. In the spring of 1942, a cadre of Texas and Oklahoma oil field workers was added to the company of "Technical American Forces" under my father's command, a group of workers known in the business, and for good reason, as "roughnecks." Still, it occurred to my father that with a minimum of discipline, it would be possible to celebrate the American Fourth of July holiday, and he organized a lawn party on the grounds of Rosneath Castle, complete with parade, a softball game between the Texans and the New Englanders, and a soccer game between the Irish construction workers and the crew of a Canadian corvette which had docked at Rosneath pier for refueling and minor repairs. He threw the first pitch in the softball game, in dress blues, and a good time, and a reasonably sober one, was had by all.

As summer came to a close, the office of the O.I. in C.C. (which had always been based at Base 1, Londonderry) was transferred to Scotland:

7 October, 1942:
  Lt. Commander M. R. Montgomery, C.E.C., U.S.N.R., took over duties of O. in C.C. replacing Commander H. P. Needham, C.E.C., U.S.N. Lt. Commander R. E. Jenkins, C.E.C., U.S.N.R. became R.O. in C.C. Office of O. in C.C. moved from Londonderry, North Ireland, to Helensburgh, Scotland.

There is a habit among construction men, whether supervisors or mechanics (we tend to use the word "mechanic" today as a shorthand for automotive mechanic, but a construction tradesman has always been a mechanic, and a good one is more likely to be described as a good mechanic than as a good carpenter or a good mason or some other specialty), to take verbal credit for a construction project, to say, "*I* built that." So, I remember, my father said *he* had built a base in Scotland, had built a pipeline in Scotland. But this final report of contract NOy4850 was the first indication to me that in fact, he had. As Roink and Oink, he did it.

There were few enough Scotland stories in my childhood. I suspect my mother was not very fond of them, for they would remind her of a solid two years of separation and the six months of secrecy that sent us back to Montana. But I remember a few, and one anecdote in particular that—and I think I understood this when he told me—summed up my father's frustration with the management of this isolated project, so dependent on unenthusiastic contract labor. It would have been around 1952 or 1953 that he told it, after I had started to work for his construction company as a kind of general laborer and carpenter's helper during high-school summers. He got me working on small jobs where union jurisdictions were not rigidly enforced, and I learned how to do a number of mechanic's jobs: framing, finishing cement, building forms for concrete, mostly rough work for small renovations. You never forget how to do them, but you do run out of enthusiasm, over the years.

I'd spent a day helping form up a footing for a small addition to an existing building, and my work included placing the reinforcing bars, which would have been an ironworker's business on a larger job and probably should have been on this one, but we did it ourselves, the carpenter and I. You tie the rods together in an open gridwork, so that they stay where they belong when the concrete is poured. The wire ties are not for strength, but simply to hold the reinforcing bars in place until the concrete sets. You use a soft, malleable, ductile iron wire to do it, pulling it off a reel or, on a small job, from a coil about two feet wide that you carry diagonally across your shoulders. It is a repetitive but mildly interesting task. You take the side-cutting pliers and form a U in the end of the wire, push it through the grid of re-bars, pull back, twist the U closed around the intersection of two bars, cut it, and push the sharp ends in toward the re-bars. It's a male equivalent of crocheting, and pleasant enough work if the bars aren't thick and heavy.

When I got home that evening, my father asked me what we'd gotten done (at the time he was supervising a massive ten-story

hospital job across town from the little addition where I was learning the trade), and I told him I'd been tying iron all afternoon and
that we were ready to pour in the morning. It was one of those
wonderful southern-California evenings, with thunderheads building up over the Laguna Mountains, off in the eastern distance,
and we were sitting on the porch watching the clouds start to color
up in the sunset's alpen glow. It was also one of those rare inter-
sections between his memory and my readiness to understand a
story, and I write here what he said as if I remember it exactly:

"When the Irish labor showed up in Scotland, I went down one
morning and they were all sitting around, not working, and I went
over to the foreman and asked him what was going on. He told me
they were getting ready to tie iron. And you know what they were
doing? They were sitting there making little hairpins out of the tie
wire and sticking them on their belt; that's how they were going
to do it. So I got a coil and put it across my shoulders and pulled
out the loose end and showed them how we did it in America. The
trouble was, you see, they never wanted a job to end."

It did not occur to me to ask him to go on. It was not merely
our usual mutual reticence; it was, I know now, simply too perfect
a moment for me to say another word. I might just have been a
high-school kid to the world at large, but, at least that evening, I
was a good mechanic who would understand the story, and I was
not about to break the spell.

So, forty and more years after that conversation, one sits in the
Quonset hut at Port Hueneme and reads the Log of Events in the
Final Report of NOy4850 with a different eye:

13 August 1941:
    First contingent of Irish labor arrived, approximately one hundred
and fifty men.

And not a one of them knew how to tie rods.

16

"A Severe Disappointment to Them"

On August 2, 1941, two ships of importance to this narrative set sail from Atlantic ports. One was a dumpy cargo ship, the other a millionaire's yacht.

A telegram copy in the Port Hueneme files reports the departure of the *Gretavale*, a British merchantman, from Quonset Point, Rhode Island, with the first shipment of materials for Base 2, Rosneath, including a very large rock-crusher which would turn into a logistical monster when they attempted to unload it at ill-equipped Rosneath. And the presidential yacht *Potomac* left Washington on a well-publicized "fishing trip." Off Rhode Island, out of sight of land, Franklin Roosevelt and his advisers transferred to the heavy cruiser *Augusta*. On that ship were the American chiefs of staff, including General George C. Marshall and Admiral Stark, plus attendant admirals and generals and staff. They were headed for Placentia Bay, Newfoundland, to meet secretly with Winston Churchill and his advisers, to formulate plans for the further defense of Britain, and, as it turned out, most especially the defense of her colonies. It was, after all, Winston Churchill who would later swear that he was not the Prime Minister who would preside over the dissolution of the British Empire.

The results of the negotiations at Newfoundland were substantially different from the public announcements that followed. It was there, the public would learn, that Roosevelt and Churchill subscribed to the Atlantic Charter, the famous "Four Principles of Freedom," which were to make up the prologue of the United Nations Charter. The secret and complex military agreement, should properly be thought of as the "Pacific Charter."

Churchill and the British staff pleaded for immediate action in the Atlantic—specifically, port-to-port escort of war materials and Lend-Lease goods by American ships, presumably by the so-called Atlantic Support Force, which was designated to take up the burden of cross-Atlantic convoy protection on "M-Day," the date of expected war between the United States and Germany. This was refused, the President fearing the political consequences of entering into what would amount to a state of war, if not with Germany, at least with the German fleet. There was some irony in this refusal, for it was given to the British aboard their flagship *Prince of Wales*, which had arrived in Placentia Bay still scarred from her successful gunnery duel with the German battleship *Bismarck*. Indeed, the *Bismarck* had been discovered and brought to bay by a Lend-Lease PBY Catalina in May 1941, a plane based at Lough Erne in Northern Ireland, where, in June 1941, the construction of seaplane Base A was begun by U.S. Navy Civil Engineer Corps officers.

If Churchill failed to get the immediate implementation of Rainbow 5, including convoying, and therefore the full use of the four

British bases then under construction, he was more successful in getting Roosevelt's agreement on matters in the Western Pacific. The exact nature of the agreement, even after fifty years of declassification of documents and innumerable biographies of the participants, is still, frankly, unclear. But there was complete agreement on one matter, that the United States would cooperate with the British in opposing Japanese movement toward British colonies on the Malay Peninsula. Isolationists later argued that Roosevelt had agreed to join Britain should she be attacked by the Japanese. Pearl Harbor conspiracy theorists argued that Roosevelt's plans for the Western Pacific showed he would do anything to get a shooting war going with the Japanese, including, in the "infamy" theory, letting Pearl Harbor sleep away in the face of known, certain attack. (This is not the place, nor this the author, to settle such questions, but one thing has become clear in declassified documents. Roosevelt expected that war with Japan would occur, and even attempted to provoke it, but he expected it in the Philippines, not the Hawaiian Islands, and he was under the great illusion that the choice as to the timing of the outbreak of hostilities would be his.)

The Americans apparently promised to the British that no capital ships of the U.S. Navy would be withdrawn from the Pacific fleet and sent to the Atlantic. Instead, they would remain in the Pacific, and support Britain's defense of her Asian colonies. In effect, and to the relief of the Pacific commanders (and, not surprisingly, to the relief of the commander of the Atlantic fleet, the Anglophobic Admiral Ernest J. King), there would be no Atlantic Support Force, and the British would remain responsible for the naval defense of the British Isles and for convoy escort east of Iceland. (Since World War I, it had been assumed that in the event of future war the United States would defend the Western Hemisphere and the British would support their home isles and the approaches to Western Europe. Rainbow 5, after all the talk, remained nothing but a temporary, paper change in that policy.)

As the *Gretavale* neared Scotland, the meeting at Placentia Bay broke up, and the Prime Minister returned to Britain on the *Prince of Wales* with the assurances about the Pacific that he so much desired. The Americans understood that they, in order to make the commitment of ships to defend Britain's Far East colonies, had abandoned Rainbow 5. But it was not discussed in these blunt, horse-trading terms. As far as the British knew, Rainbow 5, including port-to-port convoy protection and the Support Force, remained the war plan of the United States. Convoy escorting was, as the British imagined the results of Placentia Bay, only delayed until "M-Day." They believed, sailing home, that they had acquired an *additional* measure of support from the United States, not a swap.

The Roosevelt-Churchill agreement on cooperation in Asian waters was never published, perhaps never even written down. But there is one bit of public evidence for its existence. On January 17, 1942, Churchill defended himself against a censure motion in Parliament: the charge was an allegation that Britain's Asian colonies had been left to fend for themselves against the Japanese. Churchill told the Members, in open session, that he had made arrangements with the United States, that he and Roosevelt had agreed during "the Atlantic conference . . . that the United States, even if not attacked herself, would come into a war in the Far East." His "expectation" of mutual aid was "reinforced" as the days passed between the August conference and the December debacle, he explained to the Members. "As time went on . . . one had greater assurance that if Japan ran amok in the Pacific, we would not fight alone."

The American isolationists did "pick it up," as Harry Hopkins predicted, and they were led by our Montana Senator Burton K. Wheeler. Until his death, shortly after the end of the war, Wheeler hammered away at the implications of Churchill's speech to Parliament, though the actual record of the Placentia Bay meeting was not available to him or to the Joint Congressional Committee that spent the greater part of 1945 trying to assess blame for the Pearl Harbor disaster. Curiously, but I think understandably, Montana was a proper ground for generating fears of war, and Burton's response was to fight against American involvement in it. Other Montanans, including my father, accepted and tried to anticipate it.

The most problematic question about the apparent junking of Rainbow 5 at Placentia Bay is, who knew about it? It is extremely unlikely that the civil engineers, the Special Naval Observers at the four British bases, had any clue that they were engaged, after August 1941, in what was a sideshow to the real war plans of the U.S. Navy. Shortages of materials and delays in delivery could be ascribed to general scarcity and the exigencies of shipment across the Atlantic without looking for a subtler, hidden cause. Certainly, as is clear from the records, both the British government and the navy engineering staff kept pushing forward on the bases, anticipating their full use by Americans when "M-Day" inevitably arrived and Rainbow 5 went into effect.

What was apparently operating here was that old military, and particularly that old navy, principle, "need to know." It would have done no good at all—it would have been disastrous, in fact—to include the naval officers in Northern Ireland and Scotland in the understanding that the British bases had suddenly lost their significance, just as ground was being broken.

It is not even clear when Admiral Moreell came to understand this reality. In his miscellaneous incoming correspondence file one very exotic piece of paper lays out the matter of Rainbow 5, but unfortunately does not show any date stamp to indicate when Moreell received it; there is, moreover, nothing to explain—and this may be quite deliberate—*how* he managed to get his hands on it.

It is a typescript, clearly labeled "copy," of a memorandum dated October 9, 1941, from the First Assistant to the Special Naval Observer, London, Commander Paul F. Lee, to an otherwise unidentified "Mr. Biggers." Fortunately, Mr. Biggers had sufficient ego to respond to a request from the publishers of *Who's Who in America*, which tells us that John David Biggers was a Lend-Lease officer, in civilian life a manufacturer of glassware in Saint Louis, Missouri, employed by the War Department as a specialist in "production, coordination and Lend-Lease"; he was in Britain in regard to a proposed Lend-Lease program to assist in building what the memorandum called "British Ship Repair Facilities in Red Sea Area."

Construction of the four British bases had just begun when Commander Lee settled down to brief Mr. Biggers. The galley (kitchen facilities) for the first construction workers had been completed; the troublesome rock-crusher was being unloaded in Greenock, and arrangements were being made to truck it the forty miles by narrow road to Rosneath. The dock construction was being planned, and the first load of wooden piles for the waterfront was still on a ship, somewhere in the Irish Sea. American naval officers were beginning to lay out the outward and visible signs of the phantom "North Atlantic Support Force" that would ensure the delivery to England of war materiel and food under Lend-Lease. Given that background, Commander Lee's memorandum for Mr. Biggers is worth citing in its entirety:

1. In connection with possible discussions which you may hold with our Navy Department regarding the erection by us of ship repair facilities [for the British Navy's use] at Port Sudan, the following background may be of value:

(a) When the original decision was made last March to construct ship and air bases in Northern Ireland and Scotland it was then the plan of the Navy Department that should we become involved in the war our ships would operate from these bases and they would be, in fact, taken over in toto by the United States Navy.

(b) The broad basis for the agreement regarding the construction of these bases was that all materials coming from the United States would be paid for out of Lease/Lend, but that all labour used in Ireland and Scotland would be paid for by the British Government. In addition the British Government was to requisition all land necessary for the erection of these bases. I have no definite information regarding the total cost of the material and labour involved [Commander Lee evidently has a British typist; note the spelling of "labor"], but it does represent a large sum of money [fifty million dollars] which, while not directly out of the British Treasury, has had the effect of decreasing the money available under Lease/Lend for other urgent British requirements.

(c) It now appears that should we become involved in the war the Destroyer Repair Base now under construction at Londonderry and the combined Destroyer and Submarine Repair Base at Gareloch [Rosneath] will not be used by U.S. Naval Forces, but that our ships will continue to base on the Western Atlantic.

[Now comes what in horse-trading parlance in Montana is known as a "kicker":]

When this knowledge is conveyed to the British it will, no doubt, be a very severe disappointment to them for two reasons: First, they were most anxious that our ships operate from this side of the Atlantic: Second, that large sums of money will have been spent on bases which will not, in fact, be used by us and may not be fully used by them. This latter represents a direct decrease in the amount of money which would have been available to the British under Lease/Lend.

[And now, the real kicker:]

2. Para. (c) above is due, apparently, to a basic change in our strategic plan for co-operation between the two Navies. In so far as I am aware it is *our* change and not the British. In view of this it is considered that the Navy Department should attempt to soften the disappointment of the British by whole-heartedly supporting the development of facilities in the Red Sea Area.

So, there it is. The unwritten, unrecorded result of the conference at Placentia Bay appears to have been this: the American agreement to support the British in the Southern and Western Pacific had the result, *from the American point of view only*, of abandoning the concept of convoy support from North America to the British Isles. One copy of one memorandum is not enough, perhaps, to justify rewriting this small corner of history, but there is some further indication that the official histories, which blame Pearl Harbor for the temporary abandonment of the British bases

and the permanent abandonment of the paper-only "Support Force,
North Atlantic," are simply wrong, if not duplicitous.

And Sam Morison, in his volume on *The Battle of the North
Atlantic*, is only half right. He thought, perhaps was told in interviews, that the U.S. Navy's decision to escort convoys only to the
waters just east of Iceland was understood and agreed to by the
British sometime in the early summer of 1941.

A few small details, however, completely correspond with Commander Lee's understanding that it was a unilateral American decision, not conveyed to the British until Pearl Harbor gave them
the public, understandable excuse. The most obvious is the recruitment and training of the destroyer repair unit that was, the-
oretically, to be deployed at Rosneath and Londonderry as soon as
possible after "M-Day." The unit was pulled together out of some
experienced navy ratings and a large force of new recruits at San
Diego, not at any of the half-dozen Atlantic navy shipyards where
destroyers were based and repair facilities were in place. Why it
should be a part of the Pacific fleet if it was truly intended to
support an Atlantic operation is inexplicable, even given the military's habit of moving things around randomly. And although the
construction at Londonderry and Rosneath and at the two seaplane
bases went ahead expeditiously, there were constant problems with
minor supplies. Quonset units and temporary warehouse units were
regularly pulled out of the supply line to Britain and shipped either
to Newfoundland (for convoy-escort repair facilities) or to Iceland
(for PBY bases); other items were sent to the Caribbean and South
America. The industrial capacity of the United States was not yet
the overwhelming machine it was to become by 1943 and 1944,
but manufacture was not a bottleneck, and the civil engineers in
Britain might have suspected that something more than ordinary
difficulties in transatlantic shipping was holding things up. Even
something as simple as getting the right size wooden pilings for the
docks was a problem. The nature of the underwater soils at Rosneath required seventy- and eighty-foot pilings, but most of what
was shipped was shorter, in spite of regular pleas, and construction

of the destroyer and submarine piers was slowed by months because the workmen had to drive short piles, then splice on an extension and continue driving to a hard bottom.

There is no indication, in any of the files, that any of the civil engineers knew they were engaged, in the rainy fall of 1941, in a great project with no apparent purpose.

17

"A Long and Weary Job"

The Rosneath engineers understood that their half of the twinned destroyer/submarine bases was second in priority to the Londonderry facility, and while they waited impatiently for various construction materials and equipment, a more difficult construction project was soon added to their already considerable task.

On November 14, 1941, the embassy in Washington sent a "most-secret" memorandum to the British Supply Council in North America. This joint British-American agency was in charge of allocating Lend-Lease to the British and, equally important, of assigning Allied merchant shipping to carry Lend-Lease goods across the Atlantic. The memo concerned a deceptively simple project—in the imagination, at least. British oil supplies in the Firth of Clyde on the west coast (Glasgow) and the Firth of Forth on the east (Edinburgh) were linked by a pipeline. Because of the extreme danger from German submarines and aircraft based in occupied Holland, France, and Belgium, the easterly end at Edinburgh could be reached only by slow, coast-hugging convoys, so shipping to the Forth was delayed by at least ten days' extra time in each direction, adding to the turnaround time for the desperately needed tankers. The Glasgow end of the pipeline, safer and quicker to reach, depended on tankers from the Americas' coming up into the narrowest and most congested part of the Clyde estuary.

The Americans now proposed, and the British agreed, to spend Lend-Lease funds for a twenty-five-mile pipeline from Loch Long to the existing oil terminal at Old Kilpatrick, on the north side of the Firth of Clyde, opposite Glasgow. Loch Long, which runs along the western side of the Rosneath Peninsula, was totally undeveloped in 1941 except for a small submarine ordnance depot. (Loch Long had been used since World War I as a practice area for submarine torpedo practice, since it was narrow, deep, and isolated, allowing for secrecy, safety, and the easy retrieval of the dummy torpedoes, which would almost always run ashore in the narrow upper end of the loch, even if wildly inaccurate and out of control.) The navy civil engineers would be able to supervise the building of the moorings for the incoming tankers, the pipeline to Old Kilpatrick, and the installation of the necessary high-pressure pumping stations to lift the oil some six hundred feet above sea level as it crossed the highlands between Loch Long and the Gare Loch, following the course of the only highway and the western line of the highland railroad. From there it would rise again, through Glen Fruin to the banks of Loch Lomond, and then run southeastward through Balloch to Old Kilpatrick. That none of the officers had ever built a pipeline, and that most of them were totally unfamiliar with marine waterfront construction, was no obstacle. Civil engineering had been a generalist's business in the 1930s, when they

were trained. And because American civilian labor had been im-
ported to build the bases, it was assumed that American oil-pipeline
workers could be sent from the American Southwest to Scotland
to provide the hands-on expertise.

From the U.S. Navy's position, the addition of the pipeline project in behalf of the British Navy was potentially beneficial to the
Americans. As the line crossed the Highlands and descended to
the upper end of Gare Loch, it would come within five miles of
the Rosneath base. The second paragraph of the cipher-encoded
message to the British Supply Council explained:

> [The] project has now been examined in relation to American
> Naval Base at Rosneath and if executed with arm running to Ros-
> neath would provide valuable increased facilities for U.S. Navy and
> reduce amount of tankage (?planned) for base. [The parenthetical
> question mark indicates the cryptographer's best guess as to the
> intended word in the coded letter group.] This integration of plan
> for pipeline with plans of Naval Base will place at disposal of U.S.
> Navy all oil stocks on Clyde.
>
> 3. The whole question has now been discussed with Commanders
> Flanigan and Bragg [Flanigan is an unknown quantity; Bragg was
> the Civil Engineer Corps R.O. in C.C.] on the basis that American
> authorities should undertake on Lease Lend terms execution of the
> project as complete and undivided accepting responsibility for gath-
> ering material and equipment.

The sense of cross-purpose is palpable. This is one month after
Commander Lee had informed Lend-Lease's Mr. Biggers that the
navy had no intention of taking over Base 2 at Rosneath, and nearly
a month before the attack at Pearl Harbor gave the United States
an express reason for telling the British that Rosneath would not
become an operating naval base and that the alleged Support Force,
North Atlantic, would never protect the North Atlantic convoys.
It certainly does confirm Lee's statement to Biggers that the abandonment of the Support Force was "our change, not the British,"
and makes it clear that the British were still in the dark.

Indeed, although the funds for the pipeline project (finally totaling ten million dollars) were appropriated in November 1941 as an addition to the basic Fuller-Merritt contract, no work began on the line until June 1942, at which time Rosneath was a British base, designated in the quaint system of the Royal Navy, which regarded all installations as ships, H.M.S. *Rosneath*.

What may have stirred work on the pipeline into action was the American plan to retake Rosneath from the Royal Navy, which transfer took place on August 24, 1942, in anticipation of using it as the staging base for American troops involved in the joint British-American "Torch" invasion of North Africa. Although there is no direct mention of it in any of his few surviving letters, I suspect that by then my father was beginning to understand that he was very possibly involved in a sideshow. Construction of Base 2 was virtually complete by January 1942, but it was July before the first pipeline equipment and construction mechanics arrived. His offices, in the "Princess Louise" (Rosneath Castle) by May 1942, at the sufferance of the British Navy, were moved three times to locations along the pipeline route: first to Finnart on Loch Long; then to Tullichewan Castle, near the Old Kilpatrick terminal; then back to Helensburgh, about the midpoint on the line, and directly across the Gare Loch from Rosneath. At one point, while moving from Tullichewan Castle to Helensburgh, he was completely without either an office or a bed. For those several weeks, he was guest of a Sir David MacGowan, lord of Lomond Castle, on the banks of Loch Lomond, about halfway between Old Kilpatrick and Helensburgh.

How he met Sir David is unknown to me. I do remember him saying, so long ago now, that he had "lived in a castle in Scotland." In any case, Sir David introduced my father to Scottish angling, on Loch Lomond itself, of course, but, more important, Sir David owned fishing rights on the river Leven, the outlet of Loch Lomond to the Clyde. The Leven leaves the Clyde just a few miles downstream from the Old Kilpatrick oil station. It was not difficult for an American officer to return hospitality, even to the lord of a castle, because the American commissary had several otherwise absolutely unavailable items in it, including fresh fruit. My father used to bring grapefruit, among other things, to Sir David.

While the civilian contract force, under his direction, did what they could to prepare for the operation of the pipeline, vital material from the United States was unavailable. They built platforms for the pressure tanks at Loch Long, and laid in the concrete dock there, but it was the spring of 1943 before the piling for the tankers' deep-water berths was made available. Not, perhaps, that the work could have proceeded much faster than it did, given the difficulty of the terrain, but it was evident to all of them that they were involved in laying a pipeline that would not be quickly put into use, since none of the terminal gear, piers, pumps, or pressure tanks was even on the way.

Ditching operations were delayed until the winter of 1942–43, the one in which monthly rainfall averaged nearly ten inches, and the civilian work force, knowing their contract was about to be terminated, worked with agonizing slowness. It was, by every official account, a miserable job, partly because of the weather, the terrain, and then the soils. Hard rock would have almost been a blessing, for much of the line traversed either peat soils or beds of marine clay that had been laid down during the great Ice Age and then lifted, along with the main landmass, as the weight of the glaciers was removed by melting. These marine clays, blue and soft, are pre-shales, not unlike the Bear Paw shale through which the Fort Peck spillway was constructed, and, like the harder Bear Paw, are made up of sediments so fine that you cannot feel any grittiness when you rub the wet material between your fingers. Work went reasonably well on the five-mile branch line from Rosneath to Garelochhead, a job completed in July and August 1942, before the rains came; the crews had yet to deal with the rugged cross-mountain terrain from Loch Long to Garelochhead, from there, via Glen Fruin, to the highway along Loch Lomond, and thence to Old Kilpatrick on the river Leven.

Commander Swarthout's typescript history sums up the problem well enough:

> On the 15th of August [1942] work finally got under way on the actual laying of pipe on the main lines. . . . It was almost concurrent with the return of Base II to the U.S. Navy, and the necessity for returning contract personnel to the Base to undertake the maintenance again and to construct the new facilities required did not lessen the difficulties on the Pipe Line job. But good progress had been made in the long daylight hours on some of the projects and the 1st of September saw most of the work on the branch down the Rosneath peninsula done, and by the 19th the Tanker Dock [but not the deep-water moorings] on the shore of Loch Long had been finished. Meanwhile the flow of materials from the States had been considerably accelerated [no doubt, because it was again a project that would serve an American base] and with the completion of the main construction camp at Balloch and the one at the eastern end of the line at Bowling [Old Kilpatrick] it was possible to build the force up to 1800 men and broaden the job out by starting work on 8 September on the Finnart Tanks [on Loch Long] and on the Pumping Stations at Old Kilpatrick and at Finnart on the 5th and 19th of October.

The sudden retakeover of the base from the British Navy, and its use as a staging area for the North African invasion, marks a very unhappy period in the relations between Britain and the United States. The invasion of North Africa itself caused the problems: the Americans had pressed hard for some kind of "second front" against Germany (the "first front" being the Russian front), and an Allied invasion of Western Europe being out of the question, everyone agreed, the show in North Africa became the Americans' much-hoped-for second front.

As we noted, the abandonment of Rainbow 5 and thus the abandonment of a U.S. Support Force in the North Atlantic put the burden of convoy escorting and antisubmarine warfare east of Iceland on the British and Canadian navies. Now the long convoy to

North Africa would pull even the Royal Navy's Support Force away from these existing duties. Indeed, "Support Forces"—cruisers, airplanes, destroyers, and frigates able to move about freely, rather than tied to the slow-moving convoys—had just come into being in the North Atlantic, and were just becoming successful, even as they had to be redeployed to the North African invasion. The Germans were quite aware of their disappearance in the North Atlantic, and convoy losses doubled almost immediately. In October 1942, 619,000 tons of convoy shipping were sunk, and another 729,000 tons in November. By the end of the year, 7.79 million tons had been lost, including a ship carrying pumps for the twenty-five-mile pipeline. Early in the winter of 1943, the Support Forces returned and the battle against the U-boats turned in favor of the Allies, as, simultaneously, Base 2 Rosneath reverted to the British and again became H.M.S. *Rosneath*. In March 1943 Admiral King, as COMINCH, removed the last U.S. naval forces from the eastern North Atlantic, where they had participated in joint-command support groups. Just as the British bases were completed, the last vestige of the never-realized North Atlantic, Support Force, was canceled, and the entire burden fell on the British, Canadians, and Free French, who had no difficulty working in the combined command that the Anglophobic King so detested.

If the British bases were just a back-burner project on the world's stage, the Bureau of Yards and Docks took them very seriously. In early December 1941, the local commanders dismissed Fuller-Merritt's general superintendent and put day-to-day operations under the direct command of the navy civil engineers. This was entirely contrary to long-established procedures, where Officers in Charge of Construction acted as inspectors and contract officers, not as hands-on construction men. And it was a decision not taken lightly. The problems with the civilian supervisors ran the gamut of everything that can go wrong on a job: payroll fraud, lack of experience in heavy construction, inability to keep the civilian labor force (particularly the Free State Irish) from slacking, and the poor quality of American craftsmen. In November 1941 there were 225 Americans at Rosneath, and seventy were sent home: twenty-eight for sickness, nineteen for drunkenness and shirking, another nineteen for the general cause of "would not work"; two diagnosed as insane, and two for unspecified reasons.

The Fuller-Merritt men in Rhode Island were no more enamored of their staff in Rosneath than was the navy. Lengthy cables listed tradesmen making two and three times the expected wages because of excessive overtime. It even provoked sarcasm, a rare quality in civil engineering and even rarer in expensive cablegrams:

> You advised us to discontinue sending truck drivers yet they must be a scarcity because badge seventy (Bishop) payroll indicates he worked fourteen hours Sunday twenty-four hours Monday and Tuesday seventeen Wednesday. . . . We believe it is physically impossible for men and more so truck drivers to work twenty-four hours a day. In this particular instance a personal investigation is requested.

Admiral Moreell summed up a long list of cabled complaints about the contractor and compliments to his own men with this blunt reminder to the Officer in Charge in late November: "I want to get it into the contractor's mind that you are running this operation, and that when you say you need something we will do our best to get it through, but I want to be sure that you are the one who is establishing the need and not the contractor." Within a few weeks, there was no question who was in charge. The new role suited my father perfectly: he was a construction man, not an accountant or a lawyer.

After Pearl Harbor, all of the regular-navy civil engineers were pulled back to the United States, leaving the very junior reservists in charge. My father got a promotion to lieutenant commander and complete responsibility for finishing up the bases' contract and completing the twenty-five-mile pipeline in the summer of 1942.

Part of the recommendation for promotion notes his need for rank
as well as his readiness for it:

> Because of the intimate contacts which these officers must have
> with high ranking British Naval and civilian officials . . . it is deemed
> essential that [Lieutenants Montgomery and Dailey] be given tem-
> porary promotions to the rank of Lieutenant Commander in order
> to more effectively prosecute their work to completion.

The nature of the intimate contacts is not clear in the record.
The only instance I recall of my father's telling me about British-
American military cooperation was an anecdote concerning the poor
nature of the Scottish roads, which twisted and turned to avoid
historical sites and ancient trees (in Britain, a tree is frequently
designated as a historical monument). He and I were having a
problem in southern California getting permission to cut a street-
side shade tree for access to a job site. He remarked that during
the war he had become friendly with the Dunbarton County road
commissioner, whose cooperation he needed in regard to building
the twenty-five-mile pipeline. "You see," he explained, "I had the
authority, as an Allied military officer, to order the straightening
out of curves in the county roads that jogged around things like
old trees and, in one place, a bit of Roman wall. So I'd sign off for
cutting the trees or bulldozing the wall, and he'd sign for any
damage I caused to his roads." He said this all rather more reticently
than usual; I think he must have been a little embarrassed about
the wall, if not the trees.

When I think of my father today, more often than not I imagine
him in Scotland. It was such a perfect match between the demands
of a practical job and a very practical man, all suffused with the
patriotic glow of wartime urgency. He was far enough from Washington, D.C., to find his own way. He was even better off than
Tocqueville's democratic man: he had more than the illusion that
his destiny was in his own hands. He completed the bases, and
kept the pipeline moving as fast as it could, given the weather and

lack of essential parts. For him, the winter of 1942–43 passed into the long days of the Hebridean summer, and he continued at his assigned task, mopping up the contract and the pipeline. Meanwhile, the tide of war turned at Midway in the Pacific and Alamein in North Africa. He was both far from home and far from the action.

18

"Serving the Country by Teaching"

When summer returned to the Colorado mountains in 1943, my father-in-law was apparently beginning to lose some enthusiasm for his job as advanced-class instructor at the Naval School of Oriental Languages. I am obliged to say "apparently," because the last thing he would ever do is either complain at the time or look back ruefully. But he was beginning to lose touch with the practice of medicine, and when all was said and done he was a doctor, not a language instructor. He could accept the disruption of the war, but to have his profession taken away, to be denied his Hippocratic duty, was certainly part of the unbearable that must be borne.

Changes in the management of the language school in 1943 would have exacerbated matters for any of the one hundred and more ethnic-Japanese instructors and the half-dozen Caucasians. For one thing, some of the incentive had been removed for the students to suffer through the twelve-hour days of study and classes. The original classes, in 1941 and 1942, were composed of either civilian "naval agents" or enlisted yeomen who were commissioned into the navy only after successfully completing the fourteen-month course.

Because of complications inadvertently caused by changes in the Selective Service System, beginning with the January 1, 1943, class, students were commissioned ninety days after enrollment at the school. (Although they had a minimum of military drill and instruction, they were, like their counterparts outside the school, all "Ninety-day Wonders.") Further changes in the draft system, taking effect in the summer of 1943, resulted in a need to commission them *prior* to enrollment at Boulder, with a predictable loss of enthusiasm for studying by some of them, since they had reached the elevated status of officers and gentlemen (and gentlewomen) before dipping into the first book of the Naganuma Instruction System. Several letters from ex-Dean Hindmarsh complain bitterly about this development, and point out the demoralizing effect of having flunked-out students go off to the relatively easy life of a noncombat naval officer while their more successful classmates struggled with the Japanese language.

As the school swelled to maximum size in the summer of 1943, the women lived separately, in requisitioned sorority houses, and more than a hundred married men lived "off campus" with their wives in civilian housing, breaking down the cohesion that had marked the classes of 1941 and 1942, who had lived, dined, played, and studied together in a single dormitory where no language but Japanese was allowed, and where all the service staff, including waitresses and other dining-hall employees, were ethnic Japanese.

The Navy Department in distant Washington had developed enough of a bureaucracy, by 1943, to start trying to impose some order on its hundreds of specialized schools scattered across the continent at colleges and universities. Japanese-language students were occasionally, and then frequently, hauled out of class to meet Washington-created obligations for parades, close-order drill, venereal-disease lectures, seamanship and navigation instruction—whatever form of universal curricula was thought up in the Navy Department.

Dr. Watanabe attempted to practice medicine in Boulder in 1943, but with no more success than when he had applied to study in the postdoctoral program at the Cook County Medical Center. Three years after the war, when congressional legislation was pending to allow resident Japanese to apply for U.S. citizenship, he described a few of the difficulties he faced in a letter to the lobbyist for the Japanese-American Citizens' League:

> During the recent war, I wanted to serve in the U.S. Armed Services as a medical officer but was automatically denied that privilege because of my citizenship [status]. Instead, I was treated as an enemy alien. However, I did the next best thing in serving the country by teaching on the faculty of the U.S. Navy School of Oriental Languages at [the] University of Colorado from 1942 to 1944.
>
> When I wished to return to [the] practice of medicine I discovered that it was absolutely impossible to obtain [a] medical license in the state of Colorado simply because of my citizenship status. And this was true in practically all of the states in the Union. Then, too, various county medical societies—the constituents of the American Medical Association—required U.S. citizenship for membership. And as the membership in the County Medical Society is prerequisite for staff appointment in most of the reputable hospitals, practically speaking, non-citizens are denied the right to practice medicine and consequently deprived of their livelihood, regardless of their education and training. This in the greatest Democracy on the face of the earth!

He was, of course, a dues-paying member of the Santa Clara County Medical Society (and a past chief of medicine at San Jose Hospital), but that was a long ways away, in a state then wholly cleansed of ethnic Japanese, let alone enemy aliens.

Life in Boulder looks idyllic in the few old black-and-white snapshots that survive. Picnics in the countryside are duly documented, and pictures show Dr. Watanabe and his brother-in-law, Ari Inouye, fishing for trout in one of the small brooks above the campus. My wife remembers volunteer hollyhocks and columbine growing wild along the fences in the alley behind the rented house that the Watanabes and Inouyes shared. And my mother-in-law remembers, of course, that "most people were very nice." Mrs. Watanabe is listed in one of the few surviving copies of the language students' newspaper as "giving lessons in *ikebana* [Japanese flower-arranging] for the wives." This was, I suspect, an exercise requiring as much courage and patriotism as anyone had to produce in Boulder, Colorado. She is a marvelous and bold flower-arranger, and also very shy. The idea of her telling a group of women that *this is how it ought to be done* is quite beyond my imagination; it is simply out of character. I do not mean she is unsure of her judgment in such matters as how long to cut the stems or how to trim the leaves, only that she is always more interested in your opinion than her own.

By the winter of 1943–44, the need for Japanese translators and decryptologists was considerably less urgent. The tide in the Pacific had turned at Midway in 1942, a great success essentially due to the intelligence efforts of the few Japanese-language specialists who had trained in Tokyo before the war. It was not that there was little work for the four-hundred-plus Boulder graduates stationed in the Pacific and in Washington, but, rather, that the intelligence gathered was that of fox hounds on the scent of a beleaguered and doomed enemy, not the glamorous intelligence that would decide a battle between two equal forces, as had happened at Midway. Victory at sea and on land now turned on the productive capacity of the United States, not on superior intelligence or crafty strategies.

Boulder graduates were dedicated students and officers, but something about their recruitment, training, and deployment kept most of them from expressing any interest in a full-fledged career in the navy. Indeed, when Lieutenant Commander Hindmarsh visited the Joint Intelligence Command, Pacific Ocean Area, in early 1944, he could only find three JICPOA Boulder graduates who would admit to even a mild interest in a commission from the regular navy. They were not, by and large, conventional Americans to begin with, for Hindmarsh had culled them from membership lists of Phi Beta Kappa and other honors lists at major universities.

A tiny black-and-white photograph of my father-in-law taken at Boulder shows him sitting cross-legged on the campus lawn, with four young navy students standing behind him, towering over his much foreshortened figure. They all signed the photograph when it was given to him: Ed Downing, Frank Rowley, Bill Mattison, Val Deale. They graduated with the summer class of 1944, guaranteeing that they would miss most of the action at JICPOA. Very few of the Boulder graduates played any role in Occupation Japan, where MacArthur relied on his army language officers for occupation duties. Deale, however, a lawyer before entering the Naval School of Oriental Languages, had one of the more peculiar responsibilities of any of the school's alumni. When the Tokyo war-crimes trials got under way in the winter of 1946, it was necessary, in order to preserve at least the illusion of a fair trial, to find bilingual defense attorneys. Deale was, very briefly, assigned to defend General Tojo, but resigned after realizing that, whatever the facts of the case, there was no defense to be offered, given the nature of the judicial proceedings. Not to belabor the obvious, but it is curious that, when it came to finding defense lawyers for the war trials, the army-run court looked to a hapless navy lieutenant.

At the memorial service when my father-in-law died, twenty-five years after the war, nothing at all was said about Boulder. I would have thought, considering his patriotism, that his war service, however accidental, would have been part of the public accounting, part of the message sent, whoever might choose to receive it. Instead—and, on long reflection, I think properly—his memorial-service eulogy dealt almost entirely with his service to his thousands of patients and his Japanese-American community in San Jose.

I was not included in the composition of the eulogy, a task assigned to his senior son-in-law with the help of the other "survivors," as they say in obituaries. The sense of family responsibility and the assignment of roles were peculiarly and appropriately Japanese in that time of trouble. I was something of an outsider, there was no escaping that reality—I had written enough obituary notices in my time to know who was "immediate family" and who wasn't. And I was also the son-in-law married to the *second* daughter. Still, I wish there had been some mention of the Naval School of Oriental Languages—not to document his personal patriotism, and certainly not to include the navy, an institution that regarded my father-in-law and uncle Ari as necessary evils to be tolerated for their ability in this most foreign and malign language, but as an important fact of my father-in-law's life: he was not only a doctor but a capable scholar of the language and culture of Japan.

We tend, I fear, to think of scholarship as something that happens in great institutions—we speak of a "Bronx High School of Science graduate," or a "Harvard man." What fascinates me about Dr. Watanabe was that he had sat for less than ten years in a rural school in the Appalachia of Japan—Matsue Province—and a generation later, after his mind had been filled with biochemistry and the anatomy of the human body and the rebarbative English language, he was still one of the most capable instructors of Japanese that could be found on the North American continent. And best of all, he was diffident about it. He would much rather have been removing appendixes and gall bladders than drilling students in the subtle differences between polite Japanese and military Japanese. I would have been wrong to talk about this, had the opportunity arisen, to an audience of his patients and friends. But not to you.

Here was a man who in 1962, nearly fifty years after he left Japan, could pick up an ink stone, rub it on the watered slate, take a brush, and effortlessly, accurately, and beautifully write any of the hundreds of Chinese characters of the so-called Toyo Kanji on three-by-five flash cards, so that his second daughter could study the Japanese language. I will not swear to the entire eighteen hundred flash cards he made, but I watched him for hours, and I never saw him make a single mistake, not even for the most multiple-stroked and complicated of characters. Some of his work did not please him, and these were replaced by more esthetic, not more accurate, calligraphy. It would have been rude, perhaps, to mention this special skill to the audience at the memorial service, of whom only a handful of the second-generation Japanese, and not many of the first, could take up the brush so confidently.

I might also have been moved to mention the only time he was ever mildly displeased with me—to my knowledge—and the memorial service was not the appropriate time to discuss that, either, although it provided an insight into his general character and attitude toward life that would have resonated in the ears of his friends and patients. We were playing golf—or, to be more precise, his son Ken was playing golf, and Dr. Watanabe and I were hacking our way around the San Jose Municipal Golf Course to make up the threesome. I came up to my ball, which was, as they say in golf, "lying four" on a four-par hole and still a good mid-iron from the green, and I took a halfhearted swing at it, leaving it lying five, and not much closer to the hole. I turned back toward the golf cart he was driving for what would have been a very short ride to my ball, but he started off slowly, leaving me afoot on the fairway, so that I would have to walk up to the ball, saying firmly: "You must try to do your best."

Nor did we mention fishing at his memorial service. It is usually the case, when we come to sum up someone's life and contributions to the community, that we neglect the significance of his preferred recreation. This is a mistake, although correcting it might conflict with the expectations of the audience. Any reader, however, who is familiar with the pleasant surroundings in which wild trout are found and the methods by which they are caught will understand that to be an angler is to be appreciative of nature's gifts in a manner consistent with, but more developed than, mere enjoyment of scenery. The angler's connection with nature is palpable and kinetic, rather than merely intellectual or esthetic. Some physicians—as we all have learned to our dismay—do most of their diagnosis without much touching of the patient, as if X-rays and laboratory tests and interviews somehow solved the mysteries of the human body. My father-in-law was not that sort of doctor, and somehow, if it could have been said properly, there was a connection to be made between his enjoyment of trout fishing—especially the sensation of the subtle tug of the deceived fish—and his skillful doctor's hands.

The days at Boulder were long and onerous, made more so by his sense that he was being denied his real chance to contribute by practicing medicine. Perhaps that is why the weekend picnics along the trout streams of Colorado seem so important now. In all the madness, the water still moved, birds sang, and trout came to the lure. My father and my father-in-law once fished together, on the McKenzie River near Eugene, Oregon. Except for our wedding, it was the only time my wife and I were able to bring them together.

I think the Greek philosopher was wrong about the inconstancy of life: if you fish, you *can* step in the same river twice. Moving water is everywhere subject to the same rules of physics. It binds time and place together and makes the world continuous again. I do not fly-fish for trout without thinking of fathers.

19

"A Grand Bunch to Go Out With"

I have wondered, lately, what my father's mood must have been, when the summer of 1943 began to soften the cold spring weather on the banks of Loch Lomond. He would have known, and surely understood, by then that the bases had been an exercise in futility as well as redundancy. Base 1, Londonderry, was busy serving the Royal Navy and the Royal Canadian Navy, with only occasional visits by American ships that had ventured into the British Coastal Command sector. If not directly supporting convoys, it did see heavy use throughout the remainder of the war as the U.S. Navy's European center for radio communications.

Base A, the Lough Erne facility for seaplanes, had been taken over by the United States Army as a training base. Loch Ryan's seaplane Base B was occupied by Coastal Command's Lend-Lease Catalina seaplanes, and remained in British hands for the duration. Base 2, after the temporary flurry of staging the North African amphibious assault team, was once again H.M.S. *Rosneath*, although on August 20, 1943, after my father had returned to the United States, it again became an American base, serving as transfer point for American servicemen and for a few small units who trained there in those two antithetical modes of operation, fire support and fire fighting—that is, shooting and putting out the results of shooting. The huge hospital complex at Portkill, on the west side of Base 2, was lightly used, mostly for casualties suffered by the merchant seamen of the British-escorted North Atlantic convoys. After D-Day, almost overnight, it acquired twenty-four hundred casualties. For the remainder of the war, the hospital served as a primary screening area for determining who were shipped home, physically and mentally disabled servicemen, both army and navy. Thus it served not the anticipated casualties from the nonexistent convoy escorts, but the casualties of the land war on the Continent. (At the end of the war, by the way, the hospital was not stripped of its equipment and shipped home. It is well remembered by older citizens of Dunbartonshire as the source, in late 1945, of the most technically advanced medical equipment they had ever been privileged to use, for the X-ray machinery and operating theater equipment were acquired by the local hospitals. The array of Quonset huts that housed the hospital were, naturally, scrapped.)

My father had two tasks in the spring of 1943, one official, one personal. He had to close out the, by then, sixty-five-million-dollar contract NOy4850, and he had to get back into the war. These two endeavors produced letters, lengthy for him. One was a final field report on NOy4850, written on February 15, 1943, just as the last civilian employees were leaving and the 29th Construction Battalion was taking over the remaining tasks. This letter survived because it was copied by the King Bee, Admiral Moreell, and for-

warded to the Advance Base Depot, Davisville, Rhode Island, for
their information, and filed with the miscellaneous "Final Report"
materials. The question of a new assignment produced briefer,
more personal letters on April 2, 1943, sent to his former boss,
Commander Harry Bolles; these survived in Bolles' "Bio File," held
at the operational archive in Port Hueneme.

I am going to quote the official letter at length now, with some
parenthetical explanations and comments. For in spite of the official
tone, it's a good letter about the reality of building a war machine
out of that intractable material the human being.

When my father wrote about the pipeline construction, he made
it abundantly clear how low on the priorities Contract NOy4850
had slid, following those heady days in March 1941 when it was
the very symbol of British-American unity:

> At the present time the entire contract organization, including
> those transferred from Base One are now concentrated on the com-
> pletion of the tank farm area at Loch Long and the tie in at Old
> Kilpatrick. . . . Some modifications have been made in the Standard
> Oil plans at all stations to comply with requests of the [British]
> Petroleum Board and the Admiralty, to ensure smooth working with
> existing facilities. [The "tank farm" at Loch Long was simply to
> hold oil being unloaded until it could be pumped to the functional
> tank farms on the Clyde and Forth estuaries. The pipeline pumping
> capacity was somewhat less than the unloading capacity of a tanker,
> and delays at port were thus avoided.]
>
> The two secondhand riveted tanks [which constituted the Loch
> Long tank farm] have been completed. It was found necessary in
> many cases to weld as well as rivet, and caulking has been very
> extensive. These tanks have been tested under full water load.
> However, some leakage may develop, particularly with diesel fuel.
> [What the Americans had found to ship to the British Petroleum
> Board were two abandoned crude oil storage tanks from the once-
> famous Teapot Dome Navy Oil Reserve Field in Wyoming, which
> were dismantled and shipped to Scotland. As the next paragraph
> indicates, the civil engineers in Scotland got little more than the
> recycled tankage.]

The lack of valves, flanges and particularly tube turns [what plumbers, talking about domestic supply, call "elbows"] has resulted in very costly slow fabrication. It is highly recommended that all possible prefabrication be accomplished by competent factories in the States before shipment to any similar installation in foreign theaters. It has been entirely practical to use the prefabricated manifolding at Londonderry despite many discrepancies between plans and actual installations.

My father then turned to what had been constant problems since the day the first civilian employees arrived in Great Britain: discipline and governance.

Approximately 90 American employees will leave on first available transportation. Some of these are excess police, commissary and supervising personnel, due to reduction of number of camps. [To speed construction of the pipeline, the civil engineers had established four separate small camps, each self-sufficient, along the twenty-five-mile route.] Some are personnel who we still need but who refuse to carry on in a satisfactory manner.

It is understood that there is a bill before Congress giving authority to the Navy to place all civilian personnel employed in foreign theaters under Navy regulations. It is strongly recommended that this procedure be followed in any undertaking similar to Contract NOy 4850. Added to the normal trouble of handling construction personnel, without the ability to immediately dismiss and replace any non-producer, is the fact that these personnel are under the direction of the Contractor and the Navy twenty four hours a day. Camp discipline is very difficult to handle, particularly in Scotland, where local Constabulary have practically a "hands off" attitude. The reason for this is that the Crown Prosecutor—who corresponds to our Attorney General—has issued instructions to the effect that under the Visiting Forces Act, no American civilian attached to our contract is to be prosecuted without prior authority from the Crown, which in effect means that local police will ignore anything short of serious crime from our personnel.

This condition has made it necessary at times to place employees in protective custody of our own brig. Our Contractor's police have been extremely shaky on this point for fear of suits for false arrest. However, they have never failed to carry out orders of the Officer in Charge. Several threats of suits against the Contractor have been made. However, I believe none of them have materialized. Had the various Resident Officers in Charge [at the four bases] been able to enforce the Articles for the government of the Navy on civilian employees, it is believed that less than one fourth of the men who had to be sent home would have been lost to the job and the general efficiency increased at least fifty per cent. The Royal Ulster Police in North Ireland were not handicapped by any such instructions and were most co-operative.

The most serious problem was apparently drunkenness. This is tolerable, almost expectable, off-hours, but drinking on the job or before a shift used to be, and still ought to be, grounds for immediate dismissal. Construction is inherently dangerous, and the smallest and briefest lapses of judgment, timing, or coordination can hurt not only the drinker but anyone in his area. In just a few years of working construction for my father, on very sober crews, I managed to accumulate two or three permanent minor injuries, and am sometimes reminded, when getting out of bed in the morning, of a long-since completed job that took care of one vertebral disk or another, or the ladder that made one kneecap permanently some-what loose on its moorings.

It had been, I am sure now, two very curious years for my father, who was capable of firing a man on the spot—to be trapped two thousand dangerous miles from home with a crew made up in large part of people who drank too much and otherwise annoyed the local population. You expected to have to bail good men out of jail after a pay-night spree up in Montana, or you expected to replace them if they were only ordinary hands, but the lack of discipline caused by the contract situation in a foreign country made life miserable for all the navy officers in charge. When I was seventeen, and running a concrete-pouring gang for my father, he fired the best crane operator I, or anyone, had ever seen. The man came back from lunch with the smell of beer on his breath. Even drunk, I think he would have been safer to work with than his replacement, but no one asked me.

This problem with the crew and the local constabulary, added to all the other "diplomatic" chores that the O. in C.C.s and R.O. in C.C.s had to handle, gave my father a sense that he was somehow being trained, if accidentally, for some larger purpose than simply pouring concrete or supervising a gang of notoriously rough Texas pipeline workers. That much is clear from the pair of letters he sent on April 2 to Harry Bolles, who was back in Washington, troubleshooting construction projects directly under Admiral Moreell. The first is a very clearly out-of-the-chain-of-command letter, with the salutation

Dear Harry,

On my last trip to London my attention was called to Procurement Directive No. 7/43, dated January 28th, 1943, which you have no doubt seen, stating that a special group of Officers was being procured and trained for duty with Military Governors of Occupied Territory and stated that amongst other groups some Engineers were desired.

I am very much interested in this Branch for reason that I fully intend to seek employment with some of the Companies operating overseas when I am released from the Navy. You are fully familiar with what I have been doing since I came on active duty, and while I do not know whether this duty here in the British Isles would be considered Foreign Service with native population—certainly when you have North Irish, South Irish, Americans, British and Canadian Armed Forces all in one group, it is not exactly simple. Certainly it has taken a bit of diplomacy this last year what with the feeling against Irish neutrality and changes in Command at Bases happening about every two months.

Before coming with the Navy I had experience in practically every line of engineering construction, including Railways, highways, irrigation, drainage, land reclamation, flood control, Dams and tunnels, some mining, dredging, harbour facilities, miscellaneous building construction and most of them large.

Any information you might be able to procure for me with regard
to the possibility of such an assignment would be greatly appreciated.

He prefaced this semiformal inquiry with a long personal note
to Bolles, which began with references to the ill-health and ability
of some of the junior officers returning to the United States, summarized the construction at the four bases, and then turned to less
formal problems:

The Pipe Line has been a long and weary story, averaging 10
inches of rain per month throughout the first four months of work
and we are still waiting almost a year after for certain materials to
be shipped. . . . We are having considerable trouble with the Labour
Board and the Unions in Londonderry since the C.B's are doing all
the work there, the local labour has nothing to do but think up
claims. We have had no labour trouble in the sense of claims with
the Scottish Labour and practically none aside from two or three
strikes with the Free State. The Scottish Ministry of Labour seems
perfectly willing to make a decision and stay by it, but I cannot say
so much for the Londonderry outfit. . . .
I see most of the old gang occasionally. Had a stag party last
Sunday night for the crowd that I have been shooting with—Chief
MacIntosh, Ronald Teacher, Kenneth Barge. . . . They are a grand
bunch to go out with and always ask about you.
I am enclosing a separate letter to you with regard to future
assignment. The proper route for it would be I suppose via my
Commanding Officer to Bupers [Bureau of Personnel, replacing the
old personnel section in the Bureau of Navigation], however I have
never been officially notified by Admiral Stark of this Bupers Procurement Directive, so I am wondering if you might be able to drop
a word to whomever represents the C.E.C. in Bupers.

Bolles responded quickly, but without any real encouragement:
no decision had been made on my father's next assignment, and
there didn't seem to be any harm in his applying for military-
government school, but only after returning to Washington. "I have

hopes of making a visit to see how the 29th Battalion is getting on," Bolles added, "perhaps around the middle or latter part of May."

In the first week of May, Harry Bolles and two other civil engineers were killed in a weather-induced plane crash while on an inspection trip to the Bering Sea. And with him died, although it is a small thing, my father's direct connection to the highest levels of the Bureau of Yards and Docks. It was Harry Bolles, sportsman and Academy graduate, who had taught him how to wear his full-dress uniform, who had, as R.O. in C.C. in Scotland, introduced his first assistant and protégé to, in no particular order, the local gentry, Scotch whiskey, and grouse shooting. Bolles had written to my father that, before departing for Alaska, he "talked over with Comdr. J. R. Perry the question of your next duty." Within a year, Commander Perry was my father's direct commander, and, it seems possible, Perry may have remembered this rapidly promoted lieutenant commander who intended to go into the international construction business when he was "released from the Navy." I do not think, now, that my father was wise to be so frank in a letter to a friend.

You may be curious about this "shooting" business. There was a war going on, wasn't there? But he had time, and he was a long way from Miles City, Montana, where two small children and a wife might have interfered with his weekend recreation. The shooting was organized in the proper manner, given the exigencies of wartime. On the bare, sheepshorn hills above Rosneath, the shooters took their stands, and a gaggle of small children recruited from the nearby villages would be sent in a skirmishing line toward the stands, beating at the gorse and heather and bracken with walking-sticks, driving the grouse and the hares before them. On one occasion, my father once told us, a small roe deer had materialized in front of his stand, and he failed to shoot it, much to the consternation of the other hunters, who would have regarded venison as a distinct improvement over rationed tinned meat. He was ac-

customed to Montana mule deer the size of small ponies, and
thought the roebuck was a fawn, and not to be killed. Good manners
are not perfectly transportable.

Of all the souvenirs he brought home from any station, the
double-barreled shotgun he managed to buy in Scotland is the most
important relic. That is the gun with which I fully expected he
would shoot the deer that were eating the petunias, on the night
when no one really understood what I was crying about. And it
was the gun, I think, when he finally gave it to me, along with
his golf clubs, once neither sport was possible for him, that symbolized Scotland. As I said, sometimes I will go down cellar, and
unscrew the lid of Alex. Martin & Co.'s Famous Rangoon Oil for
the Preservation of Rifles and Shotguns, and smell it.

Everybody has to go one place or another; after Fort Peck, I had
to go to Scotland.

20

"A Bit of Local Color for Your Book"

So, I went to Scotland. You can fly directly from Boston now, on a jet that goes there only every other day and therefore is guaranteed to be completely filled: awash with returning British tourists and temporary workers and shirkers, all of them freighted down with something duty-free and most of them quite thoroughly drunk on expensive airport-lounge drinks that must, after all, still look like a bargain. I armed myself with your Manila Bay belt buckle that some Seabee had made for you during an idle hour at the machine shop, the buckle the right size to take a regulation navy web belt. You kept it in the desk drawer,

and mother gave it to me, or I took it, and had a belt made to go
with it. There were two buckles once, which I suspect you would
have forgotten long ago. Mine was just like yours, except with the
abbreviated "Jr." incised at the end of the name. I don't know
where I lost it. On my bow arm, I had your old navy wristwatch,
the Hamilton with the genuine-radium glowing numerals and
hands. I had taken to wearing that, too, these past few years.

For knowledge, I packed the 1939 edition of Muirhead's *Blue
Guide to England, Wales, Scotland, and North Ireland*. It was the
one they gave you in 1941, because the U.S. military had not yet
cranked up the great Troop Information and Education bureaucracy
that would provide our fighting men and women with the necessary
information on local customs and indigenous personnel. The *Blue
Guide* would explain about the important houses, castles, and Points
of Interest in Rosneath, Helensburgh, Glasgow, and also about the
Castle of Montgomery, in Tarbolton, just north of Prestwick Airport, to which, on arrival, I would proceed by rented automobile
to observe the environs described by Robert Burns in "Highland
Mary":

> *Ye banks and braes and dunes aroun'*
> *The castle o' Montgomerie*
> *May your skies be e'er fair,*
> *Your waters ne'er drumlie.*

You once remarked that you had never had the opportunity to go
there. It seemed as if someone should.

It was not a satisfactory beginning, this Montgomery Castle
business. Tarbolton was quiet on that Sunday morning, and as
difficult to drive to as are most places in rural Scotland, where road
signs are small, uninformative, and located exactly on the intersection where the turn must be made, so that visitors are always
flying by the road they want and then pondering how to make a
U-turn while driving on the left side of the road. There were no
signs in or near Tarbolton to lead the tourist to the Castle o'

Montgomerie, but there was a small grocery store open on the corner of High Street and Montgomerie Street, so it seemed possible that the proprietor, with the very name on the blue-and-white enameled sign on the shop's brick wall, would be able to give directions. And so she was able, after this fashion: "Well, I know where it was, but I think it's caravans now. It burnt, you see."

I followed her directions, past the World War I memorial, and down to the place where the road, as she put it, "rather comes into a hole," and then turned up the gravel track. The site of the familial palace was made quite clear by the sudden appearance— in an otherwise completely sheep-eaten landscape with no growth higher than your shoe tops—of several great rhododendron bushes the size of one-bedroom cottages and, towering over them, enormous evergreen trees of the sort one expects around a castle, except that one did not expect to find *Sequoia gigantea*, the giant redwood, which is what they were. In Britain, they are called *"Wellingtonia"* after the victor of Waterloo, not *Sequoia* after the Cherokee linguist.

Of the castle, quite thoroughly burned or bulldozed, or both, nothing remained except a scattering of brick and cut sandstone blocks overgrown with fireweed and prickly gorse. The three caravans, with attendant outhouses, were not vacation-travel trailers but, rather, of the mobile-home sort, and seemed deserted, except that dogs—large dogs, by the sound of them—set up a ferocious barking from the inside, as best I could tell, of all three trailers. The small creek below the castle site, beyond the sequoias, was lightly sprinkled with jettisoned durable goods, including tin cans, bottles, and abandoned bits of domestic furniture. Other than that, the water did not seem particularly drumlie.

It was not a propitious beginning, but, after all, I had a few more days to see Rosneath Castle, Tullichewan Castle, and Lomond Castle, where you had lived and worked.

The roadways from Prestwick to Dunbarton, via Glasgow, would be, I think, totally unfamiliar to you, could you see them. Although Scotland has not been a place of great industrial and civic growth since you left, it is more altered, from the look of it, than, say,

Chinook or Glasgow, Montana. But from Dunbarton to Helensburgh to Rhu, which was as close to Rosneath as I could find a
hotel, the road seemed to be early-twentieth-century at best: narrow, lined with ancient stone walls that pinched in on the shoulders. Potato fields, harvested now in early October, sheep-grazed
pastures, and fields of limp, green-leaved plants that I did not
recognize lay behind the walls and fences. The green plants, I
found out a few days later, were yellow turnips—what we call
"rutabagas" in Montana—waiting for a hard frost to set them up
for harvest.

In Helensburgh, toward dusk, I consulted the *Blue Guide*, which
described ferry service to Rosneath, just across the Gare Loch.
There indeed, just past High Street, was Ferry Street, but without
a ferry any more. The parking is municipal, rather than naval, and
serves the somewhat tourist-oriented shops along the waterfront,
including, thanks to the broad reach of the postwar migration from
the colonies, one Indian tandoori restaurant, and one Hong Kong
Chinese restaurant. Looking across the darkling water toward Rosneath, I could see a scatter of streetlights, just coming on in the
evening, and a speckle of small structures, back-lit in the twilight,
just about where Base 2 would have been.

The Rosslea Hall Hotel in Rhu, just up the Gare Loch from
Helensburgh, and thus a few miles closer to Rosneath, is, as the
old one said, a clean, well-lighted place, with a business built on
summer vacationers on their way to the Highlands and, in winter,
company meetings and weddings. The service is outgoing, friendly,
and just slightly muddled. The Scots mentality, I judged after a
week there, makes a distinction between hospitality and efficiency,
as if these were antithetical qualities, which judgment, in the long
run, I think is probably correct.

I was not the first American who had arrived in Rhu on the way
to Rosneath, but the first for several years; the previous curiosity-
seekers had been veterans stationed at Rosneath, according to the
hotel manager. There had been quite a flurry in 1984, having to
do, we agreed, with the fortieth anniversary of the Normandy

invasion. For most of them it had been an enjoyable trip, he thought, except that there wasn't much left to look at. I didn't expect much—forty-five years is a long time, I believe I replied.

Mr. Dick, the hotel manager, thought that the one person in Rosneath who would have a good sense of the place was the caravan-park manager, a Mr. Quibell, although, Mr. Dick said, Quibell was not from here. On reflection, I was not prepared for another caravan park, but ventured forth anyway.

The road from Rhu around the Gare Loch to Rosneath, Father, is one you must have driven a thousand times; you would be able to separate the new from the old, and so, I think, could I. A few houses, churches, and two small hotels are clearly of the wartime age and more. The old British submarine base at Faslane, dating from the war, is utterly changed from whatever it was, now all concrete high-rise offices, with huge drydock and pier construction going on two shifts a day, as they gear up to become Britain's base for the Trident submarines that will give the British an opportunity to incinerate someone in return. The base is completely surrounded by the sort of razor wire one associates with the Berlin Wall, not the old-fashioned barbed-wire-and-chain-link fencing of World War II navy bases and Japanese-American relocation camps. They not only top the fence with razor wire, but unroll a loose coil at the bottom, inside the fence. This takes all the fun out of jumping the fence, which is the standard method of protest against Britain's nuclear forces.

Driving from Garelochhead down the peninsula to Rosneath, a veteran would not recognize Clynder. Whatever the village had been, it is now a County Council creation, with public housing of a perfectly respectable sort, low-rise garden apartments and a bus service to take people to somewhere—Faslane Naval Base, or Helensburgh, or on to Dunbarton or Glasgow by train, where there is work or an unemployment office. Additional new and private housing is being put up for better-off employed persons and retirees.

It is easy to tell where the base began. Some still-standing wire fence, with the leaning triple strand of barbed wire at the top, appears along the roadside, and then, on the water side, a series of small boat-building shops, some of them in the rusting corrugated-metal buildings that, along with the half-round Quonset huts, were the standard portable units of World War II. And just as the main road veers right, to cross the peninsula above the Rosneath Castle grounds, the old road into the camp is marked with a tasteful sign announcing the Rosneath caravan camp.

And the road in would look familiar, lined on both sides with the same monstrous rhododendron bushes that one sees at every respectable British estate, although these are getting rather badly overshadowed by weed trees growing up between them and through them—rowans, mostly, holding their red berries in the early fall. And one drives around the curve, across the series of three speed bumps—or "sleeping policemen," as they call them in the Bahamas—past the display area for new house trailers, and onto the grounds of Rosneath Castle, now, Father, fully arrayed with vacation homes on wheels and a few larger house trailers used year-round. Mr. Quibell, who is tall and friendly and a Brit by his accent, is happy to show anyone where Rosneath Castle used to be. He discovered some of the foundations while digging a septic system. And this is what happened to the castle, as far as Mr. Quibell was aware: "It just fell into a ruin, you see, and they cleared it off. But that was long before I got here."

I said something to him about its not seeming quite right that you just let the house of the Duchess of Argyll, the Princess Louise, eldest daughter of Queen Victoria, simply fall into a heap, and Mr. Quibell allowed as how the Duke and Duchess of Argyll had plenty of other houses to worry about; but, he said, "You must see Mr. Calderwood, if you can. He knows about it all, you see, if he will speak to you."

I asked if he was hard to speak to, and Mr. Quibell said that he could be, "if you see what I mean. He lives at the Croft, which is just up the macadam road, on your left, just before the main road."

I thanked him and suggested that it was hard to find someone

who really did know what it was like, back in the war, and I hoped
Mr. Calderwood could help. "Yes, it is," answered Quibell, who
was certainly old enough to remember, but was, after all, not from
here. "All sliding away into folklore, isn't it?" said Quibell.

The name Calderwood was not unknown to me. I have the final
report on Contract NOy4850, and a poor copy of the final "drawn-
as-built" blueprint of Base 2, and each lists the land temporarily
taken over from civilian owners and leaseholders, of which the
greatest number of small parcels, mostly for access roads, are controlled by "E. Calderwood & Sons." The surviving son is Matthew
Calderwood, and although he is not easy to talk to, he is, making
a distinction that does matter, easy to listen to.

And they remembered you. Mrs. Calderwood, who was baking
a cake for Sunday dinner—actually, stirring a cake—remembers
you. I introduced myself and explained that I was just trying to
get some sense of where the base had been, and she took me into
the parlor, where Mr. Calderwood, complete with green Welling-
ton boots, muttonchop sideburns, and a deerstalker hat on his head,
was sitting by a small wood fire that was burning in a patent
fireplace, one of the iron types. And I told them both that I was
interested, not because I had been there, as they first thought (sons
do grow old and gray, Father), but because you had been there.
And I said it more clearly, "Lieutenant Commander Montgomery,"
and Mrs. Calderwood, who is a dumpling, broke into a smile quite
a bit warmer, all in all, than the wood fire. "Ay," she said, "a
lovely man." Worth the trip, it was, to hear her say so.

They are retired now. A son runs the dairy farm and plants the
potatoes and rutabagas on those clear fields above the base, the
ones from which you could see across the firth to Greenock. They
remembered you all, including those three names on the letter to
Harry Bolles, the "gang" you had been shooting with. Chief
MacIntosh, who I thought was some sort of clan chieftain, perhaps
the Tosh of MacIntosh himself of that ilk, was, they said, the
Dunbarton County chief constable, whose men were so unwilling

to arrest your miscreant workers. Ronald (MacNair) Teacher—
well, he was one of the whiskey teachers, with a castle in Cove,
and perhaps I could drive over and look at it, they thought. And
Kenneth Barge—surely he was from Rhu, near my hotel.

And they were the ones who really knew what had happened to
the Princess Louise, to Rosneath Castle itself. After the war, the
price of lead was very high, Mr. Calderwood recalled, and some
Royal Navy sailors started stripping the lead weatherproofing off
the roof, at night, picking it up in a Royal Navy truck, and selling
it to a junky in Glasgow. And the water got in, and finally they
had to scrap the building. They took away the rest of the lead and
the slates and the oak beams and the paneling and the Adams
fireplaces and the marble mantels, and then gave the hulk to the
British Army, which blew it up for a demolition exercise, and then
they buried it. You had something to do with where they buried it.
When your rock crusher couldn't be unloaded, you had to substitute
local glacial gravel, and made a great hole, down toward the beach
from the castle. Rosneath Castle lies in your gravel borrow pit.

They quite remember the delay with the rock crusher, which is
understandable because the gravel was for all those access roads
that crossed their property, and the rock quarry, when you did get
the crusher, was also on their property. The odd thing—and I
suppose it was always that way during the war, when no one
explained anything—was that they thought the crusher had been
lost on a submarined ship; they did not know it had to be taken
across the firth to Greenock to be unloaded.

And they certainly remember the civilian construction workers.
"A rum lot," Mr. Calderwood said. And I hope you won't be of-
fended, but they didn't think much more of the CBs. "Construction
Bums," Mrs. Calderwood said firmly, "that's what *we* called them."
They used to steal flowers out of the castle garden, she added, and
"come up here and wave them at me through the window—and
me just a new bride, mind you."

But not the officers. "We think they were good about sending
people like your father," said Matthew Calderwood, "the better

class of people, if you see what I mean. We never had any trouble with the American officers, which can't be said for the Brits."

The old Victorian summer house on the castle's farm is theirs now. They run pigs and cows in it now. It's quite a lovely Victorian folly for all that, with some of the stained glass still in place, but with cows in the parlors. And they salvaged three of your Quonset huts, and have them stuck onto the stone summer house at odd angles, also for the cows. It is like that line at the end of *The Seven Samurai*, "The farmers always win."

They chatted about things you had seen. How one could tell when the *Queen Mary* or the *Queen Elizabeth* was coming in with troops. It was all supposed to be a great secret, said Calderwood, "but, you see, they would get these hundreds of small boats out waiting, off the point here and over across from Greenock, before dark. And, come morning, we'd look out the window and they'd all be gone. I mean, you knew what had happened, didn't you?" And they told me to look in the hay field for the big round spots where the weeds grew. That was where the German mines, intended for the Firth of Clyde, had fallen. "We called them land mines," said Calderwood, "but of course they were regular sea mines, except they missed. We filled the holes in, but the grass never caught on right. This was the first land to be bombed in World War II." But that was before you came.

Such a selective memory have the Calderwoods. I think the most vivid they have is of one of the American naval officers, long after you were gone, who rented hunting from them and shot rabbits— or hares, properly speaking ("A hare is something like your American rabbit, but much larger," Calderwood explained). And he had an enlisted man carry them, dozens of them, the hares being quite plentiful during the war, the enlisted man almost bent double under the weight of these great, dead hares. "Wrong sort," Mr. Calderwood summed him up.

And then Mr. Calderwood had to drive to the post office and that was the end of that conversation. Not easy to talk to, this Calderwood.

Your friend Ronald MacNair Teacher is buried in the Barbour cemetery, overlooking Loch Long, across the peninsula. I found the family plinth quite by accident, having decided to look at the Barbour cemetery simply because that is my old high-school girl-friend's last name. Everything connects. Mr. Teacher made it to seventy-five years of age, dying in 1976. Everyone in Cove seemed to know where his house was, and thought it not a very good idea to try to look at it. It belongs to a Dutchman, or maybe he's Belgian, with an Iranian wife who never comes out. Better not to go, they thought. The Teacher Castle is, viewed from the Barbour road above it, quite clearly of the late-Victorian, decorative period: post-Balmoral, like hundreds of other Scottish grand houses, and a suitable backdrop for a Pre-Raphaelite painting: Girl holding a long bow or petting a roe deer—that sort of thing.

And I found your pipeline dock at Finnart, still in use by British Petroleum. They occasionally bring in large tankers headed for Rotterdam, and unload part of the cargo, if they draw too much for the Dutch port. The concrete seems in excellent shape, some-what weathered with the gravel aggregate showing, but not spalled, cracked, or honeycombed. The two tanks from Teapot Dome must have been replaced years ago; all the storage is quite new-looking, above the dock. The pipeline now serves the Trident base at Fas-lane, but the spur line to Rosneath has been disconnected. It wasn't used for years, and finally leaked, and people along that shore found bunker oil bubbling up in their gardens. Apparently someone forgot to shut the valve where it connected with the main line. It is known locally as "the Yankee pipeline," as opposed to the main line, which is "BP's line."

That left just two more castles to find: Lomond Castle, where Sir David MacGowan had put you up, and Tullichewan Castle, where you had your headquarters during part of the pipeline job. Neither one of them, it turned out, showed on the extremely de-tailed Landranger maps, which do mark castles. I took your small black-and-white snapshot of Lomond Castle to a real-estate agent's office in Helensburgh, on the odd chance that it would be recognized. The man knew it immediately. It is now the Lomond Castle Hotel, and he gave me driving directions that were almost accurate. And he said: "I don't think you'll find the grounds so grand to look at now," as if—and he, too, may have misinterpreted my gray hair for a veteran's grizzle—I had been there, not you. It is a fine hotel, and the grounds are covered, more or less, with identical wooden summer cottages, not much bigger than travel trailers. In the hotel bar, well-dressed young Scots discussed real-estate deals. None of the help in the hotel was familiar with the name MacGowan, by the way.

Tullichewan Castle is supposed to be in Balloch, which is where the river Leven leaves Loch Lomond, upstream from the pipeline connection at Old Kilpatrick. The woman at the Scottish travel-and-tourist bureau (a busy one, for Balloch is the place from which tour boats leave to see the bonnie banks) said that she got hundreds of people in looking for Tullichewan Castle and was always sad to report that it, too, had been vandalized, de-leaded, and, finally, demolished. I questioned the "hundreds," considering it was just a headquarters for a few civil engineers, and she explained that it became the largest basic training camp for WAAFs, Women's Auxiliary Armed Forces. "A lot of the girls come up," she said, "and are always quite disappointed."

I am not sure I was so disturbed. There seem to be three possibilities for castles in postwar Scotland: hotels, rubble, or purchase by Middle Eastern oil moguls. There is a certain cleanliness to demolition, which is the last chapter of most civil engineering, sparing only structures of historical or cultural interest.

On the last day, I had nothing better to do than try to kill a bird, it being shooting season, and the visit to Scotland seeming to need some ritual to end it. (A single cock pheasant. I gave it to my host. Any respectable ritual has a gift involved in it somewhere.) High above Helensburgh there is still a grouse moor. It was not, you understand, possible to re-create one of those hunts for driven grouse you had taken with MacIntosh, Teacher, and Barge. That would now cost us Yanks about four thousand dollars a day, but I did climb the hill between Helensburgh and Glen Fruin with the man who owned the shooting, and from the top we could see Rosneath. Mr. Calderwood's fields gleamed plow-brown or turnip-top-green, and from that distance the summer castle was just visible, although the Quonset-hut additions, in their fading military-green paint, blended into the distant landscape. The caravans at Rosneath were just specks of reflected light, and could just as well have been Base 2.

Ian MacGregor, who took me hunting, was aware of my interest in Rosneath, and he pointed it out, lying west of us in the afternoon sun, across the Gare Loch. The high ground, including Calderwood's farm and the site of the Princess Louise, is almost separated from the upper Rosneath Peninsula by a water-cut valley, the same one that the road to Ronald Teacher's castle runs through. "We call it 'the Green Isle,' " he told me. "That's a bit of local color for your book, the Green Isle." So it was, with the sparkle of low sunlight on both the Gare Loch and Loch Long almost merging across the valley between the peninsula and Base 2, almost cutting it off from the mainland. Rosneath was quite green with trees and turnip fields, except for Calderwood's plowed ground. In clear contrast, the upper peninsula was all gray and brown, covered with heather, bracken ferns, and gorse.

It was altogether worth the climb. Your base had disappeared, like Avalon sinking into the sea, like Brigadoon into the mist, and the green almost-isle of Rosneath looked as though it might, any moment, separate itself from the peninsula and float away into the Irish Sea.

On the way back to the hotel, I looked at my watch, your old Hamilton, and it had stopped. It doesn't run at all any more. It stopped dead, at three-fifteen in the afternoon, just about the time, I would guess, that I was looking at the Green Isle. I may get it fixed, perhaps not. For now, I am content to live with the coincidence.

A postscript: Back at the office, the next week, someone asked me how it had gone. "Did you find your father's base?" And I said, "Yes. But the odd thing is, I went all that way, and he was still dead."

Silly thing to say, I suppose, but the boy always had some screwy ideas, didn't he?

21

California and the Pacific Theater

My father's return from Scotland was, as you can imagine, a much-awaited moment in our family and for me, although in fact I had literally only one distinct memory of him, and that one did not, and does not, include a clear visualization of his face. It was of a moment from the time when we were living north of Los Angeles, after he was called to active duty, when he came home wearing his dress-blue uniform.

I had tripped, going up the brick stairs to the front door, and raised a terrific bump over my right eye. It didn't hurt that much but was, from the point of view of a three-year-old, spectacular.

And he asked how I did it, and I said, "I'll show you." We went back outside together, so I could show him, and I started up the stairs, and deliberately tripped, hit my head on the brick landing again, and raised another egg-sized bump over my left eye. I tended, for many years, to take everything pretty literally, and had no great capacity for explaining things without going through the motions that accompanied an explanation. The head bumping was one slightly more dramatic example of a lifelong habit of, as relatives would remark, "talking with your hands," a behavior associated with people of certain ethnic extractions not including the Scotch-Irish. My sister, when she thought I was deserving of it, would tell me that I was adopted. In addition to talking with my hands, she would point out, I had brown eyes, and everyone else in the family had blue or green. Much later, when I discovered the general principle of dominant and recessive genes in an encyclopedia, I was somewhat comforted by it, although I would have preferred to have my mother's green eyes and keen eyesight.

When my father came home from Scotland, my mother, sister, and I went to the nearest airport, probably in Oxnard, adjacent to Port Hueneme. This was the airport where I had concluded that that stranger in the khaki uniform could not possibly be either a naval officer or my father. I don't suppose, on long reflection, this was the only family reunion in World War II when one child or another ran crying through a crowd, denying that the stranger was his father; of course, in other cases they may have been right. It was not an auspicious beginning for a reunion.

My father's orders and fitness reports for the summer of 1943 are good examples of both the navy's old-boy network and the capriciousness that makes that network less effective than one might imagine. While he had been finishing up the British contract, the original Officer in Charge, Commander H. P. Needham, CEC, had made captain, and was the Officer in Charge at the Advance Base Depot, Port Hueneme. An assignment to Hueneme put a civil engineer at the heart of the Seabee program. The entire Pacific Theater was moving materiel for bases through that port. My fa-

ther's fitness report for the third quarter of 1943 has this note in
Needham's handwriting: "This officer was ordered on board at the
request of the officer in charge [Needham himself] with the thought
of making him senior assistant in the Advance Base Depot. While
becoming oriented and indoctrinated for his new duties, he was
released on the request of the Supt. C. E. [superintending civil
engineer, 12th Naval District] of this area for duty on important
construction work."

Moving my father out of Port Hueneme took him out of the most
vital civil-engineering station on the West Coast, and also pulled
him out of his network. With Harry Bolles dead and Needham no
longer his immediate superior, it is apparent that his good work in
Scotland and Northern Ireland was not something directly known
to his superiors, although it remained on his record. He was no
longer, so to speak, the known quantity with the 3.9 and 4.0 fitness
reports.

The "important construction work" to which he was sent was
the sprawling Construction Battalion replacement-and-training depot at Pleasanton, California. It was actually two bases, Camp
Shoemaker and Camp Parks, with fuzzed lines of command; Shoemaker, by far the larger, eventually literally surrounded Camp
Parks, and to all practical purposes they together composed one
giant facility. He reported as Assistant Officer in Charge, with
responsibilities for supervising the civilian contractors who were
constantly adding new facilities: hospitals, barracks, recreation
centers, post-exchange supermarkets. He had to know that he had
been, at least temporarily, pulled out of the war.

Something like Mister Roberts, trapped on his supply vessel,
sailing from Ennui to Oblivion, was my father, as he supervised a
construction program to support people who were headed for the
real war. First as Assistant, then as Acting, and finally as Designated Officer in Charge at Shoemaker, he got his full commander's
promotion, and the proliferation of cap braid that goes with the
rank. Children of navy officers are quite aware of their fathers'
ranks. Among other things, sides are chosen up in navy brats' games

according to the parents' ranks. This seems cruel to an outsider, I suppose, but it did simplify things. Your status was impersonal and parental, and the pecking order among the children had a kind of objective quality, like a received religion.

His status—and it was considerable, thanks to his early acceptance of the commission and his subsequent speeded-up promotions in Scotland—had another tangible benefit besides priority in children's play. We acquired some requisitioned housing—a big house, by our standards, on the grounds of what was then known as the "Old Hearst Ranch" and later, after the war, as the Castlewood Country Club. It was a house in the woods, on a hillside above the Pleasanton Valley, with a red tile roof and white stucco walls, and was perfect for small boys and girls, for we had the run not only of the woods but of the associated golf course, which was lightly used by the few navy personnel with time and a set of clubs. The only disadvantage, and hardly troublesome to a five-year-old, was that the house sat virtually on top of the San Andreas Fault, and we had earthquakes about as often as we had company, or as often as most children would hear fire alarms in the city. They came like, but more frequently than, rain. There were showers of small quakes some days, starting in the morning and returning two or three times, like weather that just couldn't make up its mind.

This was the house where, shortly after we had moved in, the big steamer trunks full of clothes and souvenirs from Scotland arrived. My sister got a kilt, and I honestly don't remember getting anything, or much caring about it, for there were wonderful male objects in the trunk to be admired. There was the famous gun that would be used not to shoot the infamous deer; two or three fishing rods, with reels and lines that smelled of stale linseed oil; and leather wallets with artificial trout flies in them, these faintly redolent of moth repellent. There was a set of mismatched golf clubs, too long for me to swing them, but not too long to drag outside and look at. There were old golf balls, which bounced wonderfully on the quarry-tile living-room floor, and, thank goodness, a few blue wool dress uniforms, and the full-dress uniform sword and scabbard, which we were not ever, under any circumstances, to touch. I have not, since then, quite been able to imagine a proper man's closet that doesn't have wool clothes, guns, fishing rods, and golf clubs in it. Thus it is that we go armed into the world.

If it had been the end of the war, and not almost exactly the middle, I suppose we could have made the idealized, or perhaps even the merely normal, accommodation between father and child. It is curious but, although we lived at the Old Hearst Ranch through a complete school year, a summer vacation, and the beginning of another (my first and second grades), I have little memory of my father in the role of father. He was working long hours, and the navy, once you get up into even mildly rarefied air, is a service devoted to social events. There were parties at the house, and we children were trotted out to be polite children, a generally artificial role that we were both remarkably adept at portraying, and there were dinners at the officers' club, where we ate everything on our plates and did not interrupt the adults. There wasn't, however, any play at all. I mean by that that we didn't toss a ball around in the back yard. This was in part because I couldn't catch a ball; I do remember some abortive attempts with visiting adults and the occasional enlisted man who baby-sat for the family. My father was simply too busy, and perhaps too unaccustomed to the role, for walks and talks, for games of any kind. We knew, of course, that there was a war going on.

I do know, however, exactly what saved me from any real sadness or perceivable loss. It was the elementary school in Pleasanton, a formidable two-story concrete building. We went there by bus, fell into place on the grounds, and were led off into classrooms, fed lunch, and sent home on time, all in an atmosphere of utter safety.

Among other things that might have contributed to what amounted to a distance between my father and myself was that somehow I wasn't exactly the way small boys might be, in his experience at least. And something about me triggered the same reaction in the staff at the Pleasanton school. We have a problem here, they must have said to themselves, and the larger resources of the California State school system and various theories of education and special skills were visited upon me. Among other things, there was the speech therapist, who had been alerted to the fact that there was a first-grader who couldn't speak distinctly when called upon. She came once a week, and got me first thing every Friday morning. Among other tasks, she put me to making shapes with my tongue; sticking it out and making it look like a spoon was one, and so was sticking it out and rolling the sides up to make something like a tube. She demonstrated these with such enormous sincerity and seriousness of purpose that one couldn't have laughed if one's life depended on it, and then I would copy them. I did it all quite well, and she reported to my mother, in my presence, that I could talk perfectly well if only I wanted to, some day I would want to, and there was nothing to worry about.

Nobody asked me why I didn't want to talk in class; that was the only flaw in the educational program. The trouble—and it was not until the fall of 1944, when I got into the second grade, that they figured it out—was that I couldn't see anything on the blackboard, and the question "Which letter am I pointing at, Maurice?" was not only unanswerable but incomprehensible. I already knew all the letters, and, having spent years entertaining myself as best I could, I could read anything: the newspaper, my sister's second-grade books, anything that seemed worth the trouble. As mind-stretching discourse, questions about letters were silly, and, on top of that, I simply couldn't see anything on the board. My second-grade teacher figured the problem out in about thirty seconds; by the end of the first week of school, I had been to the dispensary, seen the optometrist, and returned to school with four eyes. Or, in the argot of the schoolyard, returned *as* "Foureyes." Myopia is not much of a handicap, unless you like your own name. Compared with "Maurice," I could live with it.

But if diagnosis was slow in coming, the spirit at that school was generous, protective, kind. The most important adult there was not the principal, but an upper-grade teacher by the name of Miss Allender, who regarded her vocation, in the religious sense, as literacy, and pursued the illiterate the way missionaries descend on the Indians of the Amazon. She would trap burly (everything is relative, but she wasn't much taller than I was) sixth-graders between classes, after school, at lunchtime, and sit them down on the steps, or a playground bench, pull out a reading primer, and set them through it. Without any pretensions, and without any very strict control of the small wild Indians who roamed the school yard at every free moment, she did, somehow, set the tone for the whole place. The purpose of school was to learn, and learn you would, even if it took a pair of eyeglasses, or Miss Allender running you to ground like a dog after a rabbit.

A few times, I have driven through Pleasanton and looked at the school, which was immediately recognizable, though it carried a few one-story temporary-looking additions—some sort of semiportable classrooms. The Old Hearst Ranch is wholly altered. The wooded hillsides and the old eighteen-hole golf course are covered with new, expensive, large homes. Our old house, once by far the grandest on the ranch, is now the smallest. It is still flanked by a pair of towering black-walnut trees, but is otherwise unremarkable, almost insignificant, next to the affluent postwar structures that crowd in about it. The golf course has been relocated, down into the valley, where, during the war, the flat farmland was covered with tomato vines, sweet corn, and less easily identified vegetation. After they harvested most of the tomatoes, they ran sheep in the fields in the late summers of 1943 and 1944. This annoyed my mother, who had no use for sheep and considerable for tomatoes. I enjoyed it, myself, for a sheep has a particularly beatific, or soporific, expression while eating overripe tomatoes, one at a time, rolling them between its ingenious lips.

Camp Parks, technically a CB replacement depot, and Camp Shoemaker, a combination of a receiving center, training center, and major hospital facility, were built under two separate and continually amended contracts, the total records of which, located at the CB archives in Port Hueneme, occupy more than six hundred cubic feet of paper. I confess to not having opened a single box, although, no doubt, a number of memoranda and reports have my father's signature on them. But this was an ongoing construction process when he arrived, and would continue after he left, and it has no narrative significance.

His quarterly fitness reports from the Shoemaker year are favorable, with the lowest checks, once again (at the high end of "very good"), in "Military bearing and neatness of person and dress." Numerical ratings ranged from the occasional 4.0 down to a perfectly adequate 3.7, and averaged, on casual calculation, somewhere around 3.9. When the Officer in Charge of Construction, Commander Robert E. Hancock, USN, was detached, my father, who had been his executive officer, succeeded him, and thus was promoted at last to full commander himself, having the job, and the time in grade, to be ready for that promotion. There is virtually no hint in the fitness reports of any problem, except one. Although Commander Hancock gave him excellent ratings, all 4.0's and 3.9's, there is a tinge of diffidence in the response to one standard question: "Considering the possible requirements in war, indicate your attitude toward having this officer under your command. Would you—(1) Particularly desire to have him? (2) Be pleased to have him? (3) Be satisfied to have him? (4) Prefer not to have him? (An affirmative entry in item (4) constitutes an unsatisfactory report.)" Uniquely, in the dozen or so shore-duty fitness reports, only this one, from his direct superior, and the man he replaced as Officer in Charge, is marked: "(2) Be pleased to have him." One senses a faint odor of personality conflict here, a hint of a difference between competence and compatibility. My father was not a very enthusiastic team player, including in sports. He was not easily gregarious. He was a golfer, but though you play golf with friends, you play alone against the terrain of the course, when all is said and done. However, more would be mere speculation.

Camps Parks and Shoemaker, for all the tens of thousands of uniformed men about, were very distant from the Pacific war itself. It was a long afternoon's ride to the ocean, for one thing. There were all the naval accoutrements, including the pair of anchors that flanked the entrance to the officers' club where my sister and I ate dinner on several occasions, usually going up to the third-floor balcony while the adults had cocktails inside. We would salute the flag at evening retreat, not without, as I recall, some sense that we were upholding the family's patriotic reputation. There were increasing numbers of combat veterans, however, and we got occasional views, in one home or another, of souvenirs from places like New Guinea or Bougainville. Those who had brought home souvenirs had odd mixtures of Japanese weapons, seashells, primitive-looking but probably very recently manufactured war clubs or bow-and-arrow sets, all objects calculated to interest six-year-olds.

The war was hardly pervasive at elementary school. I suppose we had the same Bond Drive posters that I had first seen in kindergarten in Miles City, Montana, urging us to contribute weekly, to purchase a jeep or a gun for a tank—something within the financial capacity of an organized public school. But if you spent any time at all at Shoemaker, even just took a trip to the post exchange, you would have found it hard to convince a child that the American war effort was in any financial difficulty. There were cars and jeeps and trucks enough for any purpose, and regular traffic jams, mornings and evenings.

The anti-Japanese propaganda was restricted to the play yard, as best I remember. One boy, with that natural capacity for copying that passes for artistic ability in school days, had decorated the center of a new baseball mitt with a recognizable pen-and-ink portrait of General Tojo. (We had wooden desks with inkwells, which were filled one day a week for penmanship practice.) We small boys were, severally and individually, encouraged to take a swing at the face in the center of his glove. The reason for all this punching, he explained to me, was to help make a pocket for the ball in his new, ill-formed, and overstuffed fielder's mitt. If there was ever some more pervasive encouragement of racial hatred at school, with a less functional purpose, it escaped my attention.

I did, by the way, have a certain unexpressed empathy for General Tojo and Emperor Hirohito by the fall of 1944. They had to wear eyeglasses, too.

Such things as war souvenirs and baseball mitts reminded one that a war was going on; for my father, it was undoubtedly becoming painful to be once again managing civilian contractors, as he had been in Scotland, while surrounded by officers who were commanding men, and preparing for the great sweep up the Pacific through the Philippines and the Bonins and the atolls and the Ryukyus toward the detested and detestable Japanese homeland. To Parks and Shoemaker came the hardened veterans of what were always called, as though the gerundive were part of the official name, the "Fighting Seabees," and there, too, came the new recruits to be drilled and sent off to the Pacific islands. One problem, of course, in his getting a chance actually to command was that his prescience in taking a commission in 1936, plus his excellent work and early promotions in Scotland, had put him much too high up the ladder to command a Construction Battalion. Other reservists were called on to make invasions in the Pacific, but they were lieutenants junior grade or full lieutenants. After his promotion to commander, with four wide stripes and eagles on his shoulders, he would not be able to command anything smaller than a Construction Brigade, and those posts were going, logically enough, to Academy graduates and to the most successful and experienced Construction Battalion officers.

His opportunity finally came, however. On the day after Christmas 1944, he was relieved as O.I. in C.C. at Parks and Shoemaker and sent back to Davisville, Rhode Island, where he had trained for his British assignment, for four weeks of indoctrination and training as a regimental commander. It did not seem to anyone, at this point in time, that the war was anywhere near completion. The various Philippine Islands were still held by Japanese forces, and Iwo Jima, Tinian, and Okinawa were yet to come, along with such peripheral actions as Borneo. Ahead, for all that anyone knew, was the invasion of Japan itself. He was allowed annual leave, between assuming duty as Officer in Charge and reporting to Davisville, during a part of which we must have moved. Once he was no longer O.I. in C.C., we did not rate the fancy home at the Old Hearst Ranch, and we moved into a small bungalow in nearby Livermore for the duration. This meant changing schools, which was the only painful part of the process for me.

My father's personnel record is fairly complete for the winter of 1944–45, although it begins to lose content rather quickly after he was sent overseas. On January 12, 1945, he reported to Davisville for training, and returned to San Francisco on February 9 for assignment to the Pacific, "air priority three." How long it took to get transportation, and what happened in the meantime, is most unclear, but he is next recorded as having reported to the Commander, Service Force, Seventh Fleet, on February 27, 1945.

A service force is exactly that, although its myriad details are difficult to comprehend. These would include construction troops (the Fighting Seabees), hospitals, recreation, transportation, and everything else imaginable to supply and carry fighting forces. The dates of his movements are quite clear, but, as happens in wartime orders when secrecy, or the effort at secrecy, is paramount, the orders did not specify duties, so I cannot imagine for what specific purpose he was sent to the Seventh Fleet, then operating in the Philippines. (Curiously, the only overseas assignment in his file with a specific location and title is one that he did not get. While he was on leave, just before going to Davisville, a telegram came through requesting he be assigned as public-works officer, Eniwetok Atoll. A handwritten note on the request for orders simply says: "Montgomery not available.")

Yet the *dates* on the executed orders have been a somewhat distressing archival discovery for me. The reason they are troublesome is that they conflict with my father's recollection and retelling of a personal "war story," one of the few he shared with his children. Shortly after arriving in the Philippines, he was taken down with an intense gastrointestinal ailment that had all the symptoms of appendicitis. As he told the story, he was taken into surgery on one of the fleet's capital ships, given a spinal anesthetic (all true so far), and operated on for appendicitis; the appendix was fine, but while they were in there, they decided to take it out, anyhow (also true). My problem has to do with the timing: the intentionally amusing part of the story as my father told it was that all this happened during one of the several days of the Battle of Leyte Gulf, and the surgeons kept changing places so that they could take turns going on deck and watching the progress of the battle. (When one has a spinal, depending on the amount of preoperative medication, one is quite alert and able to chat with the doctors, if one is of a mind to.)

Students of naval history have already seen the problem. The Battle(s) of Leyte Gulf, where the ships of the line jousted and the kamikazes attacked, occurred in the third week of October 1944, while my father was O.I. in C.C. at Parks and Shoemaker. The invasion with which the appendix interfered was probably the almost uncontested amphibious landing at Palawan, so-called Victor III, on February 28, 1945, one of seven amphibious landings after the invasion of Luzon—the Philippine island on which Manila, Bataan, and Corregidor lie. (The Lingayen invasion, north of Manila, was where the last contested landing took place and the last kamikazes struck in the Philippines, but that was on January 9 and 10, while my father was in Davisville.) I have no idea why he said, and perhaps thought, that he was at Leyte. It would have been the Sulu Sea, not Leyte Gulf, in any case.

Leyte was the great victory, of course, and we should all like to have been at great victories, even if they are baseball games. Perhaps he knew that it would be unlikely that his children would recognize any other name associated with the battle for the Philippines except Leyte, and so used it as a shorthand for being somewhere on that vast archipelago. The main thing, in my mind, is that it was, as usual, a mildly self-deprecating story, even given the inaccurate association with the famous battle. There he was, a patient unetherized upon a table, with nothing but a bad stomachache, while history, of some sort, was being made above deck.

The results of his surgery were two. He missed his assignment, whatever it was to have been, and he came back to duty much too soon. My mother is quite clear on this point, being a registered nurse and having strong opinions on the capacity of most medical doctors. Although the incision had healed, the spinal tap had not, and he was put back to duty while still an invalid. His few surviving orders from that period show a sequence that confirms her diagnosis, based on his letters home and, I'm sure, conversations with her after the war. He was off-duty only from February 28 to March 8, when he came back and was sent on an inspection tour by the Commander, Service Force, Seventh Fleet: "to verbally designated bases for temporary additional duty reporting to the Commanding Officer of each base visited."

What he was doing—I know from only the most fragmentary war stories—was simple enough: he was surveying both navy-built and Japanese-built airfields for suitability. Most of the Japanese-built, due to the poor quality of the concrete (a lack of sufficient Portland-type cement in the mix), had to be completely resurfaced. Many of the American-built, especially the ones on Leyte, had to be abandoned, having been constructed without regard to the sub-soil conditions. We never talked about the war, really, but before I quit working construction, my father and I did have a number of chances to talk about dirt and concrete, and I recall that these few "war stories" always occurred in relation to some construction job then under way in southern California.

The assignment to the Seventh Fleet kept my father from being involved in the last two great American amphibious operations of the war: Iwo Jima and Okinawa. Those were Third Fleet operations, and Seventh was stuck with General MacArthur and his multitudinous Philippine operations, plus providing support for the Australian Army's invasion of Borneo. And that meant that there would be no combat commands, no whole regiment of Fighting Seabees for Commander Montgomery—much too high-ranking then in a theater of small, battalion-sized landings. If the navy had had its own way, the Philippines would have been bypassed, and

great operations taken to land in Taiwan and mainland China, and
there might have been a field command for him, but MacArthur
had to return, and the Third Construction Brigade of the Seventh
Fleet, to which my father reported, was essentially a logistics-
and-planning operation, with construction responsibilities now
somewhat removed from glorious, costly, and heroic amphibious
invasions.

The rigors of surveying airfields and supervising their reconstruction took their toll, however easy the job might have been for
a healthier officer. On April 16 he reported to U.S. Naval Base
Hospital no. 15 (Leyte) for a month's hospitalization, until his
spinal tap healed and the lost spinal fluid, which had been leaking
from the puncture, regenerated itself. On May 16 he reported for
duty on the staff of the Base Planning and Construction Division,
Support Force, Seventh Fleet. He was housed, by the way, in that
object which really symbolized the incredible economic resources
the U.S. military was able to bring to bear in the Pacific. He lived,
for the duration, on an APL, one of the dozen or so "floating hotels"
that the navy located throughout the Pacific for Officers' Quarters.
There was ice for the drinks and cold beer and ice cream. He was
reasonably comfortable, although, it seems, it was not a really happy
situation at the Base Planning and Construction Division.

A Personal Gripe

The typescript Command Histories of the Commander Service Forces, Seventh Fleet, and of the Third Construction Brigade, now in the Navy Historical Section, Washington, D.C., are of the worst sort, from a biographical point of view. They are logistical and organizational, much like the official histories from Fort Peck. But the archival material at Port Hueneme has a little more utility, just enough so I can piece together some sense of what my father was doing in the waning months of the great Pacific war.

After dusting off about twenty boxes of miscellaneous Third Construction Brigade materials, most of it unsorted records of subsidiary Construction Battalions, I did turn up a Summer 1945 table of organization for "Commander Service Force, Seventh Fleet and Staff," of which the Third Brigade was the sort of "headquarters brigade." There are two familiar names on it: Commander Montgomery is "Plans Officer, Base Planning and Construction Division" (I have spelled out what was abbreviated on the chart), and Commander Robert W. Schepers, who began the war one rank junior to my father as one of the assistant civil engineers on the Londonderry side of the British-bases project, is next to him on the table. Schepers is also a Plans Officer, but has a secondary (or collateral, as they say) duty as Executive Officer, Third Construction Brigade.

Since I had only a week to plow through several tens of thousands of pieces of paper in no particular order on the shelves at Port Hueneme, pinning down what exactly my father was doing seemed unlikely. And in fact I never turned up a piece of paper with his signature on it, in all the several thousands I glanced at. You can almost smell, pulling down a box, the faint odor of futility when you look at the first file folder inside it. Whole boxes would have nothing in them but lists of material, right down to "hammer, ball peen," that had been salvaged at one base and moved forward to another. Box after box contained records of subsidiary parts of the Service Force, including saw mills (with detailed reports on the suitability of one kind of native Philippine tree or another for structural timber or waterfront construction).

And then I found some scattered papers on something called Oboe 1. Most planning reports in the Hueneme files are addressed to a "planning officer" or "medical officer" rather than to a person, but here, quite unaccountably, was an unsigned memorandum addressed to "Base Planning Division, ComSerFor7thFlt; Attn: Comdr. Montgomery. . . ." It turned out not to be the stuff of which history is made, but indicative of what commanders end up supervising. Oboe 1 was the invasion of Borneo, specifically Tarakan Island, one of the two major oil fields in northern Borneo, which had been captured and held by the Japanese since February 1942. As far as the invasion forces were concerned, they were to

be the Australian Army, with the U.S. Navy providing the assault
ships, transports, and beach-landing parties. There were about
thirty thousand Japanese troops in all of northern Borneo, and the
assault forces brought against them were, in fact, the largest invasion fleet with the most firepower in the history of the Pacific
war. It was an operation whose logistics were controlled more by
the availability of resources than by the need to employ them.

Most of the Seabees' work at Tarakan Island involved either
portable landing docks, or the construction of two U.S. Navy facilities to support the Australian troops—a Port Director unit, and
a navy-operated base for close-support aircraft. The memo to Montgomery describes the planning and loading of the prefabricated
housing, offices, and medical buildings. The planning officer took
the Australians on faith in two important matters: their maps of
the area were assumed to be accurate, and, "after having been
informed by them [the Australians] that they would take care of
all grading, road building, etc., in the area, it was decided that all
the CBMU (Construction Battalion Mobile Unit) would need for
heavy equipment would be a bull-dozer and several trucks." There
was some confusion, and perhaps a little apprehension, about the
fact that the bulldozer and trucks were to be in the Day 1 assault
unit. The Fighting Mobile Seabees seemed to think that they could
wait until the beachhead had been secured before setting up the
Port Director's camp, but they acquiesced to the Australians'
wishes. The Seabees in charge of setting up the beach landing,
with the ramps and so forth, of course had no such choice to avoid
the hostile fire on D-Day.

The reader may find this hard to believe, but in fact, on the last
afternoon that *I* could look at papers in the Hueneme archives, I
started pulling down a few boxes of the endless supply of Third
Construction Brigade paperwork and found, in a folder of miscellaneous papers, the follow-up report on how Oboe 1 had actually
proceeded, from the Seabees' perspective. From the covering rout-
ing slip, it is apparent that it went only to Commander Construction

Troops, and not to the Base Planning Division. At Commander Construction Troops, it was read and initialed by the Plans and Operations officer and the Engineering Operations officer, and filed, to turn up, or fall out of a box, for the next time just about forty-two years later. It can be read with interest, if you have some sense of the difference between plans and reality.

The CBMU got ashore with minimal trouble, suffering no wounds from a brief moment of shelling and sniper fire. By this time in the war, the Japanese had adopted a strategy of *not* defending the beaches, but of withdrawing to prepared defensive positions in the interior. In fact, if left alone in the interior, they were making very little effort to harass the invaders. It was only on small islands like Iwo Jima, or on large islands where the U.S. forces insisted on eradicating them, like Okinawa, that the desperate suicidal last stands of legend actually occurred. When the war ended, 90 percent of the Japanese troops on Borneo were alive and reasonably well in the interior, and there were still a third of a million Japanese troops on various islands in the Philippines.

Unfortunately, and out of necessity, the CBMU planning had made two of the most fundamental errors in construction planning: they had been forced to trust someone else's assessment of the local soil conditions, and they took the Australians at their word that the Aussies would provide all the necessary earth-moving equipment to supplement the Seabees' one bulldozer and six trucks. Tarakan Island turned out to consist almost entirely of either swamp or blue and yellow marine clays, those soils of impalpability that turn to grease when wet. The few bits of high ground near the proposed harbor facility had been built on previously by the Japanese, and had been turned into twisted steel rubble by the great naval firepower brought to bear for the invasion. Every building site had to be cleared by cutting up the steel with torches and hauling it away by hand. The one bulldozer spent most of the first few weeks mired in the slippery clay, and since it was not equipped with a front-end loading bucket, it was no use at all for bringing

in fill to the construction sites. The fill had to be hand-shoveled
into the trucks. Construction memos are masterpieces of understatement, and the report on Oboe 1 is no exception:

> The area along the beach selected for the office and administration
> area proved to be the most difficult to develop. All timber posts on
> the area were used to corduroy the worst sections, the largest pieces
> of scrap iron were cut up with an acetylene torch and wenched
> [sic!] off. The remaining scrap iron and debris was walked down
> . . . and the entire area filled an average of one and a half feet.
> This required approximately fifteen hundred cubic yards of fill.
> Seventy-five percent of the fill had to be loaded by hand shovels.

A thousand cubic yards of hand-shoveled fill is, by the way, about
a hundred thousand shovels-full. The report notes that after the
CBs had finished hand-shoveling hundreds of truckloads of fill,
"The extreme hot and rainy weather combined with hard work
decreased the efficiency of the unit after the first week. . . . After
the work load had decreased . . . there was a noticeable improvement in the physical condition and mental attitude of the men."

The various landings in northern Borneo (there were Oboes 1
through 6, including particularly the west side of the island in the
sultanate of Brunei, and the oil-field area in southeastern Borneo
at Balikpapan) went reasonably well, although errors on the Australian maps and the wet terrain made for temporary delays in
establishing permanent beachheads and port facilities at every landing. The Australians, who had been spoiling for a fight with the
Japanese on Borneo, where some two thousand Australians had
been captured in 1942, suffered casualties in the total of just a few
hundred dead in all the Oboe invasions. Those imprisoned by the
Japanese had not done so well. By the end of the war, all but a
handful of the Australian prisoners had died from starvation and
maltreatment. The six survivors were escapees, who had lived with
the fearsome "headhunter" natives of the great island's interior.
The Australian Army, to whom the more than twenty thousand

Japanese soldiers in northern Borneo surrendered in August 1945, simply disarmed the Japanese and told them to march, unescorted, to the sea. The native tribesmen, the headhunting Dyaks and Dusuns and Muruts and the Moslem Malays, slaughtered the Japanese at their leisure, and not more than one hundred made it from the deep interior to the coast, where they at last found sanctuary in prisoner-of-war camps. The Australians, who do not mention the matter in their official histories, told the Americans that the natives had done all the killing.

With this, of course, my father had nothing to do, although I doubt it would have shocked him. He did see Manila, shortly after it had been liberated from the Japanese Navy special forces that held it, raping and murdering the Filipinos in one of the great suicidal orgies in the history of warfare, comparable to some of the less religious events of the Crusades. Indeed, locked into his office at Base Planning and Construction, he had much responsibility on paper but little authority in fact.

If there was a fault with the planning process, as the official history of the Commander, Service Force, Seventh Fleet acknowledges, it was overplanning. Even that dry and self-congratulatory document notes several instances where elaborate plans, including sites for various buildings, could not be "constructed as drawn," but had to be "drawn as constructed." On one occasion, apparently not Oboe 1, they were fortunate enough to have a planning-office person at the site, shortly after the invasion, and whereas "ordinarily the new data would have been sent back to planning office to prepare new plans . . . the planning representative and his assistant made new plans at the site. . . . This plan [sending a Base Planning and Construction Division officer along with the CBs] worked so well that consideration is being given to the formation of an advanced planning group which would be sent to a new base soon after the beachhead is secured." To everyone's relief, the war ended before another set of plans would have to be altered to meet local realities.

Given the time in which my father served in Base Planning—

that is, the early summer of 1945—he would also have been involved
in projects for the re-creation of the permanent, and typically lux-
urious, accommodations on naval bases in the Philippines. These
were intended for use after the war. This type of construction,
including air-conditioned officers' clubs and air-conditioned homes
for base commanders and fleet flag officers, went on simultaneously
with the final Philippine and Borneo amphibious assaults. In the
official history of Commander Service Force, Seventh Fleet, it is
noted that: "Early completion of headquarters for Com7th was of
major importance. . . . Two seabee Battalions were sent to Manila
to work on these projects. . . . However, details of this construction
were slow to materialize due to the necessity of making this headquarters a permanent facility."

I prefer the comments offering a most unofficial historical opinion, handwritten scrawls on a document I chanced across at Hueneme. It is a teletype from COMSERV7THFLT (Commander,
Service Force, Seventh Fleet) to CNB (Commander, Naval Base)
MANILA:

THIRTY FIVE HUNDRED DOLLARS HEREBY GRANTED UNDER BUDOCKS
APPROPRIATION . . . FOR FURNISHING ADMIRAL GLOVER QUARTERS
FISCAL YEAR 1946 [that is, beginning July 1, 1945; Rear Admiral
Robert Glover, a 1915 Academy graduate, was the Commander of
Service Force, Seventh Fleet.]

And on this memorandum, some file clerk, some yeoman, has
scrawled a silent protest, before filing it:

Buy more Bonds!
Yah, for this shit!

And below, a second invisible hand has scrawled, in John Hancock–
sized letters:

Buy Bonds for the Braid
["Braid," of course, being shorthand for "field-grade officers"]

And finally (it takes a lot of file clerks to keep a navy floating) a third hand has added:

Never Lived Better in their life.

Which, grammar and capitalization aside, is probably inaccurate, for senior navy officers live very well indeed.

There is no Report on the Fitness of Officers in my father's personnel file for the period when he was working in Manila. But a curious document surfaced in the voluminous Third Construction Brigade records at Hueneme with his name typed at the top. It is a questionnaire to officers reporting on the fitness of their subordinates, with the note that "Information on this questionnaire will be used only for detail [that is, job-assignment] purposes."

The first question asks whether "this officer could be used to better advantage on duty other than to which assigned?" and the box for "yes" is checked. Other information notes that he is "in training for a higher office," in this case "regimental commander." (It was for that duty that he had reported to Davisville, Rhode Island, in January 1945.) Under "Remarks . . . special . . . qualifications as well as any defects . . ." the reporting officer notes, "This officer [Commander Montgomery] has had only a short period of assignment to his present duties as Planning Officer, and although he has performed these duties satisfactorily he is better qualified for field duty."

"Satisfactorily," in navy talk, is damning with faint praise. And, I would say, my father's interest in planning, navy-style, as opposed to going out and actually building something, or blowing it up if necessary, was probably low. He had not spent nine years in grade and five years on active duty in order to arrange the furnishings of Admiral Glover's residence, one of his tasks as Planning Officer, Support Force, Seventh Fleet. Nor would he have been happy with signing off on junior officers' shipping lists for distant invasions. But there were no more regimental commands, the war was winding down in the Seventh Fleet's sector, and the only remaining task

in the Philippines was to build and repair airfields and naval bases
in anticipation of the expected assault on the Japanese home islands. The first to be invaded, had the plan carried forward, would
have been the southernmost, Kyushu, in November 1945.

He did find a more congenial assignment, in the waning days of
the war, as the civil-engineering officer for Commander, Aircraft,
Philippine Sea Frontier. Duties included repairing of several Japanese airfields, making them suitable for heavy bombers, and building a number of smaller fields for shore-based navy and marine
fighter-bomber squadrons. His personnel records include not only
assignment to ComAirPhilSeaFron, as the abbreviation has it, but
a few detachments to the various air bases, "reporting to the commander thereof for duties which cannot be disclosed herein," meaning nothing special except that the veil of secrecy in a combat
theater is fairly opaque. Aside from his appendix operation, the
two months with ComAirPhil produced the only anecdotes, the
only "war stories," of his Pacific duty, probably because the Base
Planning office didn't lend itself to storytelling.

Once, while explaining to me why airplanes left condensation
trails (because the cold air aloft turns the water vapor produced
by combustion into ice crystals), he recalled the standard Marine
method for cooling beer, which was to throw a few dozen cases
into an F4U Corsair and take it up to twenty thousand feet, fly a
couple of lazy circles, and dive for the air strip before it could heat
up again in the tropical air. (Literally thousands of GIs and sailors
discovered that the general principle of evaporation worked just as
well, if not as spectacularly. Instead of burning aviation gasoline
to carry the beer upstairs, they just hung a few cans in a burlap
sack soaked in AvGas, and evaporation, even at humid sea level,
cooled it nicely. American ingenuity, given enough resources, over-
comes all problems.)

Also, he once mentioned a small personal contribution to the
war effort, when he designed a portable rock-crusher out of a
mixture of bulldozer engine and treads and a truck body, which
device could be used to break up coral rock into a sort of instant

concrete—the extremely fine coral dust serving the ordinary role
of Portland cement, binding together the aggregate of larger coral
fragments with its fine particles, which were chemically reactive
in the presence of fresh water. It worked, he said, nearly as well
as the real thing. There were, by that point in the war, plenty of
extra-high explosives to create all the coral rubble one would ever
need. This may seem like an odd conversational topic, but in fact,
when I lived at home and worked for him, we talked more about
Portland cement and its heat-of-reaction than about sex or education or sports or history.

His last fitness report on active duty was completed by Rear
Admiral Frank D. Wagner, Commander Aircraft, Philippine Sea
Frontier, on September 10, 1945. That same day, my father suddenly got a berth on a Liberty Ship headed home to San Francisco.
The timing is of some interest, because the ordinary process of a
fitness report involves the subject officer's reading and signing the
document, which then goes into his personnel records. The report
is as favorable as any, with all marks in the highest possible category, and a written note at the end which my father never saw:
". . . Commander Montgomery has carried out his duties in a very
competent manner. He has a keen sense of responsibility and has
demonstrated good judgment. He is qualified for promotion and is
so recommended." Admiral Wagner emphasized that he should be
retained and promoted, even if only 10 percent of the officers in
his category could be retained or promoted. At the end of the report,
in a different typewriter face, this note has been added: "He has
not seen this report." In the rush to get aboard the Liberty Ship
and get home, my father did not know that his last commanding
officer wanted him in the regular navy, or that he was thought
deserving of promotion to captain, immediately.

The reason that's important—and was, I think, important to our
relationship after the war—is explained in a letter I discovered at
Port Hueneme, and a very saddening letter it is. In spite of everything, and also *because* of everything he had experienced, from
Scotland to the Philippines, my father wanted to stay in the navy

and found out he couldn't. The letter, written in 1950 to the Chief of the Bureau of Yards and Docks, is on yellow, quarter-inch-scale drafting paper, from the kind of tablet every engineer has on his desk.

It is addressed informally enough, to Joe Jelly, Chief, BUDOCKS, and begins: "Ben Moreell told us at one time that if we had a gripe to write him a personal letter and give him the dope rather than get it into the files so I am doing the same to you." The gripe is that, as a member of the Organized Reserve, he seemed likely to be called up for active duty in the Korean War's partial mobilization, and he'd be stuck in some, from his viewpoint, unimportant job: "If it comes to Total War & Mobilization," he printed out in his best engineering-draftsman's hand, "and the Bureau has a job I can do and needs me, O.K. . . . But if I have to leave my job now for anything except all out war I will have lost my last 5 years work and I'm getting pretty old to start over again."

He was forty-six, and had just become a partner and general superintendent in a large general contracting firm. But what really rankled him was this: "I gave up a permanent job in 1940 to go on active duty and so far as I know did a fair job (I know I got a straight (4.0) from Admiral Stark for overseas duty), yet when the war was over I wanted to go into the Regular Navy when I talked to Shag Ransford [then Commander, Third Construction Brigade, Seventh Fleet] he said he felt I would be better off not to since my application would go through he and John Perry [Commodore, Commander Construction Troops, Seventh Fleet] at that time. I couldn't see much use of putting it in."

I suppose I should have guessed that he wanted to go navy, but I'll be damned if the idea ever occurred to me. He did spend twenty years in the reserve, with weekends taken out of his life, and made captain before it was over. I should have seen, on those days when he put on the uniform, that it was not just a way to get a little extra retirement income, but that's all I thought it was. Like most fathers, and probably for the best, he never told us about his failures any more than he boasted about successes. If compliments were scarce when I was growing up, so were criticisms. His deference about himself, I now believe, was the cause of what seemed like so much diffidence about my small triumphs.

The most characteristic line in that desperate letter is "so far as I know did a fair job." Once, when I was working for him full-time, I helped erect a precast concrete high-school football grand-stand, and we did it, from one twenty-yard line to the other twenty tiers high, in eight hours, and he said we had done a "fair day's work."

He did not know, of course, that he had gotten another 4.0 on his last duty assignment at ComAirPhil, and when Ransford told him not to apply, it was characteristic of him to take the hint, not to work where he was not, he thought, wanted. He did that, later, at the big general contracting firm, when ownership changed and he thought he was no longer wanted. I have no idea what was wrong between him and Ransford and Perry. He had been Officer in Charge of Construction at Camp Parks when Ransford was base commander, and something might have happened then. As for Commodore Perry (not to be confused with the man who opened Japan to America), there is one possible explanation: Three years earlier, as you know, my father had inquired of his friend Harry Bolles about the possibility of being assigned to military-government school. Bolles had run the idea past Perry, then a senior assistant at BuDocks. He had shown Perry the letter in which my father, rather ingenuously, said he wanted to go to military-government school because after the war he wanted to work for international civilian general contracting firms. That is not the kind of open and honest statement of career goals that brings a smile to the face of a regular-navy officer.

All in all, I think my father didn't talk much about the navy and the war simply because it hurt. And he was not a person, until he was quite old, capable of sharing any pain.

23

Impalpable Dust

My father came home from the Philippines in a little more style than some, as one of eight officers carried as supercargo on a Liberty Ship, with semiprivate cabins, rather than in a hold-full of folks on a troop ship.

He kept a diary, in the form of a letter to my mother, which describes in detail just how he managed to make such an early escape from a theater filled with hundreds of thousands of men looking for a way home. It had not much to do with the privileges of rank, but a lucky piece of information: there was a Liberty Ship authorized to carry eight officers, and no one had filled the levy, so a group of friends simply requisitioned the space and caught the ship just before it would have pulled out of Manila Bay without any passengers.

The letter is little more than a daily log of mileage toward San Francisco, notes on pennies won and lost at bridge games, and petty details of shipboard life. Only one paragraph, near the end, suggests how distressing it had been for him to be told he should not apply for the regular navy. "Honey," he wrote on October 5, "only 5 days until I'm with you again—have a lot of screwy plans to discuss. My head just goes round and round trying to figure what best to do."

He did get home, and this time we children knew who he was. He figured out what to do after a few weeks, and called a general contractor in San Diego, one whom he had gotten to know and like during the several months he was at North Island Naval Air Station, where the company was constructing hangars in 1940.

It would be unfair to say that when he came home he was some sort of distant figure, that the ordinary bonds between father and son had somehow come undone. But I was, as perhaps my sister was also, something of a stranger to him. And our efforts at getting together did not always succeed.

A couple of things happened that seem humorous now, but might have been less so at the time. While we were still living in Livermore, he took me fishing; it was the first day I had ever spent alone with him in my life. It seemed perfectly natural, except for getting up in the dark and driving for what seemed like hours to a small port somewhere on the Sacramento River Delta, where we boarded a charter boat and spent the day drifting in the sloughs of the tidal estuary. I fished very seriously, but without success. He caught a large striped bass. I would guess, from the photograph my mother took of the two of us holding it, that it was a hen fish weighing something over twenty pounds. My mother baked a big piece of it with fresh tomatoes and onion, and I ate plenty of it, and came down, an hour or two after dinner, with an all-night nausea-and-vomiting spell that kept the whole house in an uproar. It was probably the old-fashioned twenty-four-hour flu, since no

one else got sick. To this day, the peculiar odor of cooked striped
bass brings involuntary salivation and tears of nausea to my eyes.
When I learned about Pavlov's famous salivating dogs, it came as
no surprise at all to me that strong reinforcement combined with
a pungent stimulus brings an involuntary response.

The other curious business had to do with moving to San Diego.
We had gotten used, during the war, to moving frequently; I should
say that. And in the few weeks we had been reunited, we had not
established much communication; we didn't eat together often,
since my sister and I usually ate before the adults. I mention all
this because of the way we moved once again. One day, my sister
told me that we weren't going to take the bus home from the
Livermore elementary school; we were supposed to wait, and Mom
and Dad would pick us up. This seemed perfectly reasonable to
me and possibly fun, so we sat on one of the benches after school,
and the car drove up—it was our old 1938 Chevrolet sedan—and
we got in it, and we drove away. And I asked where we were going,
and my mother turned around in the front seat and said we were
going to San Diego to live, which explained why there was a lot
of stuff in the car, but which, I swear, no one had thought to tell
me.

Having learned that big boys didn't cry, I didn't, but I sulked
all the way to San Diego. Among other things, I wanted to say
goodbye to Dutch and Marge, who lived across North O Street
from us, and who had war souvenirs they would show me. Dutch
had been in the Pacific early on, with the Fighting Seabees. When
my puppy died, my mother let me go across the street by myself
to talk to Dutch, because she thought a boy needed a man to talk
to at a time like that. Dutch said it was "probably the distemper,"
and then showed me his souvenirs from New Guinea. It all went
pretty well, until we were going to bed that night and my sister
told me that puppies didn't go to heaven, a theological opinion that
had as much to do with my inability to come to terms with organized
religion as anything I was subsequently told. I forgave her about
ten years later, but only after concluding that neither would we.

My father and I reached a kind of amicable truce, over the years, only complicated by the usual childish behavior followed by the usual adolescent behavior. I did get terribly fat after we moved to San Diego, which distressed him, but then those pesky hormones that also make one a despicable teen-ager got rid of the fat, which pleased him. As soon as I was old enough, fourteen, summers were taken up with construction work, in the general category of "jobs suitable for a boy," followed a few years later by coming on regular gangs as an apprentice carpenter. Before I left home, finally, I had worked six summers and two solid years for him, and learned how to do a number of things requiring more energy than I have now, and more physical strength than I had then. Of all the genes I didn't get from his side of the family, the one for muscle was the most obvious absentee. I managed to get through all those dreary months without ever complaining, although getting up in the morning was an exercise in discomfort. It simply would not do, not to be a construction man—at least until I had earned my way through the last three years of college and saved up enough money to go to graduate school.

We worked out a system for cohabiting both the house and the job sites which was simplicity itself. I did what he told me to do, on those rare occasions when the general superintendent's authority came all the way down to my level, without questioning. With my fellow workers, I tried to walk a little faster, work a little harder, keep my back a little more bent, so that no one would think I was taking advantage of a relative in high places. Some days we did a fair day's work, and some days we just kept after it and said we'd give it hell tomorrow.

When I finally managed to finish college, just a year late, he scheduled some business near Stanford, and flew up to Palo Alto to watch the standard graduation ceremony in the old open-air theater at Stanford. Afterward, we drove to San Francisco, killing time before his flight back to San Diego, and walked around Union Square, trying just to enjoy being in The City, as we had learned to call it, so many years before, when we lived nearby. He wanted to buy me a graduation present, wanted me to go into the new Brooks Brothers branch on Post Street and pick out a jacket, "or something." I couldn't do it. I suppose it was some resentment, from what was then a recent and vivid past, at having to work so hard to finish out the last years of college without much financial help from him. And I suppose, too, that I needed to maintain the illusion of self-support, even though we both knew I was going to come back, live at home, and work for him for another year or so, before finally breaking away. I refused. It was, all in all, about the rudest thing I had ever done, and may still hold the record.

A few years later, I married a college friend who from my perspective only happened to be of Japanese descent. From my father's perspective that was certainly the most troublesome thing I ever managed to do. I will leave out the details, except to say that some people, entirely on my side of the family, now wish they had acted better. Acceptance of my wife came slowly in the case of my family. The race issue was hard enough for a Montanan, and World War II had done nothing to make it easier. But in all honesty, a better son, a closer son, a more overtly responsible-looking son, might have made his wife's burden a little lighter. Things between us did improve. Graciousness and simple politeness are much underestimated powers, probably equal to wind and water at shaping matters, and my father was, and my wife is, adept at both practices.

From the beginning I was totally comfortable, because totally accepted, in the Watanabes' home. It was not something I should boast of as a personal compliment, for it happened because I was a son-in-law and the family adopted me. I had been elected to the job, and that was good enough for all of them.

My father and I saw each other less and less, in some ways because of distance, after my wife and I moved to the east coast. Even then, our vacation time in California was, by our choice, weighted toward San Jose and the closeknit circle of relatives and friends of Dr. and Mrs. Watanabe. This preference continued after

Dr. Lee died, for although his house still seems empty without him after eighteen years, and the community of Nihon-machi has seen many changes in the twenty-five years I have known it, it has always felt like home to me.

And after many a summer, my father's health began to deteriorate. He had developed a weak heart, and Parkinson's disease, for which the medication was itself somewhat debilitating and psychologically depressing. It gave him, he told me, "screwy ideas," the same phrase he used in the shipboard letter, and one used generally around our house to describe people who were not the sort one could trust.

And finally sixty and more years of smoking caught up with him, and he was diagnosed as having small-cell carcinoma of the lung. He refused surgery and chemotherapy. He was seventy-six years old, already frail, and ready to die. It took three months, the last thirty days a very hard time indeed.

I flew out, alone, to see him in the late summer of 1981. He was calm, in many ways, but also fretful about small details. We went over the list of personal assets, the retirement entitlements and stocks and bonds that would support my mother, at least four times in the two days I spent with him. He was still taking his medication for the Parkinsonism, and was worried that he might do something "screwy," and finally found, tucked away in a desk drawer, the half-dozen cartridges for a .32-caliber Colt automatic revolver that he had given to Mother back in 1934, so that she could protect herself around that rough crowd that had descended on Fort Peck. It was my job to take the shells to the local police station and turn them in.

He went through his wallet, that evening, and it was completely empty, except for one credit card, which he broke in half, bending the plastic back and forth until the heat of friction from the flexing made the polymers less elastic, and it failed, structurally speaking. Some time before, he must have taken out the hundred-dollar bill that he always carried, having always carried cash for an emergency, never quite relying on the magic of plastic to provide car repairs or dry clothes or a night in a hotel. There is not an object much more impotent and forlorn than a man's empty wallet.

He did not want us to be there when he died. In fact, the day he died, I was in Rhode Island, shooting birds with an Alex. Martin & Sons of Glasgow and Edinburgh double-barreled 12-gauge game gun. My wife, and probably most readers, did not and will not understand that choice of recreation, considering that I knew he was about to die, any day. He wouldn't have minded, although he had given up hunting many years before, but might have preferred that I be on a golf course, using his old clubs, rather than killing mourning doves.

When he was dead, as he had planned for it years before, there was no formal funeral, no gathering of the clan. His body was cremated, and the ashes were scattered at sea by the U.S. Navy, which provides this service for retired personnel. It is done at the navy's convenience, from any ship headed outbound from port. The presence of a chaplain is optional, for the captain of a ship has both temporal and spiritual authority. The ashes are scattered, and the urn is retained, presumably recycled, although I have not had sufficient morbid curiosity to inquire about that detail.

After a few years, I felt compelled to retrace some of these old steps, and I learned many things, all of which I have tried honestly to tell you. Men had, and do have, many things in their lives that they cannot explain to wives, mothers, children, and, when it is all unsaid and undone, to themselves. It is someone else's job.

A few years ago, when puzzling through some of these matters, I talked with a navy commander who had conducted several shipboard funeral services, including the scattering of ashes, and I asked him what the ashes were like.

"Oh," he said, "they are very fine and they drift away on the wind and float on the surface."

"They are an impalpable dust," I heard myself saying.

"What's that?" he asked.

"Nothing," I said, "it's just an odd way of saying something is so fine that it will float on the surface of water." That is not entirely accurate, of course. It is an accidental quality of an impalpable dust that it will lie on the surface film. Its essential quality is that it is composed of such fine particles that they are imperceptible to the human touch.

A few months after this conversation, I was sitting alone in the cellar of the headquarters building at Fort Peck, reading the depositions of the survivors of the Big Slide. I did not know then, for news can travel very slowly in our family, that, in the last few days before my father died, he was worrying about things far beyond his control, and especially about the Slide. As I told you, he kept trying to get out of bed, said he had to get to the telephone and warn them, there was something terribly wrong, the dam was going to fail, he had to call them now. He died on the anniversary date of the Big Slide, having gotten too weak to talk, too weak even to want to get to the telephone. He died forty-eight years after Nelson P. Van Stone, Sr., and the seven others who were buried in the liquefied avalanche at Fort Peck.

I suppose there's a Nelson P. Van Stone, Jr., out there somewhere. As I said, there were more "juniors" back then, but Van Stone, Jr., and I were born before penicillin and polio vaccine, so perhaps he is not out there any more.

It was not until I read the deposition by Ralph Anglen, dragline oiler, that I actually remembered what my father had said to me the last time I saw him. Today, I can reach in the desk file and take out the electrostatic copy of the old typewritten signed deposition, and there is Anglen's clear and painful recollection, the same I wrote into this book many pages ago: "I started to run west and down the slope with Mr. Van Stone in front of me. . . . As I dropped, he went out of sight and I heard him say, 'Goodbye boys.' "

Then I remembered exactly what my father had said. I was standing by the driver's door of the compact rental car, about to drive down to Lindbergh Field and fly home to Boston. There was one of those silences to which we both had, so many years before, become accustomed. And then he hugged me, which was unusual. For the first time in our lives he was thinner and frailer than I was, and I could feel that in the moment of the embrace. And this is what he said:

"Goodbye, buddy."

A Note About the Author

M. R. Montgomery, born in Montana in 1938, received his bachelor's degree from Stanford University in 1960 and his master's degree in history from the University of Oregon in 1963. He has been a journalist with the Boston *Globe* since 1970, and is the author of *In Search of L. L. Bean* (1984) and *A Field Guide to Airplanes of North America* (1984). He and his wife live in Lincoln, Massachusetts.

A Note on the Type

This book was set in a digitized version of Fairfield, a type face designed by the distinguished American artist and engraver Rudolph Ruzicka (1883–1978). This type displays the sober and sane qualities of a master craftsman whose talent has long been dedicated to clarity. Rudolph Ruzicka was born in Bohemia and came to America in 1894. He designed and illustrated many books and was the creator of a considerable list of individual prints in a variety of techniques.

Composed by PennSet, Inc., Bloomsburg, Pennsylvania. Printed and bound by Fairfield Graphics, Fairfield, Pennsylvania. Designed by Anthea Lingeman.

DATE DUE

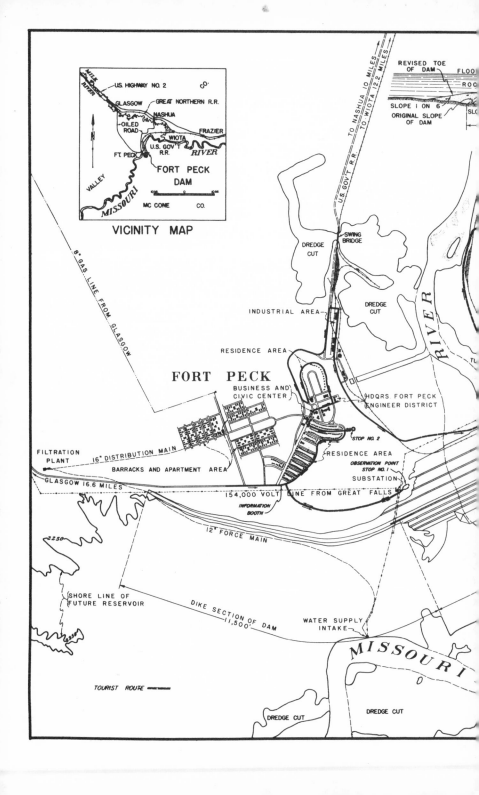